INDONESIAN
REGIONAL
COOKING

INDONESIAN REGIONAL COOKING

SRI OWEN

St. Martin's Press
New York

This book is dedicated to
the Rt Hon. JOOP AVE,
Minister for Tourism, Posts and Telecommunications, Jakarta

ISBN 0-312-11832-5

First published in Great Britain by Doubleday

First U.S. Edition: March 1995
10 9 8 7 6 5 4 3 2 1

ACKNOWLEDGEMENTS

I want to thank a lot of people for giving me their time and sharing their knowledge and skill. Some I have known for many years, others I met only when I started my work, but their support and friendship are the real foundations of this book. Many of their names will be found in the text of the book. Some of the others are named here. Many more I have no space to mention, but they too have my gratitude.

In Jakarta: Drs. Acep Hidayat, Director of Accommodation, Directorate-General of Tourism; Mrs Wage Mulyono; Tanya Alwi; Roslina and Usman Beka; Bambang Soerachim of Aerowisata Catering Services; Anak Agung Gede Rai of Hotel Indonesia International Corporation, and Ardini; Drs. Soekarno Hadian and Dra. Retno Hadian; David and Victoria Hutton; Ray Jayasakera, P. T. Rodamas Wirasakti; Prahasto Soebroto of the Jakarta Hilton; Iskandar Soangkupon and his wife Upik; Tuti Soenardi; Detlef Skrobanek; William and Lucy Wongso.

In Sumatra: Mrs Lily Abdurahman Sayoeti, wife of the Governor of Jambi; Satria Pringgodani, I Gusti Rai Tantra, Irmansyah Madewa, and Pak Baharuddin, of Hotel Pusako; Sofyan Siregar, Hotel Adian Natama, Padangsidimpuan; Desmarwita A. Adnan, Donny Yudono and Ricki Takaria of Akademi Pariwisata Bunda, Padang.

In Kalimantan: Ratnasari Haikal; Nurmalina and Anwar.

In Sulawesi: Dr and Mrs Leonard Ratulangi and members of their household at the Gardenia Homestay, Kakaskasen.

In Maluku: Des Alwi, Raymond and Min Alwi; Mrs Sitanala and her son Andre, and Stefanie Wairisal, Hotel Mutiara, Ambon.

In Bali and Nusatenggara: Kanti Bermawi and J. P. Gultom of Amanda Food Center; Otto King and his wife, at the Bali Edelweiss Restaurant; Murni; Iwan H. Rachman of P. T. Aerowisata; Stuart George-Priston and Yularso Winduharjono of Senggigi Beach Hotel.

In Java and Madura: Mr Densom Gultom, Drs. Uce Muchtar Jusuf, Drs. Suseno Kardigantara and Drs. Herman Bahar of BPLP Bandung; Ibu Etty Soeliantoro, Ibu Nina Koesnadi, Soeatminah, Janice Gabriel and Bram, Ahmad Wirono and his wife, in Yogyakarta; Sumarni and Syamsi; Dra. Harmini Djamil.

In Australia: Jan Boon, Judith Curr, Michael Dowe, Genevieve and Maggie Harris, Cherry Ripe and David Thompson in Sydney; Barbara Harman in Brisbane; Dure Dara, Diana Marsland, Alan and Yekti Morris, Nina Yusac, and Swan and Rena Sarumpaet in Melbourne; Karen Burnet and Jill Stone in Adelaide; Peter Meier, Casuarina Restaurant, Hunter Valley; Beverley and Paul Sprague, and Joyce and Charles Westrip, in Perth; Rosemary Brissenden.

In Britain: Jennifer   Smith,   of   Aerowisata   Europe;   Michael Schuetzendorff, formerly General Manager of the Park Lane Hilton, and Ronald van Weezel; Alan Davidson; Maggie Black; Silvija Davidson. And of course Caroline Davidson, my agent, and Sally Gaminara and her colleagues at Doubleday. As always, my special thanks to my husband, Roger, who has helped me with every aspect of the book, and to the artist Soun Vannithone.

I could not possibly have researched and written this book without the help and hospitality of a number of organizations. I want particularly to thank the following: P. T. Aerowisata; Hotel Pusako, Bukittinggi; Nusa Dua Beach Hotel, Bali; Nusa Indah Resort, Nusa Dua, Bali; Senggigi Beach Hotel, Lombok; Grand Hotel Preanger, Bandung; Balai Pendidikan   dan   Latihan   Pariwisata,   Bandung;   William   F&B Management, Jakarta; Hotel Indonesia International Corporation; Hotel Indonesia, Jakarta; Hotel Putri Bali, Nusa Dua, Bali; Ambarrukmo Palace Hotel, Yogyakarta; Hotel Tiara, Medan; Jakarta Hilton International; Hilton Hotels in Adelaide, Brisbane and Sydney; Grand Hyatt Hotel, Jakarta; Hyatt Regency Hotel, Surabaya.

Contents

Sweet Dishes 197

Sambal, Acar and other side-dishes 217

List of Illustrations

Pictures on pages 129 and 132 and are from photographs by Mally Kant-Achilles. The picture on page 139 is from a photograph by Janet Cochrane.

INTRODUCTION
Endangered Cuisines

This is, before anything else, a practical cookbook. Almost all the ingredients mentioned here can be bought in most parts of the world, and for those that are hard to find there are usually substitutes. Equipment and techniques, with very few exceptions, are well within the range of even a novice cook. But the book is also something of a travelogue, a history, a report on what is happening, and a manifesto for what I believe should be done.

Even before I set out on my travels, I wanted to record as much as I could of the food traditions of the past. I knew already that we are in danger of losing some very tasty dishes in the swift currents of social change, though I did not then realize how strongly these currents are running. I wanted to have some influence on the future of Indonesian food, the way it is cooked and presented, especially in restaurants. Still more, I wanted to raise people's awareness of Indonesian food and help them to know it better, whether they are Indonesians or foreigners, visiting the country for a holiday, devising a hotel menu, or cooking for themselves at home.

To write about food is to write about place. Every dish was a regional dish to start with, a response to climate, resources and custom. A book about regional food must therefore be concerned with these. I don't claim that this book is at all comprehensive. A full description of the cooking of every region of Indonesia would require a lifetime's research and fill a library shelf. But the recipes that have found their way into its pages come from many sources: memories of childhood, other books, friends, many good cooks both professional and domestic, recent journeys to areas familiar and unfamiliar.

I spent all my life in Indonesia until I was married; after many years' absence I went back to it in the 1980s and in the past three years I have travelled, with my husband Roger, through most of the larger islands and some smaller ones in quest of recipes and food lore, amazed each time at the pace of change and the underlying changelessness of Indonesian life. In some places I felt very much at home, in others almost a foreigner. But a special pleasure of our travels was the kindness with which we were everywhere greeted, and the enthusiasm with which so many people helped us. Not all Indonesians trouble themselves about good food, but all are hospitable, and enough of them know and care about food to give me hope for the future.

This is what made me want to contribute, in my own small way, to the work of saving 'traditional' foodways from oblivion. Everywhere, people are moving house, abandoning the villages to live in towns and moving from the regions to the capital, encouraged or compelled by rapid economic and industrial development. There are commercial pressures on everyone to abandon locally grown produce and eat more meat, more bread, more milk and butter and cheese, more fast food and convenience foods. Much of the flavour and variety, not to mention the nutritional value, good use of local resources, the sheer common sense of regional cooking, are inevitably lost in the process. I suspect in fact that foodways change more quickly than we realize, and leave little trace behind them. There are signs that this has happened in some parts of Indonesia, perhaps several times in the past five or six centuries.

Regional cuisines, therefore, are often endangered cuisines, and my travels in the past few years have in some ways resembled those of a collector of folk songs. It has often been necessary to seek out someone's grandmother or aged family retainer in order to find out what went into a dish that is remembered fondly as part of childhood but regarded as much too old-fashioned or time-consuming to cook today. On the other hand, some of my best informants have been young cooks, often professional chefs, who have been trained in the country's excellent hotel schools and have travelled and worked abroad. They understand what an international clientele expects from good food in hotels and restaurants, and they realize that traditional Indonesian dishes can appeal strongly to overseas visitors. This never surprised me in the least, as I have been cooking Indonesian food in England for nearly thirty years and it has always met with acclaim.

At the same time, you cannot keep foodways alive artificially any more than you can keep a language alive if no-one wants to speak it; food habits, like habits of speech, must develop. Therefore, the recipes in this book are not in any historical or ethnographical sense 'authentic'. People who know me know that nothing irritates me more than a bastardized recipe: curry powder in rendang, or coconut water confused with coconut milk, or short cuts that sacrifice quality for an insignificant saving of time. But as long as you have the essential ingredients in the right proportions, you are right to do whatever you can to make the dish attractive to your guests or your audience. An Indonesian farmer's wife, or a warung-keeper in Jakarta, will make soups and stews with every bit of the animal that is not positively unclean: bones, gristle, offal, fat, sinews are simply chopped up with a cleaver and tossed into the pot, and the cooked result is ladled out on to the diner's plate, just as it comes. I get great enjoyment from eating food like this on my travels, but even as I eat I am working out how to cook and present this dish so that I can serve it to my dinner guests in London and know that for them it will look as well as taste good.

So, if you detect a certain missionary tone here and there in the book, the convictions behind it are that we must not lose the past and that we must make old dishes popular and acceptable in a modern, sophisticated market. Foreign visitors to Indonesia nearly all praise the food, but only those who have eaten in private houses appreciate how good it can really be (and sometimes, let it be said, how bad it can become).

There are, I believe, two obstacles to Indonesian food achieving its proper stature. One is the lack of a restaurant-keeping tradition, reasons for which I shall suggest in the course of the book. Some excellent restaurants are now appearing in Jakarta and other towns, but the country needs many, many more. Overseas, the picture is even bleaker. Indonesian restaurants in the Netherlands have always been Chinese-influenced and are by now nearly as far removed from their roots as Indian restaurants are in Britain. As for London, in all my years here I have known only one or two Indonesian restaurants which, on a good night, could produce a seriously good meal, although I have been to countless parties in Indonesian London households where the cooking was excellent. In Melbourne, we went through the Yellow Pages and counted up the ethnic restaurants: the score was Thailand 32, Indonesia 4. We picked one of the Indonesian quartet at random, and it turned out to be a family business where the food was very good; but there were no other customers because the place was unadvertised and unknown.

My final conviction, then, is that Indonesians must stop apologizing for their food and learn to take a pride in it. I don't say that it is equal to French or Chinese or Turkish food, or that it has a long and distinguished pedigree. Most of the dishes in this book originate in peasant cooking, not court cuisine. Even the Central Javanese courts of Solo and Yogyakarta, which carried music, poetry and dancing to heights of the most rarified sophistication, never seem to have developed a real gourmet culture. But a high proportion of the world's classic dishes began in peasant kitchens, where they often had the benefit of the best and freshest ingredients. Indonesia, in particular, with its huge range of spices, herbs and aromatic plants, has quite naturally produced dishes that will stand comparison with those of any other country. I want to convince my countrymen and women of this. I hope to rescue the average Indonesian restaurant menu from its familiar litany of nasi goreng

5

and ikan bakar (not that there is anything wrong with these, in their right places). I would love to bury for ever the Dutch ritual of the rijsttafel. I want most of all to make Indonesians confident that their food, cooked and served as it should be, is among the best in the world.

Indonesia

If you tried to invent a country, no stretch of the imagination would lead you to anything like this one. You might think of islands and volcanoes, but never so many islands or such strange shapes, never a geography as muddled as this. Three of Earth's tectonic plates meet here in a clash of rocky shields; monsoon systems fight for supremacy in the air. As a result, Indonesia has many soils, many climates, and grows many foods.

To start with, there is the challenge of the numbers that have to be fed. Indonesia has the world's fourth largest population. China, India and the USA are all well ahead, and the next country on the list, Brazil, is quite a long way behind. On the map, the 190 million Indonesians have over 13,000 islands to inhabit, but more than half of these are too small or too dry to live on, and almost everyone is to be found on five very large islands and about fifteen smaller ones. In fact, getting on for half of the 190 million are squeezed on to Java, which is about the same size as the English (not British) mainland. The population of Java two hundred years ago is estimated to have been 3 million, so their numbers have multiplied about thirty-fold in eight generations. Compared to this, the other upheavals and revolutions they have been through seem trifling.

For a country of its size, Indonesia has managed to keep a remarkably low profile in the world. Even Australians, I suspect, do not fully appreciate how big it is, though it is their next-door neighbour in Asia. People in the West have absorbed a set of mental images of South-East Asia which obscure reality, even though they may be based on truth. I once organized a gastronomic tour of Indonesia which attracted plenty of interest until trouble erupted – two thousand miles away in the Philippines. Newspaper reports and TV pictures of something bad happening in that corner of the map caused immediate cancellation of nearly all our bookings, and of the trip itself. I am not going to paint Indonesia as a tropical paradise from end to end, but it is, by and large, a peaceful and safe country, beautiful and diverse in its scenery, developing its economy at astonishing speed and with an energy and self-confidence that its own people might not have thought themselves capable of fifty years ago.

One of its great achievements, and one that is too easily taken for granted by outsiders, is its own unity. Indonesians have paid a high price for this, but they earlier paid a much higher price for disunity. Their diversity is ethnic, linguistic, cultural – but basically it is just a fact of geography. In spite of all the trading voyages, all the skill in navigation and shipbuilding, all the inter-island raiding and invasions and vendettas, until very recently almost everyone lived almost all their lives in total isolation from the rest of the world. They knew about their neighbours, but they had no reason to trust them. Local societies and kingdoms lived separate, specialized existences, exploiting whatever natural resources were at hand and too close to subsistence to take risks with innovation. The great empires and dynasties of the past – Shailendra, Srivijaya, Majapahit – left monuments and high literary traditions but made very little mark on later society. The sultanates of the eighteenth century, one of which still survives strongly in Central Java, were quite local organizations. Yet even in Yogyakarta itself it is difficult to trace the history of any local dish or food custom further back into the past than a generation or two.

Indonesia lies right across the Equator. Day and night are of more or less equal length all the year round. There is a wet season and a dry season, but their behaviour is often unpredictable, especially in these days of global warming. Near sea level it is always very hot and very humid, but if you can climb 500 or 1,000 metres up into the hills you find that the air becomes much fresher and you start to feel chilly at night. A day without sunshine is rare, but so is a day without clouds, and when the rains come in earnest the sky is as leaden as it ever is in England. Spectacular thunderstorms bring relief from hours of brooding heat; water descends from the sky like a curtain, rivers run red with topsoil scoured off the fields and hillsides. From an aeroplane above the north coast of Java, it is sometimes difficult to be sure where land ends and sea begins. Every river mouth spews silt across a wide fan of shallows.

However, the Indonesian climate is hardly ever violent. The typhoons that do so much damage to the Philippines and sometimes threaten Australia cannot penetrate these waters, or if they do their strength is mostly spent before they arrive. Floods, it is true, often do enormous damage. Drought is a problem on some of the eastern islands and in some other areas – for example, among the hills of the Gunung

Kidul in south Central Java. Here, however, the problem is not lack of rain but absence of anywhere to store water, which disappears into underground rivers.

There are really no general truths that can be applied to the food of such a country: many Indonesians don't eat rice, they don't all like hot chillies, they are not all Muslims even though this is the largest Muslim nation in the world. (It is also perhaps the most tolerant and broad-minded.) Only a few eat dogs or snakes or sago grubs, and only a few ever, in recorded history, ate each other. Many, but not all, love to cook with pungent shrimp paste or elaborate spice mixtures. The classic Javanese or Balinese landscape of terraced, irrigated rice fields is not typical of the country as a whole.

To get a better idea of this diversity that Indonesians are now so proud of, simply look at a map. Western Indonesia is big and quite sim-ple in its design. You see at once the great curve of Sumatra and Java, which then straightens and runs eastward through Bali and Nusatenggara. This is where things get complicated, in East Indonesia, where the smooth curve scrolls back on itself through Banda and then swings north along the western half of Halmahera and up to the Philippines. This complex line marks the boundary between plates of the Earth's crust, and at weak points along it dozens of volcanoes have burst through, destroying the landscape and building it again over the course of the past million years. Many of these gunung api, fire moun-tains, are long dead, but a good number are still exhaling fumes and steam, and from time to time may explode with very little warning. The threat and mystery of the volcanoes has deeply influenced the ways of thinking of the people who grow food on their slopes, making them fatalistic, conservative, but tough-minded and adaptable. The ash that an eruption spreads over the countryside is a short-term calamity but in the long run a blessing: it enriches the soil with minerals and creates the long, evenly graded slopes that are so suitable for rice farming.

This line of volcanoes, as it curves through Sumatra and Java to Bali, also acts as a wall, facing west and south. Within it, the seas above the Sunda Shelf are warm and shallow, more like huge salt lakes, and much of the land is flat, built up by the mud left by the sluggish rivers that meander through it. Where there are mountains, they are mostly lime-stone, far older than the volcanic rock of the wall. The immense island of Kalimantan is a platform built up from the Shelf, and its only high mountains are near its northern tip, in Malaysian Sabah. But its skeletal shadow on the east, Sulawesi, is a complicated tangle of mountain chains that rise out of much deeper water, while beyond the wall the sea-bed quickly falls away to a great depth and is much colder, its ocean carried here from high latitudes that stretch southward to Antarctica.

Outside the south-eastern stretch of the volcanic wall is a broken line of smaller limestone-based islands that mark the rim of another intruding plate: passing from Sumba and Timor north-east through the Tanimbars (what name could be more romantic?), it turns tightly around to form Seram and Buru and the eastern side of Halmahera. This, in part, is the strange world of Wallacea, named for the nineteenth-century naturalist Sir Alfred Russell Wallace, who realized that the deep-sea trench between western and eastern Indonesia had once, during the last Ice Ages, been the only obstacle to free movement of animals and plants from the Asian land mass to Australasia.

Finally, throughout these seas and straits and seaways lie countless coral reefs and atolls and small islets, patches of emerald seen in the deep-sea blue as you pass above them in an aeroplane, with perhaps a few huts on a white beach, some fishing platforms offshore – but more often no sign of human life at all.

Two factors have held this mixed bag of islands together: trade and fish. Trade and seafaring have always been necessary, because the natural resources of the islands are so unevenly distributed. As for the fish, they are the true staple food of Indonesia, indeed of all maritime South-East Asia. Not everyone eats rice or soya beans or even coconuts, but they all depend on fish.

Foodways Old and New

Indonesians are sociable people who like to belong to groups. Wet-rice farming demands a great deal of social co-operation and mutual tolerance, and these are things the Javanese and Balinese have always been particularly good at; but even where there are no irrigated rice fields, family and social bonds are strong. This ought to mean that Indonesians enjoy eating together and attach great importance to food; and they do, up to a point. Until a few years ago, most people lived on the land and their calendar was that of a farming or fishing community. Communal feasts and family feasts were big affairs, often ostentatious and competitive, funded in a variety of ingenious ways. (In colonial times, the Dutch took these celebratory blow-outs as the model for their Sunday lunches at places like the Hotel des Indes in Batavia and the Savoy

Homann in Bandung, and from them developed the rijsttafel.) There were also religious feasts, which over the centuries developed a strict formality and almost, though never quite, managed to dispense with mere food altogether. Finally there were, and are, the everyday family meal-times.

The standard everyday meal for millions of country people in Indonesia consists of boiled white rice, a little dried fish, and some chilli peppers. It must be white, fully milled, rice; brown rice, with the bran still on, may be more nutritious but is reserved for very young children and invalids. There may also be lalab, raw or cooked vegetables. The midday meal in the fields will be much the same, carried in stacking enamelled containers or simply wrapped in banana leaves. The manual worker's lunch-break in town is likely to be bought from a street vendor: a bowl of soto, a dish of fried rice, or a martabak to be eaten like a big floppy sandwich. Or there are staple foods which long ago were exotic but have become acclimatized, most of them noodles in various forms or fried rice, nasi goreng, which many foreigners think of as archetypically Indonesian but which is really Chinese.

The ways families eat obviously vary enormously with their circumstances. 'The extended family' is an Asian stereotype, about which

Europeans tend to become rather sentimental. It is certainly interesting and sometimes a bit sad to watch Indonesians moving from village or small town, with relatives in the house or near neighbourhood and all the support systems of the family, to the small house or flat in the city. But it is all much less traumatic than we might expect. I think this is partly because the old life and the old routine of the household were very informal and very loosely structured. Food, for example, has traditionally been cooked and put on the table quite early in the day, and most of it stayed there till evening, ready for anyone to help themselves at whatever time they wanted to eat. It got stone cold but in the tropics even stones are quite warm. The cooking was extremely simple and required no great skill. Anyone who really cared what they were eating would have found most of the fare pretty unappetizing.

Of course, that is the extreme case, but you can see how easily that sort of eating can be transferred to city life – with the cooked food being bought in from street vendors or the local supermarket, so that the standard of materials and cooking may actually be higher now than it was before. I have to say that the family meals of my own early life were more strictly regulated. My earliest memories are of my grandmother's house in West Sumatra. It was a modern brick and plaster building, because her rumah gadang, a big Minangkabau house made of timber with upswept gable-ends, had been destroyed in an earthquake a few years before I was born. Still, the household ran on the old lines, the headquarters of a matrilineal family with many members living and eating on the premises. Food was cooked over charcoal or a wood fire in the big, bare kitchen, or outside in the yard. At five years old, I sat with everyone else on a mat-covered platform in the room next to the kitchen. We helped ourselves from the platters of food in the centre of the group, and ate with our fingers, as almost all Indonesians still prefer to do; that is one reason why we like our rice soft and a little sticky.

I could have sat at table with my father and mother in their Western-style dining room, eating with spoon and fork, but it was more fun to be with the others and the conversation was more amusing. It was assumed that even at that age I was free to choose which group I ate with. Likewise, my grandmother only cooked for all these people every day because she chose to; in most households cooking was, and is, a chore that is given to whoever can't refuse it. A family may be proud of its cooking, or of its best cooks, and they may perhaps achieve a little local reputation, but cooking has never been regarded as an art or even as a craft that demands a high level of skill. It is only in some kinds of

11

street food that you will find the cook behaving as any sort of performance artist.

How do people learn to cook if the activity is so little regarded? How did *I* learn? Mostly by helping in the kitchen, whether willingly or not. Indonesians have generally welcomed, or at least tolerated, small children of both sexes who want to come and help with the cooking; indeed, the traditional kitchen, with no labour-saving devices of any kind, has often relied on child labour. Most of the basic cookery techniques and dishes that I regard as the foundation of my knowledge today I picked up, almost without realizing I was learning, in the kitchens of my grandmothers and aunts and of course my mother – though in fact my father enjoyed cooking more than she did, and was better at it. I also accompanied whoever was to cook to market and learned about choosing meat and vegetables, shopping around, bargaining, and menu-planning on the basis of what produce was available.

Perhaps it is curious that a country which has had close contacts with China and the Arab world for so many centuries never absorbed their habit of writing down recipes and collecting them into books. For whatever reason, almost all Indonesian recipes, even in the highly literate societies like those that centred on the kraton of the Central Javanese sultans, have been handed down by example and word of mouth, and we have no way of knowing how they have changed or developed in the process. The first serious Indonesian cookbook was also the biggest, a compilation assembled in the mid-1960s by the Department of Agriculture and published in 1967 under the title *Mustikarasa*, 'The Crown of Taste'. (It was such a good name that I stole it for my shop in Wimbledon almost twenty years later.) It has long been out of print, and is hardly likely to reappear, though it remains an interesting historical document. It contains over 2,000 recipes, sent in by women's organizations from all over the country and apparently edited with a very light touch, if at all. Large numbers of recipes duplicate each other. Lists of ingredients are given, but quantities are often vaguely stated or omitted altogether, and instructions for cooking are minimal; it is assumed that the reader knows how to cook already, otherwise why would he or she be looking at such a curiosity as a regional cookbook?

Someone who is pressed for time or not interested in cooking can obviously get away with doing very little of it, but this has always been so. One reason why town dwellers have taken so readily to McDonald's and Kentucky Fried is that these are just new versions of takeaway foods that everyone has been familiar with for generations. Another is that city life really is pressured: the slow pace of the country, the somnolence of the old bureaucracy with its overmanned offices, are forgotten in the scramble for contracts and customers.

Hamburgers and Big Macs actually took longer to get established than southern fried chicken, because – it was suggested to me – people were suspicious that ground meat in a bun might conceal pork. And if a cheeseburger contains cheese, surely a hamburger may contain ham. Ninety per cent of Indonesians are Muslims. In the thirty years since the attempted coup of 1965 and its ferocious aftermath, religion has become, more widely and more deeply, a matter of private conscience and public observance. It is as though, in the twenty years after the Second World War, the nation flirted with secularism and unbelief, saw the consequences, shuddered, and withdrew to the safety of a familiar communal faith. Because I have a foreign husband, everyone I meet in Indonesia wants to know what religion each of us practises. The question is not an attempt to label or accuse anybody, but it is not idle curiosity either. If you are a good citizen, you must belong to a religious group; it doesn't matter which one, different religions can live together harmoniously under the same roof, but you are expected to identify with one of them. In one sense, there has been a great change since my student days; friends who then wore their faith lightly now take it very seriously. On the other hand, Indonesians have always been deeply interested in the unseen world, esoteric knowledge, the practices which can gain the favour of higher powers or protect you from their wrath. These practices involve, at the proper times, both fasting and feasting.

In the countryside, the great occasion for feasting was the harvest festival and, very often, the bersih desa or cleaning of the village that took place before the next crop was sown. There were also big family feasts, particularly weddings, and in some islands funerals also, which required and still require enormous communal meals. The cost of these is often borne, in part anyway, by the local community, who either give farm produce and other materials, or work in the kitchen to prepare the meal, or simply give presents of money. One of the cults the first Indonesians seem to have brought with them in their migration from mainland Asia was that of the buffalo sacrifice, and prize buffalos (and pigs) are still ritually killed and cooked at funerals in Tana Toraja. These sacrifices, like the elaborate cremation ceremonies that take place in Hindu Bali, are paid for entirely by the deceased's family, who have to save and borrow the money as best they can.

A society wedding in Jakarta today is as elaborate as that of any landowner of the old days, and no doubt costs a great deal more, though its model is usually Western. But a Muslim funeral must, by custom and religious law, take place within a few hours of death, and the meal that follows is usually an informal gathering of family and a few close friends. The Javanese have developed over the centuries an elaborate code of communal meals called selamatan. These bring family and neighbours together at fixed intervals after a death, or before and after a birth, or whenever a rite of passage has to be marked – a new house, a new job, success in an examination, recovery from serious illness. The food at a selamatan may be very plain, and may be taken home afterwards rather than eaten in the host's presence; the important thing is to establish community among people, and a relationship with God or gods, by sharing cooked food.

If food gives strength to the body, abstaining from food fortifies the spirit. Most Indonesians fast at some period of their lives, or at any rate think it would be good for them if they did. Fasting and meditation go deep down into Indonesian religion's Hindu-Buddhist roots, and perhaps deeper still into the underlying, by-no-means-forgotten animism. During the month of Ramadan, when fasting from dawn to sunset is prescribed for all Muslims, virtually everyone publicly observes Puasa, the fast. This is a big change from thirty years ago, when those who observed the rule were no more than a large minority. So close to the Equator, you can still count on nearly twelve hours of darkness out of the twenty-four, in which you can eat as much as you like, but to get through a day at your office in downtown Jakarta, commuting perhaps two hours in dense traffic morning and evening, even if you don't get a lot of actual work done, still demands physical as well as spiritual stamina. You are not allowed to smoke (most Indonesian men are passionate smokers) or to drink even a glass of water; the really strict will not swallow their own saliva, but spit it out. By the end of the day, you are thoroughly dehydrated, and as the moment of sunset approaches the traffic jams of the city are thronged by sellers of branded mineral water in plastic bottles.

Yet there is a festive air even in Ramadan, for those who can afford it. As magrib, the hour of sunset prayer, approaches, restaurants fill up with office workers, many of them having apparently just changed into their smartest and brightest clothes. Groaning trolleys of food are ordered and set in readiness by each table, and large glasses of strong, dark, heavily sweetened tea set out. The radio is turned up so that we can all hear the announcer's voice, then the heavy thudding of the drum that marks the hour. The faithful must drink at least a little, or eat something sweet, before they depart into the prayer-room at the back of the restaurant. A general air of relief rises over the city like a fountain of cool water.

There are always letters to the papers complaining that people make Ramadan an excuse for nocturnal gluttony, and maybe some of them do put on weight during the twenty-eight days, from one new moon to the next. The early morning meal has to be completed before the dawn prayer, so in a Jakarta suburb you are woken soon after 3 a.m. by a neighbour running round the streets banging a gong (or perhaps it is a saucepan) and crying *Saur! Saur!* I daresay the lethargy of the average office on Puasa afternoons is caused by lack of sleep as much as by lack of food. Still, there is very much the sense that this is a special time, and certainly not a joyless one. It ends, of course, with a feast, Idul Fitri in the local form of Arabic, Lebaran in Indonesian, or simply Hari Raya – the Great Day. This runs over into at least a second day and is spent largely in visits to family, friends, neighbours and colleagues from the office. New clothes are obligatory for everyone who can possibly afford them, presents are given recklessly. A careful order of precedence is observed, whereby the younger, junior, subordinate family calls on the senior or superior. A great deal of tea and lemonade are drunk, vast numbers of sticky rice cakes and other snacks eaten, and everyone is happy. It is also a time, of course, of big family meals and traditional Lebaran dishes.

Attitudes to Food

Thirty-five or forty years ago, Indonesia was a Third World country. Today, though it still has problems, its economy is growing quickly and it is confident of being one of the giants of Asia, or indeed of the world, in the next century. Indonesian life has become more confident, more outgoing, more cheerful and much noisier. People are taller and broader because they eat better than their parents did. And in the cities they live better, too – perhaps.

It is this confidence, expressed in the universal determination to trade and make money, that most strikes the returning exile. I write to a friend, a teacher in a provincial town, to tell him we are coming to visit and will charter a car to bring us from the capital. 'Why do you want to go all that way by road?' he asks in reply. 'I think you had much better fly.' When we get there, I telephone another old friend and ask the family to come and have traditional Javanese fried chicken with us at the place we used to go to years ago – it is still there. There is a moment's hesitation. 'Of course,' she says, 'we'd love to. Well – there's a Kentucky Fried just over the road from there; wouldn't you prefer that?'

I have to admit that I can remember when the Javanese chicken restaurant was a new business, with a new recipe. The pressures on people's eating habits today are powerful and complex. It is not just a matter of Coca-Colanization, though this plays a part. The change comes from within Indonesia as much as from without. In part, it betrays a failure of nerve; where food is concerned, national confidence seems to falter. The same ten or twelve dishes appear on every Indonesian menu; these are the ones foreigners are supposed to recognize, almost as if a gastronomic treaty had been negotiated. It is difficult for Indonesians, especially in the provinces, to offer their own local food to visitors, partly because they know that however good it tastes it doesn't always look very appetizing.

Genevieve Harris, who is now a chef in Sydney but spent a year with one of the Aman Resort hotels in Bali, told me that in Bali she spent a lot of time working with her local staff on dishes that they cooked at home every day but did not think worthy of being offered to hotel guests. All that was needed was to write down an exact recipe, so that the dish came out the same way every time, and to work out an attractive presentation. I couldn't help remembering my husband's old Javanese cook, who used to prepare bachelor suppers for him of solid Dutch dishes heavily laced with margarine. As a new wife, I asked her if she could cook a few Central Javanese sambals occasionally, give us some fresh salad with the delicious local watercress .... 'Do you really think,' she said coldly, 'that I would give the white tuan Javanese food? As for watercress, it grows in every ditch. I hope you do not expect him to eat *that*.'

She was a good-hearted old lady, and was persuaded graciously to accept a pension. That was years ago, but the attitude is still common. When I was in Jakarta in 1981, I mentioned to the editor of a women's magazine that I wanted to write about regional food. 'Regional food in this country is uneatable,' she told me. It was to be another ten years before I could travel and test the truth of this assertion; and I have to say that she was not entirely wrong. But when bad food has been set before me, its badness has been the result of careless and uncaring cooking and sloppy serving, and these vices in turn derive surely from a lack of pride in the kitchen.

This is part of a more general belief that what comes from abroad must be good. Indeed, this is a universal human trait, and contains much truth, and greatly benefits international commerce. But there is an uncritical acceptance of imported food, and ideas about food, that is having rather mixed results. Indonesians have been taking foreign ideas and beliefs and knowledge on board with enthusiasm throughout their history. Among them, in the 1920s and 1930s and still influential today, were vitamins and vegetarianism – biftek teosofi used to mean a nut cutlet. People are still very health-conscious. In taking to Western food, they are following not only the example of their own past but that of contemporary Asia; every rice-growing country that can afford it is eating less rice, more bread, more milk and butter and cheese, more fast food and convenience foods, above all more meat. What Americans eat is surely what we should eat too. Steaks, fried chicken, hamburgers, ice cream, milk shakes and cola are the staples of the urban middle class, with Japanese fast food running strongly in second place.

Crossing on the ferry from Surabaya to Madura, you have a fine view of the Bogosari flour mills, one of the biggest wheat-milling complexes in the world. A Jakarta businessman told me how its owners contracted with the government to grind flour at cost if they could keep and sell the screenings. 'They sell the screenings for animal feed all over the world,' he said. 'It's like having a bar of gold extruding from the mill, 365 days a year.' But bread, as a result, is relatively cheap and is certainly plentiful.

Even outside the cities, even in the remote islands, change is accelerating. Far more foods are now factory-processed and branded, so that basic foods like noodles are marketed nationwide. In quite small provincial towns, supermarkets are rising, old-fashioned markets disappearing and taking with them the sociable habit of haggling over unfixed prices. It will be many years of course before the pasar vanishes altogether, and changing circumstances may bring it back, but for the moment the supermarket offers standard goods, standard prices, speed, hygiene and bright lights, things which appeal to tourists as much as they do to the locals.

What percentage of a supermarket's turnover comes from imported goods or imitations of them? I have no idea; I can only say that Indonesian products take up an impressive amount of shelf space. This is not surprising, since import duties are high. People certainly have a much wider range of choice than they had twenty years ago; they are becoming more sophisticated in their tastes. Eventually they will be ready to take some traditional foods into modern life on equal terms with new ones. But by then other traditional foods will have been forgotten, along with the dishes they were used for. Good food will continue to be driven by fashion as much as by real taste, texture and nutritional value. The wide range of choice will become an illusion as processed food products drive local ingredients off the market. And fatty foods, combined with sedentary city lifestyles, will cause weight problems. In my first book, published in 1976, I wrote that it was rare to see an overweight Indonesian, almost unknown to see an obese child. This is no longer true, even though obesity is still a trifling problem here compared to what it is in the West.

Public Eating

There is still far to go if the best of Indonesian regional food is to be rescued from oblivion and given the general appeal that it should have. The classic dishes of France and China, after all, came from the regions and still, in most cases, bear the marks of their provincial origins. (This is not to say that French and Chinese provincial cooking is always good – far from it.) But these dishes had to be taken to the cities, to the provincial and national capitals, to acquire polish and sophistication, in the kitchens of wealthy families and in top restaurants. In Indonesia, this has never happened – or at least, not yet. One reason why I shall have much to say about restaurants in this book is that the overseas visitor inevitably eats in them; but the other reason, and I think just as important, is that I look to the new restaurants of Indonesia to preserve the best of traditional food and to make it appealing to everyone.

It is not easy to tell, by looking at their street fronts, which restaurants are good and which are not. Reading their menus is often not much help either. To begin with, by the time you get sight of the menu you are probably already sitting at a table, since in Indonesia no restaurant owner is compelled by any law to hang a copy of his bill of fare where you can see it from outside. I have occasionally walked out of a restaurant after carefully considering what food I am being offered, but never until I have had a talk with the waiter, and perhaps have sent him back into the kitchen, either to talk to the chef on my behalf or to bring the chef out to talk to me.

In many public eating places – indeed, in most – there is no menu anyway. Street food stalls specialize in one or perhaps two dishes.

Travelling vendors, who carry their businesses in a handcart or slung across one shoulder on a bamboo pikulan, do the same. Often, they are not producers but distributors for small businesses; much of the food is cooked by housewives in their own kitchens, and by no means all of it comes from poor households. This is one occupation in which a middle-class woman, perhaps the wife of an underpaid civil servant, can earn good money and pay for her children's education without the social stigma of being seen to do menial work. Street food is still a major component of the Indonesian scene, and has not yet been tidied up and regulated as it has in Singapore; I shall have more to say about it as we progress around the country.

The next step up from street food is the warung, a semi-permanent eating house with one or two trestle tables, benches to sit on, very simple cooking facilities and even simpler hygiene. The warung may serve half-a-dozen different dishes, or it may limit itself to one; the secret of its success is often its local reputation for cooking one dish better than anyone else in the street. Street food is cheap, it is often (but not always) cooked in front of you, it uses the cheapest possible ingredients and throws away almost nothing. It is picturesque, it helps to preserve what is best and what is worst in the country's cooking and eating habits. When I was a high school student in Yogyakarta I loved it; now I find it less tempting. Success in street eating depends on local knowledge, and the visitor rarely has time to acquire this.

The Indonesian words *rumah makan* mean, literally, 'eating house', and this is the general term for anything above the level of a warung, though the proprietor may prefer the word *restoran*. There is one type of eating house that is met with in virtually every part of Indonesia, and that is the rumah makan Padang, where cooking and service are in the manner of Padang, the largest town in West Sumatra. The instant you sit down at the table, a dozen or more dishes appear in front of you as if by magic, transported and arranged by a single waiter who balances them along both arms and deals them on to the table like a conjuror. You eat, and pay for, only the dishes that take your fancy; what you don't touch goes back into the common stock and is offered to someone else. There is obviously no menu here, and unless you can grab the waiter and interrogate him you may not know what you are eating, or how much it is costing you, until you ask for the bill.

For tourists, there is obviously a danger at such a restaurant that they will be ripped off on the spot and given food poisoning later. In fairness I have to say that most Padang restaurants are clean and honest, the

cooking can be extremely good, and even when they grossly inflate the bill for a foreigner, the total is still, by European or American standards, astonishingly low.

On my travels I met a good number of Indonesian chefs who know and respect the dishes of their country and are proud of their skill in presenting them. I ate in restaurants where the cooking was first-class, the menu varied and interesting, and the customers obviously appreciative. But such places are still exceptional. Why? One reason I was repeatedly given for the poor quality of Indonesian food in hotels and restaurants was that local people don't eat it; they can get it either at home or from street vendors, and better cooked as well. When they go out, they want something exotic and smart and fashionable, even if (to judge by the way they eat it) some of them don't really care for it much. They certainly like meat, especially the 'air-flown' beef from Australia and New Zealand, and they like anything made with milk and a lot of sugar. I see very little evidence now for the old belief that Asians lack the enzymes necessary to digest dairy products. My generation, when we were growing up, hardly ever saw fresh milk and found it rather sickly if we tasted it. Even today many people, if they want milk for cooking or to put in their tea, prefer the canned condensed sort, thick and heavily sweetened. Milk shakes are extremely popular among young people who can afford them. For a lot of rich teenagers, they have something of the fashionable allure that alcohol has for their counterparts in the West.

The idea of starting a good restaurant as a profitable investment has never held much appeal for Indonesians. If they had the capital that the project required, they preferred to put it into some other business. There was never any honour or kudos in running a restaurant, however good; cooking and selling food have always been low-status jobs. In Melbourne, I talked to Dure Dara, the ebullient Malaysian who is a partner in a famous restaurant, Stephanie's. Why, I wanted to know, are there so many Thai, so few Indonesian restaurants in Australia? She thought it was partly because there had been more Thai migrants, but mainly because 'Indonesian people are not so influenced by Western culture. The Thais have learned to be entrepreneurial, like the Chinese and the Indians, but the Indonesians haven't been led by their history to go abroad and set up businesses. They're not forward and aggressive, which you have to be to make your way in the market place.' But she thought the Thai experience had something more important to teach the Indonesians than just to be pushy. 'The Thais have been successful in showing Australia that there's a red curry and a green curry, and now every restaurant serves them, with indiscriminate use of coconut milk. The Thais live in horror at what's happened to their curries. So maybe slow is better . . .'

Views from Australia

I went to Australia partly to find out what people there think about Indonesian food. They visit Bali by the planeload, and other islands in increasing numbers, but apparently without paying very much attention to what they are eating. Cherry Ripe, who writes about food in *The Australian*, told me: 'It's quite bizarre really, because we're so close to Indonesia, yet Australia as a whole is largely unfamiliar with anything but the clichés, satay and gado–gado and nasi goreng; beyond that we don't have a knowledge of Indonesian food.' She thought this was something Australians should be 'ashamed about', but I really don't see why; even in

Indonesia itself, how are they supposed to learn? Peter Meier is chef-pro-prietor of the Casuarina restaurant in the Hunter Valley, and like many of Australia's best cooks is deeply influenced by Thai and Vietnamese food. I asked him if he ever cooked Indonesian. 'I can answer in one sentence: I don't know enough about it. When I think Indonesian, it's rijsttafel, and that's really not what Indonesian food is about.'

That is certainly true. A few days before I went to the Hunter Valley, I attended the seventh Symposium of Australian Gastronomy in Canberra, where I read a paper about the present state of Indonesian traditional food and its future, as it encountered international influences and mass tourism.

… At the top end of the market, in many big hotels in Jakarta, Bali and elsewhere, the guest is faced with a buffet groaning under an assortment of richly spiced and sauced dishes, each labelled with its Indonesian name. This is the modern version of the rijsttafel: a Dutch invention, which the tourist trade later sold back to Indonesia as the food component of the local culture. The 'classic' rijsttafel was that which was served every Sunday in the Hotel des Indes in Batavia in the 1920s and 1930s to a clientele made up mainly of Dutch planters and businessmen: an era and a society as remote now as those of Baghdad in the days of the caliphs, and very remote even then from the Indonesian population who lived and worked all around. For them, a spread like this would be associated with a great occasion: a rich family wedding or circumcision feast, or a celebration of panen, a village harvest-home supper. Especially for panen, all the women of the village who were not in the fields would be busy in their kitchens, collaborating but also competing with each other to provide the best dishes at a communal meal such as would take place once or perhaps twice a year.

Many Indonesians are still convinced that a fixed-price rice-table, often with accompanying cultural performance, must be good public relations for traditional hospitality. At such a table, the inexperienced guest tries to sample everything, piles it all on his plate on top of a mountain of rice, and ends up with indigestion but no clear recollection of what he actually ate.

My conclusion that traditional food habits were under threat, and that the future of many dishes might lie with innovative chefs, some of them foreign, was challenged by the Sydney food writer, Michael

Dowe, who maintained that regional traditions were still vigorous and the activities of chefs in five-star hotels completely irrelevant to Indonesian society – as irrelevant as the old rijsttafels had been. I don't altogether share his optimism on the first point, and he obviously does not share mine on the second – I mean, my hope that the best restaurants in the capital may create classic dishes from the Indonesian regional traditions, as Paris did in France and Beijing in China. Later, he told me something of the Indonesian restaurant scene in Sydney.

'Australia has a reputation for adopting other cuisines and preserving their integrity,' he said. 'One gets much better Vietnamese food in Sydney than one does in Paris. The French are so jingoistic they have to put their own stamp on it. Indonesian food isn't well represented here, it's largely an extension of *I've been to Bali*: gado-gado, rujak, cendol, satays predominate. Soto has been very successful – I can think of one restaurant that does a huge student trade in soto, and we're talking about Australian students. Children go to the food halls round Chinatown, and for lunch they have cendol and gado-gado. That's just an introduction, of course, but they're good gado-gados, they're rujaks which are memorable experiences.

'The Australian climate suits things like rujak. The way we eat has changed dramatically. Twenty years ago people went to work with their sandwiches in a packet. Today, they go to a Malaysian stall and have a laksa – in Castlereagh Street, near the Law Courts, all the rich silks queue at lunch-time at a laksa stall. If you go to Chinatown you'll find the Indonesians well represented there and people queueing for that sort of food. As quick food, there's a great future for Indonesian food.'

He thought the best Indonesian regional food, like much of the best Indian food, required too much time and labour. 'Just the sheer cost of preparing it makes it small-market food.' But Thai food was winning in Australia, hands down, simply because it was more readily available and people knew about it. In the end, it came back to the same problem: Australians are interested in Indonesian food, but baffled because so few of them know where to go, what to eat, how to order a good meal. 'When I was a restaurant critic, every time I wrote about an Indonesian restaurant in Sydney, and gave people a guide as to how to use it, it would be packed ... If you draw a map of Indonesian restaurants in Sydney, they're on the fringes of Chinatown and attached to the two major universities, where Indonesian students go. But the customer mix is middle-class Australians, students, Indonesian students, and then the

23

whole Indonesian community, from the doctors and the diplomats down.'

One thing that everyone I spoke to agreed about: Indonesian flavours are much more subtle than people first expect. After a cookery workshop at the Gas Cooking School in Sydney: 'What I love is the subtle blend of spices as opposed to red hot. We cooked the chicken dish and the rice – you could taste every spice that we had put in the chicken stock ...'

SUMATRA

Trans-Sumatra Highway

Sumatra is almost as big as Spain, and most parts of it are fairly empty, though there are half-a-dozen large towns and any fertile area is well populated. Mountains rise almost straight out of the sea on its western side. The high ranges intercept the monsoon clouds that come, laden with moisture, from the Indian Ocean; wherever you go in the hills you hear running water, and when it rains, it pours for hours or days. But that is a price worth paying for a landscape that sparkles and glistens in clear, cool, sunlit air. The rain feeds the big rivers that flow east through steaming lowlands to the Straits of Malacca and the Java Sea. One way or another, there is plenty of water everywhere, but most of the best soils are in the hills. Recorded Sumatran history begins with outward-looking seafaring and trading empires on the east coast, and continues with relatively isolated farming communities and kingdoms in the interior.

We started from Medan, in the Batak lands of the north. I conducted much of my research, here as elsewhere, in the dining room and manager's office of the town's best hotel. This, after all, is where you find the contemporary food experts and their customers. Svein, the food and beverage manager, confirmed that there was plenty of Batak food, but said it was virtually unknown outside Batak homes and festive gatherings. Batak recipes use local herbs and roots that are not known, or at any rate not used, anywhere else; and these, while they give the food a characteristic flavour, also turn it a uniform dull grey. He liked the food well enough himself, but would never put it on a hotel menu because no-one would order it. Apart from anything else, two of its principal ingredients are pork and dog meat, both abhorrent to the Muslim majority. Quite a few people in South-East Asia eat dogs, but they do it at home or in small restaurants that specialize in cooking them. Although I cannot see any logical reason against eating dogs that doesn't apply just as strongly against eating cows or sheep, I must admit that my own upbringing prevents me from experimenting.

Later, we set off for Brastagi and the hills, following the tourist route towards Lake Toba. A few days later, after visiting the lake and going down to the coast at Sibolga, we came to Bukittinggi and the country of the Minangkabau. This was a great moment for me, for I was returning to the hills where I was born but which I had not seen since I was a small girl. We spent a week exploring them before setting off on the long journey through the mountains and across the flat eastern side of Sumatra to Jambi.

Driving through this countryside is a continual delight, provided you have a quick eye for the passing details of life on the roadside. You also see and sample a great variety of food. Where the soil is fertile, any road attracts throngs of people, and ribbon development of small businesses extends outward from every town and village. Where brick and concrete fail, sawn timber, then bamboo and woven palm fronds take over. Eventually you reach the countryside, where fruit and vegetables are sold from the simplest of shelters, or by the roadside with no shelter at all. We stopped at one of these stalls to buy durian, whose heavy perfume lingers deliciously in the open air. Public transport and hotels ban durian because it becomes overpowering in a small space, but out of doors your nose perceives it merely as a dominant note in the chord of roadside smells, blending particularly well with that of newly laid dust after a sudden shower.

On the way into the hills, we stopped for lunch at an Islamic eating house by the roadside. Its religious aspect was merely a promise to visitors that food would be halal, the meat ritually slaughtered and nothing cooked in pork fat. There was also a room at the back where people could pray. The girl who served us wore the white headscarf that covers the hair and looks very becoming. The food was excellent, but at the end of the meal I made a bad social gaffe. Accustomed to city life, I left a tip. My own Minangkabau upbringing ought to have reminded me that in country districts in Sumatra this is not just unnecessary, it is an insult to the person who has served you. The young waitress tactfully assumed I had left the money on the table by mistake and called after me. She saw my embarrassment, and rose to the occasion. 'If you want to give something to the mosque,' she said, 'the box is here,' and she popped the cash into the slot with a conspiratorial little smile.

Our hotel in Brastagi was on the top of a green hillock, an old Dutch country club that would have looked quite at home in Surrey. They gave us a good plain dinner in a cavernous dining room and enormous, hard beds in lofty bedrooms. Only the breakfast was a little disappointing, as breakfasts often are in the tropics if you don't want to eat a plateful of rice. The trouble is the bread, which is almost universally terrible, chalky white, flabby, often sweetened, full of air in the middle but thickening to a soggy brown outside layer which takes the place of a crust. The common name for it is roti tawar, and the best that can be said about it is that it is still locally made, much of it by quite small firms, so there are at least distinctions of awfulness and perhaps hope for improvement.

Wherever we went, I naturally made a point of visiting the pasar, the

28

local market. These are generally well-organized and reasonably clean, but the finest is undoubtedly the split-level market of Bukittinggi. The name means simply 'high hill'; the town is nearly 1,000 metres above the sea, and on the edge of a canyon. Its two market places, upper and lower, pasar atas and pasar bawah, stand one above the other on the hilltop. The vegetables, fruit, meat and fish are wonderfully fresh and much of the garden produce would win prizes at any English show. The women who bring this bounty to market and preside over its sale are humorous, sharp, wide-awake and full of self-confidence. Besides the raw ingredients for cooking there are immense quantities of snacks, convenience foods, biscuits and cakes, sweet and savoury things to crunch, lick, or chew, all of which you are constantly being invited to taste and sample as you walk round. Admittedly flies are a problem, and of course the market is not enclosed or air-conditioned, so freshness depends on a rapid turnover of stock. And I am not sure that I would want to buy the ready-made spice mixes that even the kitchen staff in the hotel regarded as legitimate time-savers. But for anyone who loves food, a walk through Bukittinggi market is a reminder of how good our raw materials can be.

The landscape of these hills is rich, green and varied, a fine balance between man and nature. I am not fond of walking, and my idea of enjoying mountains is to sit in a well-placed coffee shop or restaurant and look at the view across a glass of local coffee or a plate of rice. The cooking at such places is usually quite good, even if their menus are unadventurous. My favourite coffee-shop, among many, is on the road to Lake Maninjau; it overlooks a neat green valley, with a stream and an enchanting village far below you like a toy. A little farther on, you stop in an ornamental park to see Maninjau, the entire lake, spread 200 metres beneath you within its rampart of hills. Once over the rim, the road descends by a spectacular series of hairpin bends. The earth is rich and lush with cinnamon and clove trees, coconut palms, durian, bananas and rice. The roofs of the village at the lake's edge make their way slowly upwards through the greenery, and suddenly they are above you, shading you from the intensely bright sky of midday, whose light is now reflected from the water at your feet.

Our road to Jambi followed, very roughly, the shallow valley of the Batang Hari river. The town stands on a low bluff, lined with old trees and some pleasantly decaying colonial buildings. It is famous for its weaving, and for its extensive kampong of houses on stilts on the marshy north bank of the Batang Hari, reached now by a new bridge.

After we had been shown round the city's orchid garden and bought orchids for the governor's wife, and after I had interviewed her about Jambi food, we went across the bridge and then in a tiny boat to call on her husband's niece, who lives in one of these houses and runs a batik workshop. The rooms were high and cool and spacious, beautifully made from fine timber. We sat long, talking about food, inspecting samples of superb hand-drawn batik and munching away at the succession of little snacks that came through from the kitchen. This is how casual visitors in Indonesia like to be entertained, and how the hostess likes to entertain them: an informal occasion, with just enough ritual to give it shape and significance.

Gulai itik Aceh
Duck cooked in the manner of Aceh province

The province of Aceh in the most northerly part of Sumatra is well known as the home of a fiercely independent people. They maintained their independence of Dutch colonial power in a long war that only ended in 1903. The area is now quite prosperous, not overpopulated and with no big cities. Acehnese food shows distinct Arab and Indian influence, because as early as the thirteenth century AD mariners from these countries, sailing to Indonesia in search of spices, made their first landfall here. So you have lamb korma (page 34), very much like the lamb korma of India. The Acehnese, oddly enough, don't seem to take much pride in their cuisine; if you want to eat out, you will be directed to a Padang restaurant. I have been told there is an Acehnese restaurant in Medan and another in Jakarta, but we could find neither of them on our recent visits.

The spice mixture for this dish is similar to that for lamb gulai bagar on page 43, and it takes as long to make. But I want to record the recipe before it disappears completely. There is another gulai itik on page 32, for those who do not want to slave over a hot stove.

For 4 people

---

1 duck, weighing about 2 kg/
  4–4^1/2 lb, without giblets
6 shallots or 2 onions, very
  finely chopped
285 ml/^{1}/2 pint/1^1/4 cups thick
  coconut milk

4 tbsp peanut oil
2 tbsp lime juice
4–5 tbsp freshly grated or desiccated
  coconut
570 ml/1 pint/2^1/2 cups thin
  coconut milk

For the paste:

2 shallots, chopped
3–6 large red chillies, de-seeded
  and chopped
2 tsp chopped ginger
1 tsp chopped galingale or ^{1}/2 tsp
  powder
4 cloves
6 tbsp of the thick coconut milk

3 tsp coriander seed
1 tsp ground mace
^{1}/4 tsp grated nutmeg
^{1}/4 tsp fennel seed
7–10 whole black or white
  peppercorns
1 tsp salt

Cut the duck into 8 serving pieces and trim off excess fat from each piece. Wash the pieces well in salted water, then rinse well to get rid of the saltiness. Dry the duck pieces with kitchen paper, then brown them, without oil, in a large thick-bottomed pan. Keep the browned duck in a large glass bowl. Use the duck fat, which is still in the pan, to fry the finely chopped shallots or onions until they are just slightly coloured. Take them out with a slotted spoon and then discard the fat.

Dry-fry the grated or desiccated coconut until golden brown. Put this in a blender and blend until you have an oily paste. Alternatively, this can be done with a pestle and mortar.

Put all the ingredients for the paste into a blender and blend until smooth. Transfer the paste to the bowl with the duck pieces and add the browned coconut paste, the fried shallots or onions and the lime juice, and mix well. Now add the rest of the thick coconut milk, mix it well in and leave to stand for 10–15 minutes.

Put the duck mixture into a large saucepan, heat it to near boiling point, and cook until it starts to sizzle and spit. Turn the duck pieces around with a wooden spoon, then cover the pan tightly. Let the duck cook in its own steam for 5 minutes. Uncover and add the thin coconut milk. Leave uncovered and continue cooking for another 25–30 min-

utes, or longer (depending on how old the duck is), or until the sauce is
thick. Adjust the seasoning and serve hot with plenty of boiled rice.

Gulai itik

Sumatran duck with green chillies

Most domesticated ducks in Indonesia fall into two types: in Java, one is
called bebek and the other entok. However, people in Sumatra and
Kalimantan and some of the smaller islands use the same name for both,
which is itik. Not everybody likes duck, because they consider that
these birds have a strong smell, particularly the entok. There are several
grandmother's recipes for getting rid of this. Using a lot of garlic is one
method, or soaking the birds in salted water, or covering the cut-up
duck pieces with coarse sea salt for several hours, then rinsing them well
before cooking, or washing the duck in diluted vinegar. I find that with
the spice mixture given in this recipe, just marinating the duck pieces in
the paste for several hours does the trick. In any case, people in the
West don't complain of duck odour the way Indonesians do.

Here I give two ways of cooking the duck, the traditional Sumatran
way, and my own quicker Wimbledon dinner party method. I call the latter bebek panggang hijau (see next recipe), and I use only the duck breasts.

For 4 people

---

4 duck breasts, thinly sliced

168 ml/6 fl oz/³/4 cup hot water

For the paste:

*4 large green chillies, de-seeded
  and chopped*

5 shallots, chopped

4 cloves garlic, chopped

4 candlenuts, chopped

2 tsp chopped ginger

¹/2 tsp ground turmeric

*1 tsp chopped galingale or
  ¹/2 tsp powder*

2 kaffir lime leaves, shredded

*2.5-cm/1-inch stem of lemon
  grass, outer leaves discarded,
  chopped*

*4–6 whole black or white
  peppercorns*

*4 tbsp tamarind water or
  lime juice*

2 tbsp peanut oil

1 tsp salt

Put all the ingredients for the paste into a blender or food processor and blend until smooth. Then transfer the paste into a saucepan and simmer, stirring often, for 4–6 minutes. Then add the slices of duck, and continue cooking, stirring often, for 6 more minutes. Add the hot water, and increase the heat to bring the sauce to the boil. Continue cooking on this high heat for 5–8 minutes. Adjust the seasoning, and serve at once with rice.

Bebek panggang hijau
Marinated and grilled or roasted duck

In the previous recipe, I described a traditional way of cooking a duck. This is my adaptation of it. Cooking the duck breast this way will give you a nice crisp skin and very tender, slightly pink slices of duck. Slice the meat after cooking, and serve straight away with some green salad or cooked green beans. This duck is equally good with rice, pasta, or potatoes. The marinade can be reheated with 112 ml/4 fl oz/1/2 cup of water and served as a sauce.

For 4 people

---

4 duck breasts
The paste as for gulai itik (above)

Simmer the paste for 6–8 minutes, stirring often, then leave it to get cold in a glass bowl.

Make two incisions in the skin of each duck breast. When the paste is cold, marinate the breasts in it, mixing them well so that every duck breast is well coated with the marinade. Leave to stand in the fridge for at least 4 hours, or overnight.

When you are ready to eat, pre-heat the oven to 200°C/400°F/Gas Mark 6. Drain off the marinade, and place the duck breasts, skin uppermost, on a rack in a baking tray. Half-fill the tray with hot water and roast for 25–30 minutes. Serve immediately as suggested above.

If you are going to grill the duck, whether under electricity or gas, set the grill to maximum heat. Grill on the meat side first for 20 minutes, then turn the breasts over and continue grilling until the skins are almost charred. Serve straight away.

Kambing kurma
Mutton or lamb korma

In North Sumatra, people will tell you that this curry comes from Malaysia. In fact it is very similar to the lamb korma cooked by Muslims in Central India, except that it is made with coconut milk instead of yogurt. Restaurant menus in Medan and the surrounding area often call it gulai kurma, gulai meaning any dish with plenty of sauce; the meat of course is goat. Usually, as in Malaysia, it is served with roti jala (page 35), especially as a snack or for lunch. At the evening meal, rice will come to table with the gulai.

For readers who are more used to cooking with yogurt, I explain here how to use yogurt instead of coconut milk.

For 6–8 people

---

1 kg/2 lb 3 oz mutton or lamb, preferably leg meat, cut into 2.5-cm/1-inch cubes

1 tsp salt
5 tbsp ghee or clarified butter, or peanut oil

For the dry spice mixture:
2 tsp coriander seed
1 tsp cumin seed
1 tsp fennel seed

Seeds of 3 green cardamoms
4 cloves
10 whole black peppercorns

Other ingredients:
5 shallots or 1 medium red onion, finely chopped
6 cloves garlic, finely chopped
2 tsp chopped ginger
2 tsp finely chopped lemon grass
5-cm/2-inch cinnamon stick
2 salam leaves or bay leaves
570 ml/1 pint/2½ cups hot water

450 g/1 lb/4 cups small new potatoes, scrubbed and washed
225 ml/8 fl oz/1 cup very thick coconut milk or 8 tbsp plain yogurt
More salt to taste

Put all the ingredients for the dry spice mixture into a thick-bottomed frying pan, and stir-fry for 4–5 minutes. Transfer to a bowl and leave to cool. When cold, put them in a coffee grinder and grind them finely.

(You can also do this in a mortar with a pestle.) Then mix the ground spices with the meat cubes in a large bowl. Add the salt. Leave to stand for 15–20 minutes, while you prepare the rest of the ingredients.

Heat the ghee or oil in a wok or large shallow saucepan, and fry the meat cubes in two batches, for 5 minutes each batch, stirring all the time. Keep the meat aside on a plate. Heat the remaining ghee or oil in the pan, and stir-fry the chopped onion for 5 minutes. Add the garlic, ginger and lemon grass, and continue stirring for 2 minutes. With a slotted spoon, transfer the onions, garlic, and so on, to the plate of meat, and discard the oil. Now put back everything from the plate into the same saucepan, and add to it the cinnamon stick, and the salam or bay leaves. Stir once, then pour in the hot water. Add the potatoes. Cover the pan, and simmer for 45–50 minutes.

Then uncover, and add the coconut milk or yogurt. (If you use yogurt, you will probably need to add some more hot water before you stir in the yogurt, a tablespoonful at a time.) Continue to simmer for a further 20 minutes, stirring often. Adjust the seasoning, take out and discard the cinnamon stick and leaves, and serve hot, as suggested above.

Roti jala
Lacy pancake

In North Sumatra, this pancake is eaten with lamb korma (page 34). Roti jala is not very well known in other islands, except in the capital, Jakarta, where you can find food and cooking of all the islands of Indonesia. People in North Sumatra will say that this is a Malay recipe – as opposed to Chinese; I myself am never quite sure whether the recipe first came here from Malaysia, or, like so many other Indonesian recipes, was taken to Malaysia from Sumatra. Large numbers of Sumatrans have migrated to West Malaysia, especially the states of Johor and Negeri Sembilan, from quite a long time ago.

If you wander around market places in Malaysia or North Sumatra, you may find a special roti jala cup (picture on page 38) to help you make roti jala more easily, but you can make it without the cup, as I explain in the method below. The original roti jala is made with coconut milk, but there is no reason that cow or goat milk cannot be used. Some people in Jakarta and Penang make it with canned evaporated milk for convenience, so by all means use canned coconut milk if that is available in your neighbourhood.

450 g / 1 lb / 4 cups plain/ *all-purpose flour* *¹/2 tsp salt* *2 eggs, lightly beaten*	*570 ml / 1 pint / 2¹/2 cups coconut* *milk, or full cream or* *evaporated milk*

Sift the flour and salt into a bowl, and stir in the beaten egg and the coconut milk. Whisk until you get a smooth batter.

Grease a 20–23 cm/8–9 inch flat frying pan or skillet (preferably a non-stick one), and heat the pan on a low heat. Spoon out some batter with a large serving spoon, and dribble the batter on to the pan in a continuous series of figure-eight shapes. Leave to cook for 2 minutes. Transfer the lacy pancake to a plate, and continue making pancakes until all the batter is finished.

When the pancakes are cool enough to handle, fold each one in half, and serve straight away with the lamb korma.

Piong duku babi
Spiced minced pork Batak style

This is a minced pork dish traditionally cooked in green bamboo segments. This method of cooking pig in green bamboo is found in other parts of Indonesia, among the Dayak of West Kalimantan and the Minahasa in North Sulawesi. They, too, use the blood of the pig, obtained when the animal's throat is cut, as one of the ingredients. The Dayak in fact chop an entire small pig into little pieces, innards and all, and cook the lot, with the blood, in a number of bamboo segments around a bonfire. The segments are supported between two wooden rails (picture on page 23), and frequently rotated so that the contents are evenly cooked. It takes about 3 hours and is very laborious; even in 1987, when I first watched it being done, I was surprised that no-one seemed to have thought of stuffing the spiced pork mixture into the skin of the pig to cook it. But it is only the Balinese who, for a big feast day, cook the famous babi guling, a whole stuffed pig roasted on a large bamboo spit, turning over a glowing charcoal fire in a shallow trench (picture on page 10).

I have found black pudding quite a satisfactory substitute for the fresh blood. But if you can't get a good black pudding, use the pig's liver instead. Here, I wrap the minced pork in banana leaves, then in aluminium foil, roll it up and cook it in the oven. This recipe also suggests a method for making piong duku babi with a whole leg of pork.

For 4–6 people

450 g/1 lb boneless pork chops	*112 g/4 oz/¹/2 cup black*
170 g/6 oz/1¹/2 cups papaya or	*pudding, or pig's liver*
cassava leaves, or young vine	*Salt and pepper*
leaves or curly kale	
285 ml/¹/2 pint/1¹/4 cups	
coconut milk	

For the paste:	*2.5-cm/1-inch piece of*
5 shallots or 1 onion, chopped	*galingale, finely chopped*
5 cloves garlic, chopped	*3–4 red tomatoes, skinned and*
3–6 red chillies, de-seeded and	*de-seeded, then chopped*
chopped	*(optional)*
2 tsp coriander seed	*1 tsp salt*
2 tsp chopped ginger	*6 tbsp coconut milk*

With a cleaver, chop the pork chops, or mince them in a mincer. Keep aside. Shred the leaves finely, and chop the black pudding, discarding the skin. (If liver is used, chop this also.)

Put all the ingredients for the paste in a blender or food processor and blend until smooth. Then transfer the paste to a small saucepan and simmer for 6 minutes, stirring often. Add the shredded leaves, stir these around, then add the rest of the coconut milk. Continue to simmer for about 10 minutes. Adjust the seasoning and leave this to get cold.

Meanwhile, put the chopped or minced pork together with the chopped black pudding or liver into a large glass bowl. When the paste with the leaves is cold, mix this well into the meat. Then, put the meat mixture on top of a flat tray already lined with banana leaves. Roll the meat to make a large sausage shape. Put this banana leaf roll on top of two layers of aluminium foil, and roll the foil around it. Cook in a pre-heated oven at 150°C/300°F/Gas Mark 2 for 50–60 minutes. Then reduce the heat to 100°C/210°F/Gas Mark ¹/4, and continue cooking for 1–2 hours longer.

To serve, unwrap the piong duku babi, transfer it into a large serving dish, and cut into thick slices. Serve hot with plenty of rice.

With a whole leg of pork

Carefully score the skin of the leg of pork with a sharp knife. Then cut the skin lengthways and cut it away from the meat in one piece. Keep aside. Bone the meat and cut it into large cubes; you will only need to use 450 g/1 lb of the meat for this recipe. Keep the rest of the meat for other purposes. Mince the 450 g/1 lb of the meat in a mincer or food processor.

You will need the same paste, shredded leaves and black pudding or liver as above. Mix all these ingredients together, and carefully place them along the centre line of the skin. Roll the whole lot into a large sausage shape, and tie it in three or four places with string. Rub the skin with salt. Put the rolled pork on a rack on a roasting tray and roast for 1 hour in a pre-heated oven at 160°C/320°F/Gas Mark 3. After 1 hour, turn the oven to 190°C/375°F/Gas Mark 5 and continue roasting for another 30–35 minutes. By this time you will have nice crisp crackling. Transfer the pork to a serving platter, carve into thick slices and serve straight away.

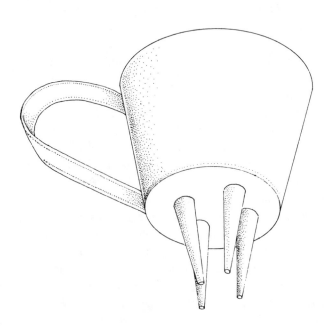

Ikan bakar Danau Maninjau
Spiced grilled fish

Wherever you go in Indonesia, especially on the tourist routes, you will find ikan bakar, and each region will claim that its ikan bakar is the best. I had this freshwater fish grilled over charcoal in a small restaurant by Lake Maninjau. It was a beautiful spot, on the edge of the lake where people could safely swim. There were several small dugout perahu, each with a single fisherman fishing with a net for pensi, which are small cockles. The fish for the ikan bakar was a gurami, not from the lake itself but from a specially constructed enclosure at the lake's edge. The gurami grow quite large, sometimes to as much as 5 kg/11 lb, though you are advised to choose a much smaller one. Ours that day was about 2 kg/4^1/2 lb. The spice mixture they used in the restaurant by Lake Maninjau was the same as that for pangek ikan (page 52).

To make this version of ikan bakar in England, I suggest tilapia or red snapper, or pomfret (ikan bawal), which is now available on most Chinatown fish counters.

For 4 people

---

4 small tilapia or pomfret, or
   1 large red snapper, cleaned
   but left whole

For the paste:

6 candlenuts, chopped	1 tsp chopped galingale
5 shallots or 1 onion, chopped	1 tsp ground turmeric
4 cloves garlic, chopped	4 tbsp tamarind water
2–4 red chillies, de-seeded and chopped	4 tbsp coconut milk or 2 tbsp peanut oil
2 tsp chopped ginger	1 tsp salt

Put all the ingredients for the paste in a blender or food processor, and blend until smooth. Divide the paste into two, and put one half in a bowl and the other half in a small saucepan.

Make two deep incisions on each side of the fish, and then rub the

39

fish inside and out with the paste in the bowl and leave to stand in a cool place for up to 2 hours. Grill the fish on charcoal or under an electric or gas grill for about 8 minutes each side, turning them several times. (Allow longer for the large red snapper.)

While the fish are being grilled, heat and cook the paste in the saucepan for 6 minutes, stirring often. The easiest way to finish the fish is to put it or them on a flameproof platter, spreading the cooked paste all over the fish with a spoon; then put the fish under the grill for another 2–3 minutes, or into a pre-heated oven at 180°C/350°F/Gas Mark 4 for 5 minutes. Serve straight away while still piping hot.

Rendang
Beef long-cooked in coconut milk with spices

Rendang probably developed out of the need to preserve the meat from a newly killed buffalo for as long as possible in a tropical climate with no refrigerators. The meat was cut into chunky cubes and was then boiled in large pots, not in water, but in spiced coconut milk, which slowly penetrated the meat and incidentally gave it a delicious flavour. It also tenderizes the meat, though I must say that real old buffalo rendang remains very chewy even after 3 hours on the stove. A good cut of beef is tender but should not disintegrate at the end of 3 hours.

This is the only dish I know which passes from boiling to frying in a continuous process. As the water in the coconut milk is driven off, the oil remains, until eventually the meat is frying in the highly flavoured oil. When cooking is complete, the meat has absorbed the oil and has become almost black, quite dry, but richly succulent, while the solid residue from the oil, the blondo (page 252), forms a kind of dry relish. (If you want to retain some of the sauce, you can stop the cooking somewhat earlier; the dish is then called kalio.) I recall that a cookery editor once wanted to describe rendang as 'a dry beef curry'. Fortunately, I was able to persuade him not to. Rendang spices are not curry spices. There are Malaysian versions which use curry-style spices, but they would not be regarded as rendang in Indonesia.

The recipe that I have used in all my books is the one that my grandmother used in Padang Panjang when I was a small child. She usually cooked about 20 kg/45 lb of meat at a time. The list of spices should not be changed, but the main ingredient can vary; you can make very good rendang nangka with unripe jackfruit, because the fibres absorb the coconut milk residue particularly well. During the Second World War, when meat was very scarce, we made rendang with very little beef, extra coconut milk and freshly picked red kidney beans. The fresh beans were added only for the last hour of cooking. If you use dried red kidney beans, soak them overnight and boil them without salt for 30–45 minutes before draining them and adding them to the still-cooking rendang. You may need to experiment a little to work out exactly when to add the beans so that they and the meat finish cooking together. The beans should be tender and just a little crisp on the outside. If they cook too long, they will become rather hard and chewy.

Rendang is traditionally eaten with sticky rice cooked in coconut milk, or with lemang, the same sticky rice but cooked in a bamboo segment. However, it is just as good with plain boiled rice. It also makes an excellent sandwich filling, especially if it has been cooked with a little extra coconut milk so that the beef crumbles easily. For beef rendang, I recommend brisket, with silverside or good-quality stewing steak as my second choice. Topside and rump steak tend to fall to pieces during the long cooking, and are too expensive anyway.

For 6–8 people

1.35 kg/3 lb buffalo meat or beef:	*6 red chillies, de-seeded, or 3 tsp*
preferably brisket, otherwise	*chilli powder*
topside or silverside, cut into	*1 tsp chopped galingale or $^1/_2$ tsp*
cubes about 2 cm/$^3/_4$ inch on	*powder*
a side	*2.3 litres/4 pints/10 cups coconut*
6 shallots	*milk*
4 cloves garlic	*1 salam leaf or bay leaf*
2.5-cm/1$^1/_4$-inch piece of root	*1 fresh turmeric leaf or 1 stem*
ginger, peeled	*lemon grass*
1 tsp turmeric powder	*2 tsp salt*

Peel and slice the shallots finely, and roughly chop the chillies and ginger. Put them in a blender with 4 tablespoons of the coconut milk, and blend until smooth. Put all these ingredients, with the coconut milk, into a large wok or saucepan. (It is generally more convenient to start in a pan, and transfer to a wok later.) Put the meat and the rest of the ingredients into the pan also, making sure that there is enough coconut milk to cover them.

41

Stir the contents of the pan, and start cooking, on a medium heat, uncovered. Let the pan bubble gently for $1^1/2$ hours, stirring from time to time. The coconut milk will by then be quite thick, and of course much reduced.

If you started in a large saucepan, transfer everything to a wok and continue cooking in the same way for another 30 minutes, stirring occasionally. By now the coconut milk is beginning to reduce to oil, and the meat, which has so far been boiling, will soon be frying. From now on, the rendang needs to be stirred frequently. Taste, and add salt if necessary. When the coconut oil becomes thick and brown, stir continuously for about 15 minutes, until the oil has been more or less completely absorbed by the meat. Take out and discard the salam or bay leaf and the turmeric leaf or lemon grass. Serve hot with lots of rice.

Rendang itik, rendang ayam
Duck or chicken rendang

Beef rendang, which is the traditional Padang dish, is not included in the many different dishes served as nasi Kapau (page 59), because beef rendang is always to be found in any warung or restoran Padang. But nasi Kapau usually includes rendang made with chicken or duck (my own favourite). There are two important differences between this and beef rendang. First, duck or chicken rendang contains tamarind, which beef rendang does not; this is another reason why nasi Kapau, with its hot-and-sour note in every dish, excludes beef rendang. Second, duck or chicken rendang is usually not cooked for as long as beef; it retains some of the luscious coconut-based sauce, and should perhaps, strictly speaking, be called a kalio. Another reason for including this as a separate recipe is that, although most of the other ingredients are the same as for beef rendang, the duck or chicken must be put into the pan much later.

The coconut milk and the paste must be cooked for at least 1 hour before the duck or chicken meat is put in. The same applies to cassava rendang, which is often made by the people of Payakumbuh, and to rendang jaring, another favourite of the Minangkabau people. Jaring is the Minangkabau word for this vegetable; in Java and elsewhere it is called jengkol (page 264).

1.7 litres / 3 pints / 7^{1}/2 cups coconut milk	*2.5-cm / 1-inch piece of galingale or ^{1}/2 tsp powder*
6 shallots or 1 large onion, finely chopped	*2 salam leaves or bay leaves*
4 cloves garlic, chopped	*1 turmeric leaf (optional)*
2 tsp finely chopped ginger	*1–2 tsp salt*
1–3 tsp sambal ulek (page 219) or 1 tsp chilli powder	*1 duck or chicken, weighing about 2 kg / 4 lb, cleaned and cut into 8 pieces*
1 tsp ground turmeric	*2 tbsp very thick tamarind water*
1 stem of lemon grass, cut into 3 and bruised	*(optional)*

Put the coconut milk and all the other ingredients, except the duck or chicken and tamarind water, into a large saucepan or a wok. Bring to the boil, stir, and lower the heat a little, so that the coconut milk will just bubble gently. Stir this from time to time. After an hour the liquid will have reduced somewhat. Add the duck or chicken pieces and tamarind water, if used, and continue cooking as before, stirring occasionally, for another 1 or 1^{1}/2 hours.

The liquid is now quite thick. Lower the heat a little, and continue to simmer, stirring often, until the sauce is very thick and appears to be oily. This is because the coconut milk, after long cooking, has become oil, with the blondo or sediment well blended with the spices. Increase the heat, and go on cooking, stirring often, until all the oil has been absorbed by the meat and sediment. Adjust the seasoning. Serve hot with plenty of rice, accompanied by any green vegetables. Or, of course, this rendang can be served as part of your nasi Kapau.

Gulai bagar
Chunky mutton curry

Not all Sumatran-style gulai can be called curries, but this is very much like one because it uses almost all the curry spices: cloves, cumin, cardamom, coriander seeds. This is also one dish that I prefer served in the original way, on top of a mountain of white rice, or in a large earthenware bowl with the gleaming rice on the side in a woven bamboo tray or basket, lined with banana leaves. It is the appropriate food for a family gathering or selamatan, as it was served during my grandmother's time, for instance on the day one of my boy-cousins was circumcised. She would have made this with several whole young goats, especially slaughtered for the occasion. Here in London I replace the goat meat with mutton, if I can get good mutton; otherwise a shoulder or a leg of lamb will do very well. Better still, if you don't want the trouble of cutting the shoulder or leg meat into large chunks, buy some chump chops or mutton chops.

For 8–10 people

3 kg/6^1/2 lb shoulder or leg of lamb, or chump or mutton chops	3 kaffir lime leaves
	3 cloves
	1 stick cinnamon
2 tbsp groundnut or coconut oil	4 green cardamoms
570 ml/1 pint/2^1/2 cups thin coconut milk	1 stalk lemon grass, cut across into 3
570 ml/1 pint/2^1/2 cups thick coconut milk	10 small round white aubergines/eggplants or 2 large purple ones

To be roasted first:

6–8 tbsp freshly grated or desiccated coconut	1 tsp cumin seed
3 tsp coriander seed	5 candlenuts or macadamia nuts, roughly chopped

For the paste:

8 shallots or 2 large onions, chopped	1 tsp ground turmeric
6 cloves garlic, chopped	A large pinch of grated or ground nutmeg
4–8 large red chillies, de-seeded and chopped	4 tbsp thick coconut milk
2 tsp chopped ginger	3 tbsp tamarind water

Cut the shoulder or leg of lamb into large chunks still on the bone. If using chops, just trim off and discard some of the fat.

If you are using the small round aubergines/eggplants, cut them in halves. The large purple ones need to be cut into several thick round slices.

44

Put all the ingredients to be roasted into a wok or a thick-bottomed frying pan on a low heat. Stir almost all the time with a wooden spoon until the coconut is golden brown. Transfer the roasted ingredients to a bowl to get cold.

Put all the ingredients for the paste into a blender or food processor. Add to it all the ingredients from the bowl. Process them until you get a smooth paste. You may need to do this in two batches. Transfer all the paste to a large saucepan and simmer, stirring often, for 8 minutes. Add the 2 tablespoonfuls of groundnut or coconut oil, and keep on stirring for another 2 minutes. Now add the kaffir lime leaves, cloves, cinnamon stick, cardamoms, lemon grass and the chunks of meat, and stir so that all the chunks are well coated with the paste. Add the thin coconut milk, lower the heat a little and simmer, uncovered, for 30 minutes. Now add the thick coconut milk, and bring almost to the boil, then simmer for 20 minutes. Add the aubergines/eggplants, and continue to cook the gulai for 15–20 minutes longer. Adjust the seasoning.

To serve, take out the chunks of meat and cut them into largish pieces. Arrange the meat on a large flame- and ovenproof dish, and the aubergines/eggplants on top of the meat. Extract from the sauce all the unwanted solids and discard them: cloves, cardamoms, cinnamon and leaves. Pour away the excess oil, which is floating on the top of the sauce, and pour the sauce over the meat. Keep the dish hot in the oven (at 100°C/210°F/Gas Mark 1/4) until you are ready to serve the gulai bagar piping hot with plenty of boiled rice or boiled potatoes.

Gulai gajebo
Brisket of beef cooked in West Sumatra style

This dish is typical of the chilli-hot cooking of the Padang area, a style that is popular all over Indonesia. Traditionally, it is made with slices of beef that have a lot of fat on them. It is made richer still by being cooked with a lot of coconut milk for a long time. The large quantity of chillies used make the sauce quite red, and the tamarind gives a pleasant sourness.

My version here is an improved recipe which was demonstrated by Donny Yudono, a senior instructor at the Akademi Pariwisata Bundo (a privately run Tourism Academy) in Padang. However, he still left all the fat on the brisket. I suggest any fat should be discarded before serving.

For 4–6 people

---

1 kg/2 lb brisket, in one piece
1.1 litres/2 pints/5 cups cold water

For the paste:
4 shallots, chopped
4 cloves garlic, chopped
4 red chillies, de-seeded and chopped
1 tsp chopped ginger

Other ingredients:
1 stalk of lemon grass, cut across into 2, then bruised
3 kaffir lime leaves

1 tsp salt
285 ml/1/2 pint/11/4 cups very thick coconut milk

2 tsp chopped fresh turmeric or 1 tsp turmeric powder
2 tbsp tamarind water
2 tbsp coconut milk
2 tbsp peanut oil

A small piece of fresh galingale
2 salam leaves (optional)
Salt to taste

Put the brisket and cold water into a large saucepan and bring to boil. Add the salt and simmer, skimming it often, for 1 hour. This can be done a day ahead. Keep the meat and stock separately in the fridge. The next day discard all the fat from the stock and measure 570 ml/1 pint/2^1/2 cups of stock for cooking the meat. Cut off all the fat from the meat, and slice the meat thinly.

Put all the ingredients for the paste in a blender and blend until smooth. Cook the paste in a saucepan, stirring often, until you get a good aroma; then add the stock. Continue to simmer for 15 minutes and add the slices of meat and the other ingredients, except the coconut milk. Continue to cook slowly for 20 more minutes, then adjust the seasoning. Up to this point the cooking can also be done in advance. Keep aside in a cool place.

Just before you are ready to serve, heat the meat in the already reduced stock, discard the galingale, lemon grass and kaffir lime and salam leaves, and add the coconut milk. Simmer and stir for 5 minutes only and serve straight away, with boiled rice or potatoes.

Sate Padang
Offal kebab with a special Padang sauce

Indonesians love offal, and sate Padang is well known as a dish that combines tripe, heart, spleen, intestines and kidneys, and more, all cooked together in the sauce and served with compressed rice or lontong. For my recipe, however, I am going to be very choosy, and use only tripe, ox tongue and heart. If you visit West Sumatra, you should make a point of going to my birthplace, Padang Panjang, less than an hour's car ride from Bukittinggi. Near the market you will find the Sate Syukur restaurant, run by Pak Djafar, long reputed to sell the best sate Padang anywhere. It is an unpretentious place, but we certainly ate well there, at a very moderate price.

The sauce must be thick and served piping hot. Nowadays, everyone – even Pak Djafar, I suspect – thickens their sauce with rice or corn-flour. I myself still prefer to do it the way my grandmother used to, with water which has been used for cooking rice by the absorption method: that is, with just the right amount of water in a single saucepan. You need to put a little extra water, say a cupful, into the pan to begin with. Then, just before all the water has been absorbed, you carefully spoon off what is still lying on top of the rice. The water itself is slightly coloured and thickened by fine powder, starch and oils that it has taken

47

from the rice grains, and these are enough to thicken the sauce and give it a particularly good flavour. However, if you are not going to eat the kebab with rice anyway, then by all means thicken the sauce with flour, preferably rice flour.

Makes 48 skewers, or more if smaller

---

1 fresh ox tongue, soaked in cold water for 2–3 hours
1 ox heart
1 tsp salt

450 g/1 lb honeycomb tripe, soaked in cold water for 10 minutes

For the paste:
4 shallots, chopped
4 cloves garlic
2 tsp ground coriander
1/2 tsp ground cumin
1 tsp chopped ginger
1/2 tsp chopped galingale or 1/4 tsp powder

1 tsp chopped lemon grass
2–6 red chillies, de-seeded and chopped
1/2 tsp ground turmeric
1 tsp salt
2 tbsp peanut oil
2 tbsp tamarind water

Other ingredients:
225 ml/8 fl oz/1 cup hot water
1 turmeric leaf (optional)
112 ml/4 fl oz/1/2 cup rice cooking water, or 2 tbsp rice flour, diluted in 4 tbsp water,

plus 112 ml/4 fl oz/1/2 cup hot water
Metal or wooden or bamboo kebab skewers

Drain the ox tongue, then put it in a large saucepan. Cover with cold water, add 1 teaspoonful of salt and bring to the boil. Simmer this for 2 hours, then leave it to get cold in the water. When cold, peel the tongue, and slice it into 6 or 7 slices. Drain the tripe and cut it into 6 pieces. With a very sharp knife, trim off the fat around the heart, also cut away the arteries and fibrous tissue of the heart. Cut the heart into halves.

Blend all the ingredients for the paste until smooth. Transfer the paste into a saucepan, and simmer for 4–5 minutes, stirring often. Add the 225 ml/8 fl oz/1 cup hot water, bring the whole thing to the boil and add the offal pieces. Continue to cook these for 45–50 minutes. With a slotted spoon take out the tripe, heart and tongue, and leave them to cool on a platter. Add to the cooking juices the rice-cooking water (or the rice flour with 112 ml/4 fl oz/^{1}/2 cup hot water), and simmer for 5–8 minutes. Adjust the seasoning, then remove the pan from the heat.

Cut the offal into cubes, ready to be put on to skewers. Just before serving, grill the skewers for a few minutes to brown them. Reheat the sauce, and serve while the sauce is piping hot, with boiled rice or lontong.

Singgang ayam
Roast or grilled chicken Padang style

A standard, everyday method of preparing and cooking chicken in West Sumatra. Very good for a barbecue, but also good for roasting in the oven. Allow half a chicken per person with rice, potatoes, or pasta and some salad.

For 4 people

---

2 free-range chickens, each
   weighing about 1.5 kg/
   3–3^1/2 lb, cut in half

lengthways, all the fat
trimmed off and some of the
bones removed

For the paste:
4 shallots or 1 onion, chopped
3 cloves garlic, chopped
1–3 large red chillies
2 tsp chopped ginger

1 tsp chopped galingale or
   ^{1}/2 tsp powder
1 tsp turmeric powder
2 tbsp peanut oil
1 tbsp water

Other ingredients:
570 ml/1 pint/2^1/2 cups
   chicken stock
1 stem lemon grass, cut into
   3 lengths
1 turmeric leaf (optional)

2 kaffir lime leaves
570 ml/1 pint/2^1/2 cups very
   thick coconut milk
Salt to taste

Put all the ingredients for the paste in a blender, and blend until smooth. Then transfer the paste to a largish saucepan, bring to the boil, and simmer for 4 minutes, stirring constantly. Add the chicken halves and 4 tablespoonfuls of the thick coconut milk, and stir the chicken around so that all the pieces are coated with the paste. Now add the stock, and all the other ingredients except the coconut milk. Bring everything back to the boil, then turn down the flame a little. Cover the pan and simmer for 25 minutes.

Uncover the pan and add the coconut milk. Give everything a little stir, and continue simmering for 20 minutes, stirring occasionally. Adjust the seasoning. Up to this point the whole thing can be prepared up to 24 hours in advance. If you are doing this, take out the chicken halves from the sauce and leave them to get cold. Keep the sauce in a bowl and refrigerate when cold.

When you are ready to serve, grill the chicken on the barbecue for about 6 minutes each side, or roast in a pre-heated oven at 180°C/350°F/Gas Mark 4 for 15–20 minutes. Transfer the sauce to a pan and heat until it is hot but not boiling. To serve, either pour the sauce equally on top of each half-chicken, or put it in a bowl and ask your guests to help themselves.

Ayam pop
A popular chicken dish

This chicken dish intrigued me, because I saw it advertised in restaurants all over Sumatra. I was told that pop is short for *populer* – and indeed there are many popular chicken dishes in Indonesia. After trying this one in several restaurants I realized that although it looked like a nice boiled chicken it was always rather oily. When I asked for the recipe, I saw it had been fried, and this too is typical; most Indonesian chickens end up in the frying pan. Many locally famous fried chickens have been franchised or imitated all over the country: there are fried chicken restaurants mBok Berek, Ibu Suharti, Cianjur, and so on, in many towns, and they all have to compete with Kentucky Fried Chicken. One ingredient that is used by all the Indonesian recipes (but not by the Kentucky version) is coconut water – not the milk extracted from the flesh, but the water of the fresh coconut.

How could I mistake a fried chicken for a boiled one? As you will see, this chicken is really simmered in oil. The recipe here is one that has been developed by Donny Yudono, but the ginger, garlic and lemon peel condiment is my own invention, to replace the traditional crisp-fried onion which, delicious though it is, is used in many other Indonesian dishes.

For 4 people

4 chicken breasts, on the bone and with skin	*570 ml/1 pint/2¹/2 cups good-quality cooking oil*

For the marinade:

The water of 1 coconut, plus cold water to make up 285 ml/¹/2 pint/1¹/4 cups	*2 tbsp mild vinegar or lime juice* *3 cloves garlic, crushed* *¹/2 tsp salt*

For the condiment:

28 g/1 oz ginger, peeled and roughly grated	*4 cloves garlic, finely sliced then cut into tiny strips*
The peel of 2 lemons, cut into very thin strips	*3 tbsp lemon juice* *A large pinch of salt* *A large pinch of chilli powder*

Put all the ingredients for the marinade in a large glass bowl and marinate the chicken for at least 2 hours or overnight in the fridge. At the same time mix all the ingredients for the condiment in a smaller bowl and keep in a cool place as long as the chicken is marinating.

When you are ready to cook the chicken, drain it in a colander, with a bowl underneath to catch the marinade. Drain the condiment as well to remove the solids, and keep the solids aside. Mix the liquid condiment into the chicken marinade.

Heat the oil in a wok or deep fryer, and heat to 160°C/320°F, or until it is just hot enough to make a piece of sliced onion sizzle straight away when dropped in. Put in the chicken breasts, and simmer the chicken in this oil for 30 minutes, turning them several times. The object of cooking the chicken very slowly is to make it, not golden brown, but white in colour and very tender. While the chicken is cooking, heat the marinade in a saucepan and keep it warm.

When the chicken has had its 30 minutes, transfer it (without the oil) into the saucepan with the marinade and cover the pan tightly. Remove from heat and leave the cover tight for 10 minutes.

Now pat dry the drained ginger, lemon peel and garlic with some kitchen paper, and stir-fry these in about 4 tablespoons of hot oil in a frying pan until they are slightly coloured. Remove from the pan and drain on absorbent paper.

To serve the chicken, bone and skin the breasts, and slice the meat thinly. Arrange the slices on individual plates with the cooking juices divided equally, and spread the fried condiment over the top. This dish can be served hot, warm, or cold, and can be eaten by itself or accompanied with boiled rice or potatoes and cooked vegetables or salad.

Pangek ikan
Fish cooked in coconut milk with fiddleheads

My Sumatran grandmother would make pangek with a dozen or more river fish in her large belanga (a round-bottomed earthenware pot), with plenty of fiddleheads (paku or pakis, see drawing on page 64) freshly picked from her own land. In England I make pangek with trout, which I can buy fresh from trout farms, and Canadian fiddleheads in

jars, which are available in the food halls of large department stores. If I can't get fiddleheads I use the small, fresh asparagus that are available almost all year round in the supermarkets. These are imported from Thailand.

For 6–8 people

6 or 8 trout, cleaned and left whole with the heads on	*each cut across into 3*
1 tsp salt	*850 ml/1½ pints/3¾ cups coconut milk*
340–450 g/12 oz–1 lb/3–4 cups fiddleheads or small asparagus	*A handful or more of kemangi, or mint or basil or equal quantities of both*
2 stems of lemon grass, cleaned,	

For the paste:

6 candlenuts, chopped	*1 tsp chopped galingale*
5 shallots or 1 onion, chopped	*1 tsp ground turmeric*
4 cloves garlic, chopped	*4 tbsp tamarind water*
2–4 red chillies, de-seeded and chopped	*4 tbsp coconut milk*
2 tsp chopped ginger	*1 tsp salt*

Rub the trout inside and out with the salt. Keep aside. If you are using fiddleheads from a jar, drain the liquid and keep aside. Trim the asparagus if necessary.

Put all the ingredients for the paste in a blender or food processor, and blend until smooth. Transfer this paste to the cooking pot (preferably an earthenware or enamelled pot, but in any case not aluminium), and simmer for 5–6 minutes, stirring often. Add the rest of the coconut milk and continue to simmer for 10 minutes, stirring occasionally. Adjust the seasoning and transfer to a large glass bowl to get cold. In the same pot, arrange first of all the lemon grass pieces at the bottom, then 3 or 4 trout in one layer, then half of the fiddleheads or asparagus. Top these with the rest of the fish, then the rest of the vegetables. Slowly, pour in the spiced coconut milk. Arrange the kemangi, or mint and/or basil, on top and cover the pan, first with banana leaves or foil, then with a saucepan lid, as tightly as possible. Simmer gently, undisturbed, for 50–60 minutes; or put in a pre-heated oven at 150°C/300°F/Gas Mark 2 for the same length of time. Serve hot, warm, or cold.

Gulai paku

Fiddleheads in coconut milk sauce

For me there is no substitute for paku or pakis, the fernshoots I used to gather with my grandmother on our way to her paddy field in the beautiful landscape of West Sumatra. And her gulai paku was out of this world; I can't pretend that I have fully recaptured it. This is partly because fernshoots or fiddleheads are only available in London frozen or in jars, packed in brine or water. However, the sauce described here is excellent, so as alternatives to fernshoots I cook yard-long beans, which are now available in the West, or curly kale in the autumn, or broccoli in the spring. If you can get frozen fiddleheads from Canada, try cooking them this way, but remember to thaw them completely before putting them in the sauce.

For 4–6 people

450 g/1 lb/4 cups fiddleheads, or yard-long beans or other alternatives	*thick coconut milk*
	2–3 asam kandis (page 275) or
	3 tbsp tamarind water or
850 ml/1¹/₂ pints/3³/₄ cups	*2 tamarind slices (page 275)*

For the paste:

1 tsp sambal ulek	*2 tsp ground coriander*
5 shallots or 1 onion, chopped	*1 tsp ground turmeric*
3 cloves garlic, chopped	*2 kaffir lime leaves, shredded*
1 tsp chopped ginger	*1 tbsp finely chopped lemon grass*
¹/₂ tsp chopped galingale or ¹/₄ tsp powder	*4 tbsp of the coconut milk*
	2 tbsp peanut or coconut oil
4 candlenuts or macadamia nuts, chopped	*1 tsp salt*

If using frozen fiddleheads, thaw them out completely. Yard-long beans need to be cut up into 2.5-cm/1-inch lengths. Broccoli should be separated into small florets. If curly kale is used, discard the tough stalks, and shred the leaves roughly.

Put all the ingredients for the paste into a blender and blend until smooth. Then transfer this paste into a saucepan and simmer, stirring often, for 6–8 minutes. Add the coconut milk and asam kandis, or tamarind water, or tamarind slices. Bring almost to the boil, then simmer for 25–30 minutes, stirring often. Adjust the seasoning and add the vegetable. Continue to simmer until the vegetable is cooked, which will take about 8–10 minutes, unless you are using broccoli, which needs to be cooked for about 3 minutes only. Serve hot.

Daun ubi tumbuk
Purée of cassava leaves

The manager of a small family hotel in Padangsidempuan told me, when I interviewed him for my radio programme to be broadcast from the Indonesian Section of the BBC in London, that I must record this recipe. This cassava leaf purée is delicious as a vegetable to be eaten with rice, or as a stuffing for fish. In fact, even if I didn't have this mission to save endangered regional recipes, I would want to publish this one. I loved it, and I remembered where I had eaten it before – in my grandmother's house, naturally, in Padang Panjang. She called it gulai daun Perancis; Perancis means France or French, and I have no idea why cassava leaves should be considered French. Anyway, I am saving this from oblivion for the sake of the younger generation in Sumatra. You cannot get cassava leaves in the West, though cassava roots or tubers can be found quite easily in ethnic street markets or Indian shops.

I have made this dish in London with curly kale or spinach. I either purée the leaves in a food processor or, as people in Indonesia would do, chop them very finely and cook them for a long time to soften them to a purée consistency. The dried fish or salt cod can be optional if the puréed leaves are to be used, as I use them, for stuffing fish. For the fish itself, I suggest boned trout or red snapper; when stuffed they should be baked in a pre-heated oven at 180°C/350°F/Gas Mark 4 for 10–15 minutes only.

For 4–6 people as a vegetable, or for stuffing 3 trout or 2 small red snappers

---

450 g / 1 lb / 4 cups cassava leaves or curly kale or spinach
225 g / 8 oz ikan asin (page 263) or salt cod (optional)

570 ml / 1 pint / 2¹/₂ cups thick coconut milk
1 turmeric leaf (optional)

For the paste:

3 shallots, chopped	*1 tsp chopped ginger*
1–4 large red chillies, de-seeded	*1 tsp salt*
and chopped	*2 tbsp tamarind water*
1 tsp chopped lemon grass	*3 tbsp of the coconut milk*
1 tsp ground turmeric	

First of all soak the dried or salt fish in cold water for at least 4 hours or overnight. Drain and rinse them under running cold water, then chop them finely.

If curly kale is used, take off and discard the hard ribs of the leaves, shred roughly and boil for 4 minutes. Squeeze the water out, and chop finely. If cassava leaves are used, boil them for 6–8 minutes, then proceed as for the curly kale. Keep aside.

Put all the ingredients for the paste in a blender and blend until smooth. Transfer the paste to a saucepan and simmer, stirring often, for 4 minutes. Add the chopped fish and turmeric leaf, if used, and the chopped vegetables. Stir, and add the coconut milk. Continue to simmer for 35–40 minutes, or until all the coconut milk has been absorbed. Adjust the seasoning, take out and discard the turmeric leaf. Serve straight away with rice; or use as a stuffing for trout or snapper, as suggested in the introduction above.

Martabak Mesir
Savoury meat pancake Padang style

Mesir means Egypt, but why the name is used here I do not know. My guess is that this is Muslim food. In fact, as I explained in an earlier book, *Indonesian Food and Cookery*, this dish came to Indonesia from India. But I am almost certain that, even further back in time, it was a Middle Eastern dish similar to what is now called borek. Somehow it reached Malaysia, Singapore and Indonesia, and its name changed on the way. Here in Padang there is also a sweet martabak called martabak Kubang (page 211), presumably because the original vendor was a man from the village of Kubang.

In my student days in Yogya, we called savoury martabak, with a beef or lamb filling, martabak daging. The sweet one, with the same filling as

I found in Padang, was martabak manis.

What follows is a recipe for making a pastry dough that can be pulled out very thin, like pastry for strudel. The alternatives are to use filo pastry, or wonton skins (kulit pangsit in Indonesian).

For the filling, most street vendors use boiled beef or lamb or goat's meat, chopped or minced. The meat must be cooked first, because the vendor only mixes it with onions, spices and eggs just before he makes the martabak in front of his customers. At home, you can either make the filling with leftovers of roast beef or roast lamb, or boil the meat first before mincing it, or use raw minced beef or lamb.

For 4 people as a one-dish meal, or 6–10 people as a snack

For the filling:

500 g/1 lb 2 oz beef or lamb, roasted or boiled, or raw, finely chopped or minced	*1 tsp ground coriander*
	1/2 tsp ground cumin
	1/2–1 tsp chilli powder
3 tbsp peanut oil or olive oil	*1/2 tsp ground turmeric or*
1–2 onions, finely chopped	*curry powder*
4 cloves garlic, finely chopped	*1 tsp salt, or more to taste*
2 tsp finely chopped ginger	

To be added later:

2 tbsp finely chopped lemon grass	*6 tbsp chopped parsley,*
112 g/4 oz/1 cup chopped spring onions/scallions or chives	*preferably flat-leaf parsley*
	2–3 hen or duck eggs, beaten

Heat the oil in a wok or wide shallow saucepan, and fry the onions for 5 minutes, stirring most of the time. Then add the garlic and ginger. Continue stirring for 2 minutes, and add the ground ingredients. Stir again to mix, and add the minced meat and salt. Continue to stir and mix for 3 minutes for cooked meat, or 8–10 minutes if you are using raw minced or ground meat. Up to this point, the filling can be made a day in advance. Keep in the fridge until needed.

Just before you are ready to fry the martabak, mix the meat in a large bowl with the rest of the ingredients for the filling, including the eggs. Adjust the seasoning. Fill the dough and fry as explained below.

To make the dough:

225 g/8 oz/2 cups plain/
  all-purpose flour
A large pinch of salt
1 egg

84 ml/3 fl oz/6 tbsp lukewarm
  water
About 2 tbsp peanut or olive oil

Sift the flour and salt into a large bowl. Make a well in the centre and break the egg into it. Using your fingers, mix the egg into the flour while pouring the water in, a little at a time. Continue working with your fingertips until you get nice soft crumbs. If the dough feels dry, add a little more water. Press the dough into a ball, and on a floured work-surface knead the dough for up to 8 minutes, picking up and throwing the dough again and again on to the worktop or into the bowl until the dough is shiny.

Now the dough needs to rest for 5–10 minutes. Leave it on the work-surface, with the bowl turned upside down to cover it. After the rest period, divide the dough into four equal balls, wet the palm of your hand with some oil, and press each dough ball flat. This dough can now be pulled out to make a very thin sheet of pastry. (The martabak vendor throws his dough on to his work surface, pulling and throwing it again and again to make it paper-thin.) At home, you may need a rolling pin to help you roll the dough to the right thinness before you can pull it further.

As you finish each portion of the dough, get the filling ready. Oil a large, flat frying pan or skillet, and put it on a low heat. Spoon the filling on top of your thin pastry, and wrap the pastry round it to make a rectangular shape. Carefully put the filled martabak into the already hot frying pan or skillet, and cook, turning it over several times, until the egg is set and the whole martabak is hot. Repeat the process until you have used up all the ingredients. Serve the martabak hot, warm, or cold. It can be reheated gently in an oven, or on the skillet. It is not suitable for reheating in a microwave oven.

To make martabak with filo pastry

You need to use a double thickness of filo pastry. Oil one side of the pastry, spread the next layer on the oiled side, and brush this top layer with oil also. Then spread the filling, and wrap it as described for the homemade dough. Continue as above, cooking the martabak on a large, well-oiled frying pan or skillet.

To make martabak with wonton skins

Put four of the small square wonton skins on a lightly floured board, and put one heaped tablespoonful of the filling on each square. Then put another square wonton skin on top of the filling, and press around the edges with a fingertip.

While the martabak are being filled, pour about 110–170 ml/4–6 fl oz/^{1}/2–^{3}/4 cup of peanut oil or olive oil into a frying pan or skillet, and heat. When hot, carefully transfer the four filled wonton squares into the pan, and press the martabak down with a spatula for a few seconds. Cook for 2 minutes or so, then turn them over and continue cooking for 2 more minutes. These small martabak will be quite crisp on the outside, but moist and soft inside. Repeat the process until all the ingredients are used up. The oil in the pan will need renewing once or twice. With wonton skins, you will get about 20–26 small square martabak from the amount of filling shown above. These small squares can each be cut into four pieces, and served as canapés with drinks.

Note: Martabak can be frozen successfully. To serve them from the freezer, thaw them thoroughly, put them in an ovenproof dish, cover with foil, and heat in a pre-heated oven at 150°C/300°F/Gas Mark 2, for up to 10 minutes.

Nasi Kapau
Bukittinggi rice platter

I have several times mentioned Padang-style restaurants, where all the dishes are set before you and you only eat and pay for what you want. Many very small restaurants and warungs simply offer rice with one meat or vegetable dish: nasi ayam, for example, is rice with chicken cooked in the local manner. A little higher up the scale are small businesses which serve rice with a number of meat and vegetable dishes, with sauces, on a single plate. Every region has its favourite variations on this simple idea. Elsewhere in the book you will find nasi rames (page 171) and nasi tumpeng (page 173), both from Java; the first is sold in countless little eating houses, the second is reserved for selamatan.

Nasi Kapau is extremely popular in the Bukittinggi area, and the classic place to eat it is Uni Lis, a small open-sided space under some concrete additions to the Pasar Atas. It has something in common with a food court or a self-service restaurant in that the various things you can eat with your rice are displayed in bowls on the counter. You choose four or five dishes from a total of about sixteen, and the young lady puts them on your plate, wielding with great accuracy a long-handled spoon made of a polished segment of coconut shell lashed to a length of split bamboo. What comes to table is just your plate, well piled with food.

Most people eat with their fingers (using the right hand only), but spoons and forks, as well as finger-bowls, are provided for anyone who wants them. The food is extremely good, well cooked and fresh, because the place is popular and nothing hangs around being warmed up. In the meat section the gulai are almost all made from offal: liver, heart, intestines, and so on. There are ten different dishes here, including pangek ikan (page 52) and gulai paku (page 54). Every dish is the same price, which is low even by local standards: in January 1993, we paid Rp 1,000 each, equivalent to about 35 pence or 50 US cents.

Uni Lis herself is a Minang lady from the village of Kapau, who came to Bukittinggi with a few friends and neighbours and started this profitable business some years ago. They have many imitators all over West Sumatra, and the name 'nasi Kapau' has passed into the culinary language. The dishes served with the rice have plenty of chillies in them, and nearly all are in sauces made hot, yellow and sour by chillies, turmeric and tamarind. The one dish that everyone has is gulai kacang panjang, a gulai of yard-long beans; this is made exactly as the gulai paku described on page 54 (but don't cut up the beans, in this case they should be cooked whole). The beans are always the first dish put on to the rice as your plate is made up, and one mark of a nasi Kapau place is the uncut beans in the gulai. Other vegetable dishes are gulai nangka (jackfruit), gulai rebung (bamboo shoots), gulai tempe and cabbage gulai, as well as boiled cassava leaves.

An interesting omission is beef rendang. I have never seen beef rendang in a nasi Kapau; however, it is usually replaced by chicken rendang (page 42), sometimes with some tamarind water added to it. Besides the meat dishes, there are six vegetable dishes, and if you don't say 'no' to any of them, all six vegetables will be on your plate. If you just have these, and no meat, your bill will be even lower.

Berengkes ikan
Grilled fish from Palembang

In Palembang this recipe is always made with ikan belida, a freshwater fish that is not obtainable in England. In London, I first tried using Spanish mackerel. However, I found the paste does not penetrate deeply enough into the flesh and the fish is too oily. I therefore use skinned and boned fish steaks. To wrap the fish before grilling, I prefer vine leaves to banana leaves.

For 4 people

---

4 white fish steaks (weighing
  about 140–175 g / 5–6 oz each)

For the paste:

5 shallots, chopped

4 cloves garlic, chopped

3 red chillies, de-seeded and
  chopped

5 candlenuts or macadamia nuts,
  or 8 blanched almonds

3 tbsp tamarind water

2 tbsp peanut oil

1 tsp shrimp paste (optional)

5-cm / 2-inch piece of lemon
  grass, inner part only, finely
  chopped

1/2 tsp salt

Blend all the ingredients for the paste until smooth. Rub this paste on the fish steaks and keep them aside in a cool place. When you are ready to grill the fish, wrap the steaks in the vine leaves and grill them until all the leaves are charred on one side. Then turn the fish steaks over, and continue grilling for about 3–4 minutes longer. Discard the burnt leaves and serve hot.

Note: If you don't want to wrap the fish in leaves, pan-fry them in olive oil or clarified butter for 2 minutes on each side, turning them over once.

61

Empek-empek Palembang
A speciality fish cake from Palembang

The real attraction of this dish is the hot, sweet and sour sauce. For myself, I like it best when I serve empek-empek in London as an exotic warm salad of fish cake with Oriental dressing. But it originated as a Palembang street food speciality, and connoisseurs will tell you that you have to go there to get the real thing. I know only two people who can make really good, authentic empek-empek at home. One is an Indonesian colleague who used to help me cook when I had my delicatessen in Wimbledon. She was born in Palembang. The other is one of my brothers-in-law, Usman, who used to live in Palembang until he moved to Jakarta. He made some excellent empek-empek for me at his home in 1987, but when we were in Jakarta again early in 1993 he introduced me to a street vendor who, he told me, is the only one left in Jakarta who can make real empek-empek. I am sure he is right because all the other empek-empek I had on this trip, including one in Padang, were tough and uneatable.

In Palembang, people always use ikan belida for this dish (*Notopterus notopterus* or *N. chitala*), a good-tasting fish but with lots of bones. So the bones and flesh, without the skin and head, are pounded in a mortar until smooth. In England I use cod or tilapia and grind it in a food processor. The salad for the Indonesian street food version usually consists of cucumber, beansprouts and cellophane noodles. There are variations on empek-empek: you can buy them stuffed with duck eggs, for example, or dried shrimps. But plain ones are much tastier, and if you make them the way I do, mixing the pounded fish flesh with the minimum of flour, and not overcooking them so that they become tough and leathery, they make a lovely summer lunch or supper dish.

For 4–6 people

For the fish cake:
*450 g/1 lb skinless tilapia or
   cod fillets, cubed*
1/2 tsp salt
1 tbsp very finely chopped garlic
1/4 tsp freshly ground white
pepper
1 tbsp lime juice
2 tbsp rice powder or cornflour
2 tbsp warm water

For the salad:

1 cucumber, peeled

112 g/4 oz/1 cup beansprouts, cleaned

112 g/4 oz/1 cup watercress, cleaned

56 g/2 oz cellophane noodles

2 tbsp chopped spring onions/ scallions

2 tbsp chopped flat-leaf parsley

For the dressing:

2 tsp dried shrimps, soaked in hot water for 10 minutes, then drained

112 ml/4 fl oz/^{1}/2 cup water

1 tbsp sugar

1 tsp salt

2 small fresh or dried red chillies

(if the dried ones are used, soak these with the dried shrimps)

2 cloves garlic, finely chopped

112 ml/4 fl oz/^{1}/2 cup white distilled malt vinegar

More salt and sugar to taste

All these ingredients can be prepared well in advance, and refrigerated for 12–24 hours. You will then need only about 10–15 minutes to assemble and serve the empek-empek.

Put all the ingredients for the fish cake in a blender and blend until smooth. Alternatively, this can be done in a mortar with a pestle. Transfer the paste into a glass bowl and keep in the fridge for 10 minutes or so, while you prepare the rest of the ingredients.

If you are going to eat straight away, soak the cellophane noodles in warm water for 5 minutes, and drain them in a colander. Keep aside. If you are going to eat twelve or twenty-four hours later, leave the soaking of the noodles until just before serving. Assemble all the ingredients for the salad in a bowl, cover with clingfilm, and refrigerate.

To make the dressing, first crush the drained shrimps and chillies in a mortar with a pestle, then put these with the water, salt and sugar in a small saucepan. Heat, and then simmer, stirring often, for 3–4 minutes. Add the rest of the ingredients, and continue simmering for another 3 minutes. Adjust the seasoning, take the pan off the heat, and leave to cool. Refrigerate when cold until needed. This is to be served at room temperature.

Now, take out the fish mixture from the fridge. Roll it into a fat sausage shape. Put it into a deep-sided plate that will fit inside your steamer, and steam the fish roll for 3 minutes only. Leave to cool and refrigerate until needed. Just before serving, slice the roll into 8 thin slices or 6 thicker ones, and pan-fry in a little oil or butter for 2 minutes each side.

To serve the empek-empek, first boil about 1.1 litres/2 pints/5 cups of water in a saucepan. Take everything out from the fridge so that it will all be at room temperature to serve. Plunge the already soaked and drained noodles into the boiling water for 10 seconds. Tip them into a colander to drain. Divide them, by cutting them with kitchen scissors if necessary, and arrange the portions on 4 or 6 plates. Put the fish cakes on top of the noodles, two each for four people, or one each if there are 6 of you. Arrange the salad around the fish cakes, and just before you bring the food to table, pour the dressing equally over each serving. Serve straight away.

KALIMANTAN

Rivers and Trees

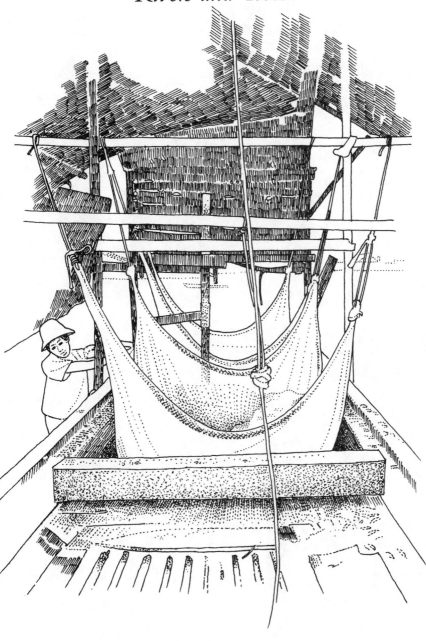

Borneo is the world's third largest island. Even when you discount the north coastal strip that is part of Malaysia, and the tiny, oil-rich Sultanate of Brunei, what's left is still about as big as France, with fewer people in it than Paris. Some are Dayak, descendants of the first inhabitants of the island, making a living in the forests of the interior or the coastal swamps. But most people live in small towns along the river banks, or cities at the great river mouths. The rivers – Kapuas, Mahakam, Barito, and many others – are still important means of transport between coast and interior.

Sanskrit inscriptions, Hindu remains, Chinese histories, show that this island has been on Asian trade routes for perhaps 2,000 years. By the fifteenth century AD, Islam had arrived in the ports and soon they were setting themselves up as sultanates. The Chinese are still here, and today there are rapidly increasing numbers of Indonesians from other islands, government people, ambitious businessmen, or farmers who have transmigrated here from overcrowded Java and Bali. Kalimantan is said to have great mineral wealth, but for the moment its economy is focused on timber and oil, with a little rubber and fish to help it out. Tourism is developing, but there are few good beaches, and no high mountains or spectacular monuments. Most foreigners come here on business. Four-star hotels, Western food and air-conditioned travel are therefore not particularly cheap.

From Pontianak, we were taken to see rice and soya beans being farmed by a Javanese village community who had moved here en masse a few years before. There is no compulsion about village transmigration; anyone who wants to stay behind in Java is free to do so, though the fact that your friends and neighbours are all leaving simultaneously must put a lot of pressure on you to go with them. There are effective support schemes to help everyone get going again in their new home. Some households were obviously doing better than others. Each family is given 2.5 hectares of land (a little over 6 acres); in Java, virtually all were landless. The people I talked to looked prosperous, by their own standards, cheerful certainly, and their houses had the fastidious neatness of the Javanese, people who carefully sweep every centimetre of their dusty front yards twice a day.

Later we crossed the Equator on the northern boundary of the town, and after two or three hours arrived at a village among low hills where local farmers were getting ready for their harvest festival. These were not wet-rice growers or peasant proprietors like the Javanese, but shifting cultivators of communal land, clearing a patch of forest, sowing rice,

67

beans, other vegetables, bananas and papaya, all together in the thin soil. They take one or two crops, and then leave the forest to regenerate for four or five years before they clear it again. Five years is barely long enough for the soil to recover, and this dry-rice cultivation can only support a very sparse population.

Another couple of hours of bumping along dirt roads will bring you, if you know the way, to a Dayak community, a single longhouse with a row of family rice barns opposite. Almost the whole structure is of bamboo, set up off the ground on massive bamboo trunks, its open verandah reached by a flight of steps chopped into another trunk. We were welcomed with great kindness by the adults and intense, but polite, curiosity from the children. Green coconuts were quickly slashed open with a machete, and we drank the juice from them as if they were goblets, sticky coconut water dribbling down our chins. Although the idea of a Dayak longhouse is romantic, suggesting war dances and perhaps a few severed heads, this longhouse, typical or not, was extremely cosy. It was in effect a row of terraced houses; each family had its own slice of the building, and when we were invited into one we found the only heads on the walls were those of Queen Elizabeth II and the Pope, in framed colour photographs.

There is little in the way of a food tradition in any part of Kalimantan. Most of the townsfolk are first- or second-generation immigrants and cook the dishes of whatever part of Indonesia they came from originally. But, as usual, you find better food in homes than in restaurants. My sister, who lived in Pontianak at that time, had a young woman in the house who was an enthusiastic and talented cook, a real treasure. I am sure she never saw a cookbook, but she had probably learned basic technique from her mother and was always talking to neighbours' cooks and watching food programmes on television. Her perfectionist approach appeared when she spent almost an entire day preparing bubur pedas for the family. You will never get real bubur pedas in a restaurant, it is much too fiddly a job. In any case, this is a special dish for occasions when the family is gathered together in private. Rice is first roasted until it is a beautiful golden colour, then ground by hand in a stone mortar. Herbs are freshly picked – daun kesum, daun kunyit, daun kecur and many others. There are twenty-four ingredients altogether, including lemon grass, galingale, ginger, fennel seeds, nutmeg and candlenuts. Our cook in Pontianak insisted that this was how her mother, grandmother and great-grandmother had all made bubur pedas, and she was certainly not going to be the first to change.

Such an old-fashioned attitude is probably rare, and was presumably not learned from watching television. I admit I would not spend six hours in the kitchen to make a hot spiced rice porridge, however delicious. In fact, the list of ingredients is similar to, though much longer than, that of the Minahasa dish, tinutuan (page 93).

We flew on to Balikpapan, an oil town on the east coast. One of the highest-profile foreign companies here is Total, and the strongest foreign influence is certainly French. To start with, a French management company runs the biggest hotel in town. I had a long talk with Gilles Tressens, who was just coming to the end of his tour of duty as food and beverage manager. He was off to Paris for a couple of months' leave, but, like almost every European who has worked in Asia, he intended to come straight back, and did not anticipate any difficulty in finding work in the hotel business.

The croissants here are perhaps the best in South-East Asia. They were a problem, Gilles said, until he realized that Indonesian butter, made by Australians in Jakarta, has too much water and salt for croissants; butter from Elle-et-Vire made all the difference. He agreed that the F&B manager has to plan a long way ahead to make sure his imports arrive when they are needed. 'But in Balikpapan, everything is imported, nothing grows here that is any good to anyone except papaya and pineapples. You are going to Samarinda tomorrow? Along the road, you will see thousands of pepper trees – a few years ago, everyone planted pepper. Then prices collapsed and the trees are worthless, no one looks after them.' We had heard exactly the same thing about copra in Pontianak, and were to hear it again about cloves in Manado.

Samarinda is an attractive and busy town on a bend of the great Mahakam. At its centre is a handsome new mosque, still being built, and an award-winning shopping centre, a little like Silom Village in Bangkok but less enclosed and much less touristy. On the way into town we stopped to buy amplang kuku macan, a fishy-tasting, crescent-shaped crisp savoury snack. Kuku macan are tiger's claws. In the shopping centre, full of rather superior warungs, we found one selling Banjar food, which is as near as you will get to an interesting regional cuisine in Kalimantan. We ought, of course, to have gone to Banjarmasin, a mere twelve hours' drive from Balikpapan, to learn about Banjar food on the spot; but one has to leave something for next time. The sea- and river-food that we ate in Samarinda was extremely good, though we couldn't bring ourselves to sample the turtle's eggs. They looked exactly like collapsed ping-pong balls.

Semur daging Pontianak
Beef in soya sauce Pontianak style

The flavour of the sauce here is different from that of any other semur. Mrs Saleh Ali, a good friend of my sister in Pontianak, made this for me with a round joint of beef, boiled first before it was sliced and then cooked in the soya sauce.

I include several suggestions for suitable cuts of beef. Brisket or silverside is obviously good if you like to cook your meat for a long time. The initial boiling of the beef will take about an hour. Don't put in too much salt – you want to incorporate the stock with the sauce later. I would make the sauce twenty-four hours or so in advance, because it tastes better the next day, and then use thick slices of the boiled beef, or thin slices of sirloin steak. I also use those very thin slices of beef which are now available in supermarkets in the West as well as in the East, and which are intended for making sukiyaki; they are very suitable for this dish.

For 4 people

336–450 g/³/4–1 lb topside or silverside, in one piece, boiled for 1 hour; or 4 thin slices of sirloin steak, or

about 112 g/4 oz per person of very thinly sliced beef (see above)

For the beef marinade:
1 tbsp dark soya sauce
1 tbsp lemon or lime juice

1 tbsp cold water

Spices to be roasted, then ground:
1 tsp coriander seed
¹/2 tsp cumin seed
¹/4 tsp fennel seed
¹/2 of a whole star anise
3 candlenuts, chopped

1-cm/¹/2-inch length of cinnamon stick
3 cloves
8–10 whole peppercorns
A tiny piece of nutmeg

Other ingredients:
1 tbsp melted butter
1 tbsp peanut oil

3 shallots, finely sliced
3 cloves garlic, finely sliced

*56 ml / 2 fl oz / ¹/₄ cup tamarind
water, plus 112 ml / 4 fl oz /
¹/₂ cup water or stock;
or 6 ripe tomatoes, skinned
and de-seeded then chopped,*

*plus 168 ml / 6 fl oz / ³/₄ cup
water or stock
2 tbsp dark soya sauce
2 tsp clear soya sauce*

The sauce should be made at least 3 hours in advance, and improves if made a day before it is needed. To make it: heat the butter and oil in a wok or saucepan, and fry the sliced shallots and garlic, stirring all the time, for 2 minutes. Add the ground or blended spices, stir once, and add the rest of the ingredients, except the chopped tomatoes (if used). Simmer for 4 minutes. If you are using tomatoes, put them into the pan now and continue to simmer the sauce for another 1 minute. Leave the sauce to get cold, then refrigerate it.

The roasting of the spices can also be done in advance. The easiest and quickest method is to put all the spices in a small thick-bottomed saucepan, and heat them gently. Stir the spices with a wooden spoon for 2 minutes. Transfer them immediately to a bowl. Let them cool before grinding them in a coffee-grinder or crushing them in a mortar with a pestle. Alternatively, put them in the blender with 56 ml / 2 fl oz / ¹/₄ cup of the tamarind water, water or stock, and blend until smooth.

Whichever kind of beef you use, marinate the slices for only 10 minutes before putting them into the sauce.

When you are ready to serve the semur, heat the sauce in a pan, and when it starts to boil add the slices of meat and cook for 3–4 minutes. Serve hot with rice or boiled potatoes.

Gang asam
Braised rib of beef from Samarinda

I haven't come across anything in England similar to the cut of meat used for this dish. The nearest was in an American restaurant in Knightsbridge, where I once had a barbecue of short ribs. In Indonesia this short rib is called tulang iga. This recipe is for an everyday dish, loved by children and adults, who would naturally eat the ribs by hand with plenty of boiled rice. If your butcher or supermarket can supply you with short ribs, use these; otherwise I suggest using back rib or thin rib, in one piece. Daun kedondong are used to give some sourness to the dish, so as a substitute I suggest rhubarb or young vine leaves.

For 6–8 people

1 kg/2 lb or a little more of short rib, back rib or thin rib	3 green chillies, de-seeded, each cut into 4 pieces
1.1–1.7 litres/2–3 pints/ 5–7^1/2 cups cold water	6 shallots or 1 large onion, finely sliced
1 stem lemon grass, crushed at the thick end, and cut across into 3	4 cloves garlic, finely sliced
	1 tsp crumbled shrimp paste
2 salam leaves or bay leaves	56 g/2 oz/^{1}/2 cup daun kedondong (page 265) or
2-cm/^{3}/4-inch piece of galingale	10-cm/4-inch stick of rhubarb, chopped, or about 10–15
4 red chillies, de-seeded, each cut into 4 pieces	young vine leaves, shredded
	1 tsp salt or a little more to taste

Cut off some excess fat from the meat, and put the meat into a large saucepan. Add the water, lemon grass, salam or bay leaves and galingale. Bring the water to the boil, and simmer for 50 minutes, skimming often. By now the water has reduced a little; add the chillies, shallots or onion, garlic, shrimp paste and salt. Continue to simmer for 25–30 minutes, turning the meat several times.

Adjust the seasoning of the liquid, which has reduced further, add the kedondong, vine leaves, or rhubarb, and continue cooking, turning the meat more often now, for about 10 minutes. Discard the salam and/or bay leaves, galingale and lemon grass, and serve hot, with the thick sauce. If one-bone rib or thin rib are used, cut the joint into thick slices.

Pecri nenas
Pineapple relish in coconut milk

This recipe is from Pontianak in West Kalimantan, though several other regions claim that the dish is theirs as well. It is normally cooked as part of a main course, to go on the table together with the meat dishes. But here, since I know from experience that pineapple will ruin any wine you drink with the meal, I suggest making it in a much smaller quantity and serving it as a relish to accompany any meat dishes. The pineapple must be fresh. Choose one that is not too ripe.

For 8–10 people as a relish

1 large pineapple, peeled and diced	1–2 tsp sugar (optional)
	570 ml/1 pint/2^{1}/2 cups coconut
3 cloves	milk
2.5-cm/1-inch cinnamon stick	
For the paste:	
3 shallots, chopped	^{1}/2 tsp ground cumin
2 cloves garlic, chopped	^{1}/2 tsp ground turmeric
1 tsp chopped ginger	1 tsp whole black or white pepper
1 tsp chopped galingale or ^{1}/4 tsp powder	1 tsp salt
1 tsp ground coriander	6 tbsp of the coconut milk

Put all the ingredients for the paste in a blender or food processor and blend until smooth. Transfer this to a saucepan and simmer, stirring often, for 8 minutes. Add the cloves, cinnamon stick and sugar if used, and the rest of the coconut milk. Continue to simmer for 5 more minutes, then add the pineapple. Cook on a low heat, stirring occasionally, for 8–10 minutes. Adjust the seasoning, discard the cloves and cinnamon stick, and serve hot, warm, or cold.

Pecri terong
Aubergine/eggplant relish in coconut milk

Like pecri nenas (page 73), this is from Pontianak in West Kalimantan. It is usually cooked as part of a main course, to be served with meat dishes. But here, since this is to come to table together with pecri nenas – or instead of it, if you are worried that your wine may be ruined by the small amount of pineapple the latter contains – I suggest that this should be treated as a hot and spicy relish. If what you need is an aubergine/eggplant vegetable dish, go for a similar recipe from Ambon on page 108.

For 8–10 people as a relish

---

2 large aubergines/eggplants,
  washed and left whole
3 cloves
2¹/2-cm/1-inch cinnamon stick

1–2 tsp sugar (optional)
568 ml/1 pint/2¹/2 cups coconut
  milk

For the paste:
3 shallots, chopped
2 cloves garlic, chopped
1 tsp chopped ginger
1 tsp chopped galingale or
  ¹/4 tsp powder
1 tsp ground coriander

¹/2 tsp ground cumin
¹/2 tsp ground turmeric
2–4 bird peppers
1 tsp whole black or white pepper
1 tsp salt
6 tbsp of the coconut milk

Boil or roast the whole aubergines/eggplants until soft. Boiling in slightly salted water will take about 8–10 minutes. Roasting in the oven at 160°C/320°F/Gas Mark 3 will take about 25–30 minutes. Leave them to cool a little, then peel them, chop the flesh, and put it aside in a bowl.

Put all the ingredients for the paste in a blender or food processor and blend until smooth. Transfer this to a saucepan and simmer, stirring often, for 8 minutes. Add the cloves, cinnamon stick and sugar if used, and the rest of the coconut milk. Continue to simmer for 5 more minutes, then add the chopped aubergines/eggplants. Cook on a low heat, stirring occasionally, for 6–8 minutes. Adjust the seasoning, discard the cloves and cinnamon stick, and serve hot, warm, or cold.

Lobster Tenggarong
A Tenggarong lobster dish

This recipe was given to me by Chef Baharuddin, a Padang man and the head chef at the Hotel Pusako in Bukittinggi. Bukittinggi is a hill resort, 1,000 metres above sea level and too far away from the coast for a live lobster to go, so the dish is not on his menu. But he created it when he was a chef in Balikpapan, the big and brash oil town in East Kalimantan. Some distance upriver is the pleasant little town of Tenggarong, once the capital of the local kingdom. Why the lobster is named after Tenggarong, which again is too far from the sea for a lobster to travel, I did not find out. But the dish is quite delicious, and also rather expensive.

You could serve this as a main course for 2 people on the half-shell, or slice the meat and serve it daintily off the shell to serve 4 as a starter.

For 2 or 4 people

---

1 lobster, weighing about
  600–700 g / 1^1/$_2$ lb

For the paste:
3 shallots, chopped
2 cloves garlic, chopped
2 tsp chopped ginger
^{1}/$_2$ tsp ground turmeric
1 red chilli, de-seeded and
  chopped (optional)

1 red tomato, skinned and
  chopped
^{1}/$_2$ tsp salt
^{1}/$_4$ tsp pepper
5 tbsp coconut milk

Other ingredients:
1 stem lemon grass, washed and
  cut into 3
1 salam leaf or bay leaf
2 kaffir lime leaves

4 tbsp brem or mirin (page 259, 268)
450 ml / 16 fl oz / 2 cups coconut
  milk

For the garnish:
2 red tomatoes, skinned,
  de-seeded and sliced

A handful of kemangi
  or sweet basil

To prepare the lobster, first of all rinse it well under the cold tap, then plunge it head first into a large saucepan just over half full of boiling water, and leave it there for 10–14 minutes. Take it out and leave it to cool a little before cutting it in half, from head to tail, with a very sharp knife. Remove the gut and stomach sac and discard. If you can find the coral, keep this to be put later into the sauce. Take out the meat from the shell, slice it, and keep aside. Crack the claws, take out the meat, and keep together with the rest. Wash and clean the two halves of the shell under the cold tap, and dry them with kitchen paper. Put them on a flameproof platter and keep them warm in a pre-heated oven at 100°C/210°F/Gas Mark 1/4 until you are ready to serve the lobster in the shell.

Put all the ingredients for the paste in a blender and blend until smooth. Transfer this paste to a frying pan or a shallow saucepan. Cook on a low heat for 4 minutes. Add the lemon grass, salam or bay leaf, kaffir lime leaves, and brem or mirin. Simmer for 2 more minutes, adjust the seasoning, and add the sliced lobster meat, including the claw meat. Cover the pan and simmer for 4–5 minutes. Now, with a slotted spoon, take out the lobster meat and keep it warm on a heated plate. Add to the sauce the rest of the coconut milk and the coral, if you have it, and cook, stirring often, for 5–8 minutes.

Adjust the seasoning again, and pass the sauce through a sieve. Arrange the lobster meat in the shells and place these on large dinner plates (or, for 4 people, slice and arrange the meat without the shells). Pour the hot sauce over the lobster meat. Garnish with sliced tomatoes and basil and serve straight away.

Masak habang, masak hijau, masak kuning

Cooking red, green and yellow: meat dishes from Banjar

Banjar is short for Banjarmasin, a large town in Kalimantan Timur or East Kalimantan. We made the mistake of not visiting Banjarmasin, and went to Balikpapan and Samarinda instead. The whole area around Banjarmasin is reckoned to be the real centre of Kalimantan food. Dishes like soto Banjar, sate Banjar and ikan asam pedas Banjar are known all over Indonesia.

The title of this section refers to meat dishes cooked in sauces that are red (habang), green (hijau), or yellow (kuning). The yellow colour comes from turmeric, the red sauce is cooked with lots of red chillies and the green with green chillies. Again I have adapted these three dishes so that they can be cooked anywhere in the world, and I have toned down the hotness to suit everybody's taste. Here I use chicken with the red sauce, duck with the green and beef for the yellow dish.

Masak habang
Chicken in red sauce

For 4–6 people

4 chicken breasts and 6 thighs, boned and skinned	*850 ml/1¹/2 pints/3³/4 cups water*
1 tbsp lime juice	*5 ripe red tomatoes, skinned, de-seeded and chopped*
1 tsp salt	
For the paste:	
5 shallots or 1 large onion, chopped	*nuts, roughly chopped and roasted until light brown*
4 cloves garlic, chopped	*1 tsp shrimp paste*
3–4 large red chillies, de-seeded and chopped	*1 tsp palm sugar or demerara sugar*
1 sweet red bell pepper, de-seeded and chopped (optional)	*3 tbsp tamarind water*
5 candlenuts, or 6 macadamia	*2 tbsp peanut oil*
	¹/2 tsp salt

Cut the meat from each thigh into 4 pieces, and the breast into pieces of the same size. Put all these in a glass bowl and mix in the lime juice and salt. Keep aside.

To roast the candlenuts or macadamia nuts, just put them in a frying pan and stir them around with a wooden spoon until they start to colour.

Put all the ingredients for the paste in a blender or food processor, and blend until smooth. Transfer the paste to a large saucepan and simmer, stirring often, for 4–5 minutes. Add the chicken pieces and stir-fry for 3 minutes, then pour in the water. Bring to the boil, then lower the heat a little and continue cooking the chicken for 15 or 20 minutes until the sauce is reduced by half. Add the chopped tomatoes, adjust the seasoning and continue cooking for another 5 minutes. Serve hot, with plenty of rice or potatoes or pasta, accompanied by your favourite cooked vegetable.

Masak hijau
Duck in green sauce

For the duck, I have slightly changed the method of cooking; the original method calls for the whole duck to be chopped up into as many pieces as are needed to serve all the members of the family. It also makes the sauce very oily, which my method avoids.

This dish should be hot, aromatic, and yellowish-green in colour. The yard-long beans can be replaced with fresh green peas (but not frozen or mushy ones). Naturally we eat this duck with rice, but boiled new potatoes and green salad will also go beautifully with it.

For 4 people

---

4 duck breasts
5 tbsp coarse sea salt

For the paste:
2 shallots, chopped
4 cloves garlic, chopped
3–5 large green chillies,
   de-seeded and chopped
2 tsp chopped ginger
1 tsp chopped galingale or
   1/2 tsp powder

Other ingredients:
2 kaffir lime leaves
4 spring onions/scallions,
   cleaned and cut into thin
   rounds
1 sweet green bell pepper

570 ml/1 pint/2¹/2 cups water

1 tsp chopped kencur or
   1/4 tsp powder (optional)
1/4 tsp turmeric powder
1 tbsp chopped lemon grass
1 tsp shrimp paste (optional)
3 tbsp tamarind water
2 tbsp peanut oil

225 g/8 oz/2 cups yard-long
   beans or 112 g/4 oz/1 cup
   fresh, shelled green peas
112 ml/ 4 fl oz/¹/2 cup hot water
Salt and pepper

Rub the duck breasts with the coarse sea salt and keep in the fridge for 4 hours or overnight. Put all the ingredients for the paste into a blender or food processor and blend until smooth. De-seed the green pepper and cut it into 4 lengthways, then slice it thinly crossways. Wash the yard-long beans, then cut them into thin rounds, just like the spring onions/scallions.

When you are ready to cook, rinse the duck under running cold water to get rid of the salt, and put it with the cold water into a saucepan. Bring to the boil, and simmer for 30–35 minutes, skimming often. This boiling of the duck is primarily to get rid of the fat under the skin. Discard the cooking water. Slice the duck breasts diagonally, cutting them thin. Set aside.

Transfer the smooth paste to a saucepan and simmer for 4–5 minutes, then add the kaffir lime leaves and the hot water. Stir, add the sliced duck breasts and the rest of the ingredients, and continue cooking for 3–4 minutes, stirring occasionally. Adjust the seasoning, and serve hot straight away.

Masak kuning

Beef in yellow sauce

For 4–6 people

---

900 g/2 lb topside or silverside,
    cut into cubes about 2 cm/
    3/4 inch on a side

570 ml/1 pint/2 1/2 cups water
570 ml/1 pint/2 1/2 cups very
    thick coconut milk

For the paste:
5 shallots or 1 large onion,
    chopped
2 cloves garlic, chopped
3 candlenuts or 4 macadamia
    nuts
1 tsp ground coriander
1 tsp chopped galingale or
    1/2 tsp powder

1/2 tsp chopped kencur or
    1/4 tsp powder (optional)
1 tbsp chopped lemon grass
1 tsp shrimp paste (optional)
1 tsp turmeric powder
1 tsp brown sugar
6 tbsp of the coconut milk
1 tsp salt

Put all the ingredients for the paste in a blender or food processor and blend until smooth. Transfer this mixture to a saucepan and simmer, stirring often, for 4 minutes. Add to it about 4 tablespoonfuls of the thick coconut milk, and continue simmering and stirring for another 2 minutes. Now add the meat, and stir it around so that every piece of meat is well coated by the paste. Add the water, bring to the boil, and simmer for 45–50 minutes. By this time the sauce has become thick.

In another saucepan, heat the coconut milk gently, and when it boils transfer it into the meat saucepan. Stir and simmer for about 20 minutes. Adjust the seasoning, and serve hot, with rice. Alternatively, like most meat dishes in this book, it can be served with potatoes or pasta.

SULAWESI

Water Music

Sulawesi, Celebes as it used to be called in the West, is an island that seems, on the map, to be all coastline. Its shape has been likened to that of a windblown orchid, but it more closely resembles one of John Wyndham's triffids. We landed at Dr Sam Ratulangi Airport, Manado, near the end of the outflung north-eastern arm of the island, up by the triffid's sting.

This is hill country, well populated but not overcrowded, with good soil and plenty of water to irrigate the rice fields. Around these intricate coasts and offshore islands are rich feeding grounds for fish, and shoals of tourists come to dive and snorkel among the coral gardens of Bunaken and Manado Bay. There are many Christians here, and the extravagant designs of whitewashed churches, inspired at least partly by a wish to see how far the architect could go with reinforced concrete, reminded me of those of the Philippines, not very far away across that ultramarine sea.

Dr Sam Ratulangi was a charismatic leader of the nationalist movement in this part of Indonesia. After independence, he became the first governor of the province. Every Indonesian town of any size has a street named after him. A member of his extensive family still practises medicine in the town of Tomohon, about 20 kilometres south of Manado and 700 metres up, on the saddle between two active volcanoes. It was the doctor's wife, Ibu Bernadeth, who met us at the airport, put us into her Kijang and drove us up the winding road to their house just outside Tomohon. Soon we were sitting on the broad verandah and eating a late lunch. It was 4 o'clock in the afternoon. We started with panada (page 95) as an appetizer. Then came a splendid fish soup or stew, chilli-hot and sour, and a dish of pakis or young fernshoots, also with a lot of chilli. The main course was ayam rica rica (page 90), a grilled chicken, brought to table whole, spreadeagled on its serving plate, and accompanied by plain white rice.

We wondered nervously if we were going to be faced by an equally large dinner in a couple of hours' time, but by now it was dark, the party had been gossiping about places and people and recipes for nearly four hours, the clouds had returned and it was pouring with rain. Everyone was ready to call it a day, and we were lulled to sleep by the plash of water from the bamboo conduit outside our door and the relentless thump and rattle of the downpour above our heads.

Breakfast was a huge bowl of tinutuan (page 93), from which we all helped ourselves. The doctor pointed out how healthy it was, and added that this is the favourite breakfast of President Suharto. We also had tai kuda (page 201), which means, politely, horse droppings, though it refers only to the shape of these rather delicious fried sweet-potato cakes. For breakfast we ate them stuffed with palm sugar, for tea with cheese.

Pak Dokter announced that he was taking the day off and would drive us to Lake Tondano and other local sights. We stopped to eat at a little restaurant that, he told us, is one of the last in the neighbourhood to cook in the traditional way. As a result it has a small but appreciative clientele and is doing good business where some of its trendier competitors are finding life hard. We saw the cooks setting up a row of short, stocky bamboos beside a line of smouldering charcoal; the top segment of each bamboo, open at the end, contains a packet of meat or fish which will be cooked by the heat of the fire. This process takes time, however, and they were preparing for the evening meal, so for lunch we had grilled tilapia from the lake and drank saguer, unfermented juice tapped from coconut flowers. It is a pleasant, quite mild-tasting drink, which, if it is allowed to ferment naturally for a day or so, becomes palm wine. It can then be distilled into tuak, at about 70 per cent proof. We were to drink excellent tuak a week or two later, in Tana Toraja; it is not, of course, encouraged in Muslim areas (that is, in most of the country), but this and rice wine are, as far as I know, the only forms of alcohol that can be bought cheaply in Indonesia.

Next morning we felt we could face Tomohon market. It sits on the side of the hill, its network of alleys made more confused by a one-way system that is compulsory for motor vehicles but not for horse traffic. The place is well crowded, as a market should be, and the people are relaxed and friendly, with faces that often show strong personality and even eccentricity, something one rarely sees in conformist Java. I admit it is not altogether as clean and well-regulated as Bukittinggi's pasar bawah, and the hi-fi systems blasting out the wares of the cassette sellers are as noisy as anywhere else.

But I could shop there very happily; the vegetables are profuse and splendid, the flowers gorgeous (Tomohon likes to call itself 'the city of flowers'), and the smoked tuna is a gourmet's reward for a long journey. There is a wide-ranging fish department in which many of the stock are still gasping for oxygen, and only the meat section gave me any qualms. We did not see (I think we were not taken towards) any recognizable dogs, cats, rats, bats, and so on, all of which are eaten here; but the flayed limbs of cattle hanging by the heels from gigantic hooks in the roof were impressive enough.

A day or two later we flew south-west to Ujung Pandang, where we impressed taxi drivers by telling them that on our last visit, thirty years before, the town had still had its old name of Makassar. In Ujung Pandang we hired a Colt to take us to Tana Toraja. The road north runs parallel to the coast, but always a kilometre or two inland, so that we rarely saw the sea. But the plain is a sea of rice, uniformly emerald green, bounded on the east by an extraordinary range of contorted limestone hills, looking like geological soufflés that have failed and flopped. Every 20 kilometres or so we crossed a girder bridge over a small river estuary, with handsome white-painted sailing ships tied up below us, rafts of green bamboo being floated to market or simply left to soak and season, and a busy little town nearby.

Between the towns, we passed farmers' houses built high off the ground, and roadside stalls selling fruit and dried fish — there were always a few large flatfish, split in halves and then opened out and hung from the eaves of the stall like bony grey-brown or silvery shop-signs. There were limekilns and brick furnaces, and sawpits where teams of men sliced forest trees into planks with two-handed or four-handed crosscut saws. A buffalo luxuriated in a deep roadside ditch, munching fresh grass from the hedgerow. A man in a coolie hat fished with a long pole in a rice field, the rice thick and green around him. We had a glimpse of sea, with mangrove trees teetering below high tide mark as if testing the water to see if it were warm enough for wading, and immediately above the tide mark the rice, presumably a salt-tolerant variety.

This long road north from Ujung Pandang is now in good condition, having been resurfaced and upgraded as part of the Trans-Sulawesi Highway that will run all the way to Manado. The journey to Rantepao, the centre from which most people explore Tana Toraja, is nowadays an easy and comfortable one, taking seven or eight hours, provided there are no floods or landslips on the way. The trip through the mountains is still spectacular. At Kotu we stopped to admire the mountain view and met a friendly cat in the coffee shop. We ate bajek, a sweet made like most sweets from palm sugar and glutinous rice flour but wrapped up most ingeniously in dried sweetcorn leaves. Four little cylinders were gathered together by the ends to make a kind of tetrahedron. I wanted to take some to the Symposium of Australian Gastronomy that we were going to attend in Canberra, but I didn't think the Australian Customs would ever let those leaves into the country. At Salubarani the road crosses the Sa'dan river and we entered Tana Toraja, with its extraordinary houses and still more extraordinary burial customs.

Next morning everything was silvery in early mist, and at this height —

about 800 metres – the air was fresh. It was February and the hotels were empty, apart from the occasional party of retired Germans or Dutch. The Toraja villages we went to see therefore treated us more reticently than they might have done in the high season; we still had to pay to enter each village and admire the tau-tau (and I think it is quite right that visitors should do so), but otherwise we were left pretty much to ourselves.

A tau-tau is a carved and clothed wooden effigy of a deceased relative, set up outside his or her rock-cut tomb. Naturally art collectors of all kinds love them, and they became some years ago magnets for any thief with a ladder. The tau-tau in the cliff face at Lemo village are almost all recent replacements. In other villages the originals have been taken in and locked up by their families for safe keeping, which means of course that they cannot do their job of guarding the dead; this is taken over by inferior copies of tau-tau, not worth stealing. However, if the copies fulfil their function as guardians, or if people believe they are doing so, how are they not genuine? And if people don't believe the 'real' tau-tau are effective, they surely are fakes just as much as the bad copies? My diary contains a string of questions, ending, a little exasperatedly, 'What is a "genuine" tau-tau? It's like asking, What is an "authentic" recipe?'

Sate babi Manado
Pork satay Manado style

Pork satay in Indonesia is usually made to a Chinese recipe, except in Bali and North Sulawesi. The Balinese have their own bumbu lengkap or 'complete' spice mixture to marinate the meat. In North Sulawesi the spice mixture is the rica rica mixture which is always very hot, because it is made with a lot of chillies. This is usually eaten with a sauce called dabu-dabu manis (page 88), not the usual satay sauce made with peanuts.

The pork can be boiled first together with the paste, then cut up and put on skewers to be grilled on charcoal. In London I use spare ribs of pork if I am going to boil the meat first, but if you use the more tender parts, such as tenderloin, just cut the meat into small pieces, marinate the pieces in the paste, put them on bamboo or metal skewers, and grill on charcoal or under an electric or gas grill. With the ribs, of course, you don't need the skewers.

For 4–6 people

1 kg/2 lb spare ribs of pork, cut into 10-cm/4-inch lengths	*568 ml/1 pint/2¹/₂ cups hot water*
For the paste:	
3–5 red chillies, de-seeded and chopped	*4 cloves garlic, chopped*
	2 tbsp peanut oil
5-cm/2-inch piece of ginger, peeled and chopped	*2 tbsp tamarind water or lime juice*
4 shallots, chopped	*1 tsp salt*

Put all the ingredients for the paste into a blender and blend until smooth. Transfer this paste to a saucepan and simmer for 4 minutes. Add the spare ribs, and stir until all of them are well coated with the paste. Then add the water, bring to boil, and simmer for 1 hour. By this time the water should have reduced considerably.

Continue to cook the spare ribs on a higher heat until all the water has evaporated. Take care not to burn the ribs. Up to this point the dish can be prepared in advance. Keep the boiled ribs in a cool place. When you are ready to serve them, grill them for a few minutes on each side or until they start to char. Serve hot with the sauce as a dip.

Dabu-dabu manis
Sweet and hot sauce

2 shallots, finely sliced	*3 medium tomatoes, skinned*
2 large red chillies, de-seeded	*and de-seeded, then quartered*
and finely sliced	*and thinly sliced*
2 tbsp kalamansi juice or lime	*1 tsp salt*
juice	*2–3 tsp sugar*
	2 tbsp chopped basil leaves

Mix all these ingredients in a small glass bowl, and serve immediately.

Ayam dibulu
Chicken cooked in bamboo segments

This recipe is from Tana Toraja in central Sulawesi, where chicken and fish are often cooked in this way. So too is pork, since the Toraja people are not Muslims. If you are in Toraja-land and want to eat this in your hotel, you will need to give the kitchen 24 hours' notice. The flavour and texture are excellent, but note that the chicken and fish are cooked with all their bones, so that the enjoyment of eating is rather spoilt by the necessity of picking these out. The menu in the hotel where we stayed called this dish pakpiung, but a friend who is an expert on Minahasa cooking says that pakpiung is the Toraja word for glutinous rice cooked in bamboo, the equivalent of what in Minahasa is called nasi jaha (page 97), and in West Sumatra lemang. Elsewhere in Indonesia dibulu has a final -*h*, but the people of Sulawesi don't pronounce the *h*, so they don't write it either. The same is true of tana (land), which also has a final -*h* in Indonesian.

Unfortunately, the right kind of bamboo is not available in the West, so at home in Wimbledon I wrap the meat in banana leaves, with an outer layer of aluminium foil, and either bake it in the oven or steam it. Alternatively, you can cook it in ramekins, also wrapped tightly in foil. I am not giving the fish version of the dish here, as it is very similar to what in Java is called pepes ikan, and there are several versions of pepes in the Java chapter of this book. Naturally my recipe is for chicken without the bones. The green vegetables I use here are substitutes for the cassava or papaya leaves used in the original recipe.

For 4 people

The meat and skin from 1 small
chicken, or from 2 chicken
breasts and 4 thighs, with all
the fat discarded; then
chopped into small cubes

2 tbsp lime or lemon juice
1/2 tsp salt

For the spice and herb mixture:
1–2 tsp sambal ulek
1/2 tsp salt
1 tbsp very finely chopped ginger
1 stem lemon grass, outer leaves
discarded, finely chopped
2 kaffir lime leaves, finely
shredded (optional)
A handful of basil leaves or
mint, or both

3 shallots, finely chopped
1 turmeric leaf, very finely
shredded (optional)
225 g/8 oz/2 cups cos lettuce or
spinach or curly kale, finely
shredded

Put the chopped chicken meat in a glass bowl, and mix in the lime or lemon juice and salt. Keep aside for 1 hour. Then add the rest of the ingredients and mix well together by hand. Leave the chicken to marinate in the fridge for 4 hours or overnight. Divide the chicken mixture into two portions, and wrap each portion in banana leaves. Roll each portion to make a sausage-shaped parcel, and pin the ends of the banana leaf wrappings with wooden cocktail sticks to close them.

Wrap each banana leaf packet in a layer of aluminium foil, and bake in a pre-heated oven at 180°C/350°F/Gas Mark 4 for 60 minutes, or steam the packets for 40 minutes. Alternatively, divide the chicken mixture among 4 ramekins. Wrap each ramekin in foil and bake them in the oven as above for 50 minutes, or steam for 40 minutes.

Serve hot, warm, or cold, with salad. Naturally, in Indonesia this dish will be served with plenty of rice, and in central Sulawesi the salad would consist of slices of ripe tomatoes.

Rica rica
A Minahasa dish with chillies

This can be made with chicken – ayam rica rica; or with fish – ikan rica rica. The three recipes below are ayam rica rica, ayam bakar rica and ikan bakar rica. (Remember the letter *c* is pronounced *ch* as in chilli.)

Although the Minahasa people use different names to distinguish between methods of cooking, the bumbu or paste is the same for all. Ayam bakar rica is roast or grilled chicken. In ayam rica rica, the chicken is boiled first, and tomatoes are added to the paste. Ayam bakar rica and ikan bakar rica are quite familiar to people in other parts of Indonesia, but the Minahasans also make rica rica with beef and pork. In my experience, the best cut of beef is rump steak, and I marinade the steak with the paste, then grill and serve it as medium-rare steak with salad. For pork, see sate babi on page 87. Here I give the ingredients for the paste, enough for one recipe.

For 4 people

For ayam rica rica and ayam bakar rica, you need a free-range chicken weighing about 1.7 kg/3¹/2–4 lb

For ikan bakar rica, I suggest 1 red snapper or 2 tilapia weighing altogether about 1.5 kg/ 3–3¹/2 lb (in Indonesia, we usually use ikan mas or gurami)

For the paste:

3–5 large red chillies, de-seeded and chopped
5 shallots or 1 onion, chopped
4 cloves garlic, chopped

2 tsp chopped ginger
2 tbsp lime juice
2 tbsp groundnut oil
1 tsp salt

Other ingredients:

112 g/4 oz/1¹/2 cups canned chopped tomatoes (only for chicken)
2 large red tomatoes, skinned,

de-seeded and sliced
4 tbsp chopped spring onions/ scallions
More lime juice and salt

Put all the ingredients for the paste in a blender or food processor, and blend until smooth. Transfer the paste to a small saucepan and cook over a low heat, stirring often, for 5–6 minutes. Leave to get cold.

To make ayam rica rica

Cut the chicken into 2 lengthways, and clean the inside part of the chicken well by rinsing in cold water. Put the halves of chicken in a saucepan and add to it the cold paste and about 600–900 ml/1–1^{1}/2 pints/2^{1}/2–3^{3}/4 cups of cold water. Bring the water to the boil, add the canned tomatoes, and simmer, uncovered, for 50–60 minutes or until almost all the water has been absorbed and the paste has thickened. Up to this point, the dish can be prepared several hours in advance.

Just before serving, take out the chicken, leaving the paste in the saucepan. Grill the chicken under a gas or electric grill, or put it on a rack in a pre-heated oven at 240°C/475°F/Gas Mark 9, for 8–10 minutes. Transfer it to a heated serving platter. Add the spring onions/scallions to the paste in the saucepan and heat for 2 minutes, stirring all the time, then spread the paste over the cooked chicken. Arrange the sliced tomatoes as a garnish and serve straight away.

To make ayam bakar rica

Cut the chicken as for ayam rica rica, but dry the two halves with kitchen paper after washing them. Put them in a large bowl and rub them all over with the juice of 1 lime and 1 tsp salt. Leave in a cool place for at least 2 hours. Then rub the chicken halves with half of the already cold paste, wrap them loosely in aluminium foil and cook in a pre-heated oven at 160°C/320°F/Gas Mark 3 for 45–55 minutes. Up to this point the dish can be prepared several hours in advance.

Just before serving, open up the foil wrapper, mix the canned tomatoes and spring onions/scallions with the remaining paste, and spread this mixture on top of the chicken halves. Then put them under a hot grill and grill for about 6–8 minutes. There is no need to turn them over as they have already cooked in the oven. Garnish with sliced tomatoes.

To make ikan bakar rica

Clean and scale the fish if this has not already been done by the fishmonger, and rub the cleaned fish all over with the juice of 1 lime and 1 tsp salt. Leave in a cool place for 1 hour. Add the spring onions/scallions to the cold paste, then rub the fish inside and out with the paste. Cook on a rack in a pre-heated oven at 240°C/475°F/Gas Mark 9 for 10–12 minutes, or under a very hot grill for 14–15 minutes, turning them over several times.

Serve straight away, with or without the tomato garnish as preferred.

Ikan kuah asam
Fish soup from Manado

This is another soup that can be served as a liquid stew with plenty of plain boiled rice if you want to serve it as a one-dish meal at lunch- or supper-time. But of course it can equally well become the starter for any three- or four-course meal.

This recipe is similar to the Ambonese ikan asam pedis (page 109), except that in Ambon they use tuna fish, which they call cakalang or tongkol. I have discovered that there are several other recipes which are very similar in both places; sometimes only the names are different. In Manado, Bernadeth Ratulangi, who gave me this recipe, uses garupa (grouper). In London, my choice is grouper or red snapper (in Indonesian, kakap merah or tambak merah), or maybe sea bass when it is not too expensive. Whichever fish you choose, it needs to be filleted and skinned, and the head, skin and bones are used to make the stock.

For 4–6 people

2 tbsp butter or peanut oil	*1 or 2 red snappers, altogether*
2 shallots, finely sliced	*weighing 750 g–1 kg/*
1–2 red chillies, de-seeded and	*1¹/₂–2 lb, filleted and*
very finely sliced	*skinned*
1 tsp finely chopped ginger	*2–3 red tomatoes, skinned,*
1 tsp finely chopped lemon grass	*de-seeded and chopped*
2 kaffir lime leaves, very finely	*2 tbsp finely shredded basil*
shredded	*4 spring onions/scallions, cut*
1 turmeric leaf, very finely	*into thin rounds*
shredded (optional)	*Salt and pepper*
850 ml/1¹/₂ pints/3¹/₂ cups fish	*2 tbsp kalamansi or lime juice*
stock	

Cut the skinless fish fillets into small pieces, rub them with about ¹/₂ tsp salt and set aside. Heat the butter or oil in a saucepan and sauté all the chopped and shredded ingredients, except the basil and spring onions/scallions, for about 2 minutes until they are all quite soft. Add the fish stock, simmer for 5 minutes, season with salt and pepper and add the fish slices. Continue to simmer for 3–4 minutes, then add the basil, spring onions/scallions and kalamansi or lime juice. Give it a stir, adjust the seasoning, and serve hot straight away.

Tinutuan

Manadonese sweetcorn, cassava and pumpkin soup

This is a very substantial soup, or a very good breakfast or lunch dish. For best results all the ingredients used should be fresh, but if you live in a place where sweetcorn is seasonal or does not grow at all, then by all means use canned or frozen corn kernels. If pumpkins are not in season, any yellow-coloured squash can be substituted. But traditionally, in the Minahasa region of Sulawesi, tinutuan has to be made with cassava. In the West, cassava is obtainable from Asian grocers.

For 4 as a one-dish meal, or 8 as a soup

---

225 g/8 oz/2 cups cassava, peeled and cut into largish cubes
225–340 g/8–10 oz/2–2^1/2 cups pumpkin or butternut squash, peeled and cubed
3 corn cobs, shaved, or 175 g/ 6 oz/^{3}/4 cup canned or frozen corn kernels

56 g/2 oz/^{1}/4 cup white rice, soaked in cold water for 30 minutes
112 g/4 oz/^{2}/3 cup bamboo shoots, sliced (optional)
1.1 litres/2 pints/5 cups cold water
1 tsp salt

To be added a few minutes before serving:
1 stem of lemon grass, outer leaves discarded, finely chopped
About 20 leaves of sweet basil
1 turmeric leaf, finely shredded (optional)

225 g/8 oz/2 cups young spinach, thoroughly washed
225 g/8 oz/2 cups water spinach, trimmed and washed
More salt to taste

First of all put the water in a large saucepan and bring to the boil. When boiling, add the cassava and rice and cook for 8 minutes, stirring occasionally. Then add the sweetcorn, pumpkin and bamboo shoots, if used, and the salt. Continue to simmer all these for 20–25 minutes. This mixture is now ready to become the base of the soup, and can be prepared and cooked up to this point well in advance. Refrigerate or keep in a cool place until ready to serve.

Just before serving, heat the thick soup, and when hot add the rest of the ingredients (except the basil leaves and additional salt). Simmer for 5 minutes only. Adjust the seasoning and add the basil leaves. Simmer for 1 minute more and serve straight away.

Binte bilo huta
Tuna fish and sweetcorn soup from Gorontalo

Gorontalo lies west and a little south of Minahasa, but their food crops are quite similar. This is another substantial soup made with sweetcorn, not unlike tinutuan (page 93), although here the only vegetables are beansprouts. Another difference is that this soup is actually a fish soup, or more accurately a fresh tuna soup. Alternatively, if you put in much less water, the dish can be served as a fish-and-vegetable dish to accompany plain boiled rice or boiled potatoes.

For 4 people

225 g/8 oz/1^1/3 cups sweetcorn – freshly shaved, or canned or frozen	*225 g/8 oz fresh tuna fish, cubed*
1 tbsp peanut oil	*4 tbsp chopped spring onions/ scallions*
4 shallots, finely sliced	*Salt to taste*
570–850 ml/1–1^1/2 pints/ 2^1/2–3^3/4 cups water	*2 tbsp chopped basil or mint*
^{1}/2 tsp sambal ulek	*2 tbsp chopped turmeric leaves (optional)*
3 tomatoes, skinned, de-seeded and sliced	*112 g/4 oz/1 cup beansprouts, cleaned*

Heat the oil in a saucepan and fry the shallots for 2 minutes, stirring constantly. Add the sweetcorn, stir for a few seconds and add the water. Cover the pan and simmer for 5 minutes. Now add the rest of the ingredients, except for the basil or mint and beansprouts. Continue to simmer, uncovered, for 4 minutes. Season with salt, and add the basil or mint and the beansprouts. Cook for a further 1 minute, and serve straight away as suggested above.

Panada
A Minahasa pasty

This recipe is from the Minahasa region of northern Sulawesi; the name is probably Portuguese. The pasty is filled with locally smoked tuna fish, which is a speciality of the area. Smoked tuna is available in some London delicatessens, but it is very expensive. So I use fresh tuna fish instead, though canned tuna in oil, now also available smoked (in Thailand, over sugar cane) is a good substitute. Panada are delicious as hot snacks with drinks, or cold for a picnic. Incidentally, this dough makes deliciously light, slightly sweet bread – bake it in a loaf tin for 30–35 minutes at around 200°C/400°F/Gas Mark 6.

Makes 36–40 panada

For the bread dough:

500 g/18 oz/2¹/4 cups plain/all-purpose flour or supermarket bread flour
300 ml/11 fl oz/scant 1¹/2 cups coconut milk

1 egg
4 tbsp sugar
1 rounded tsp dried yeast

For the filling:

4 tbsp vegetable oil or olive oil
250 g/9 oz/generous 2 cups shallots or red onions, finely chopped
10 cloves garlic, finely sliced
1 tbsp crushed ginger
1 tsp salt
450 g/1 lb tuna steak, chopped, or canned smoked tuna, drained

5–8 hard red tomatoes, skinned and de-seeded, then chopped
112 g/4 oz/1 cup chopped spring onions/scallions
3 large red chillies, de-seeded and finely chopped
112 g/4 oz/1 cup chopped basil or mint
Pepper to taste
Oil for deep-frying

Place the flour and yeast in a large bowl, sifting the flour around the side of the bowl to make a well in the middle. In another bowl whisk together the egg and the sugar. In a small saucepan, heat the coconut milk to blood temperature. Add the milk to the egg and sugar, then pour the mixture into the well in the flour. Gradually draw the flour into the liquid, using a wooden spoon, to make a stiff dough. Knead the dough by hand until it no longer sticks to your fingers; this will take at least 10 minutes. Cover the dough in the bowl with a cloth and set it aside while you make the filling. It will take about 45–60 minutes for the dough to rise to twice its original volume.

Heat the 4 tablespoonfuls of oil in a wok or frying pan and fry the shallots, stirring them often, until they are soft. Add the garlic and continue stir-frying until the shallots and garlic are just turning brown. Scoop them out with a slotted spoon and discard the oil except for about 2 teaspoonfuls. Put the wok back on a very low flame and put the shallots and garlic back in the oil. Add the crushed ginger and salt. Cook for 2 minutes, stirring all the time. Add the chopped tuna and continue stir-frying for 2 more minutes. Then add the tomatoes, spring onions/scallions and chillies, and cook for a further 2–3 minutes, stirring often. Adjust the seasoning, adding pepper to taste as well as the chopped basil or mint, and leave the mixture to cool to room temperature.

When the filling is cool, cut the dough into portions. With floured hands, or a rolling-pin, flatten each portion and make it more or less round. Put 1–2 teaspoonfuls of filling in the middle of each round, then fold the dough over and pinch the edges together to seal them, as if you were making a Cornish pasty. When all the panada have been filled and sealed, deep-fry them in hot oil (165°C/325°F) in a wok or deep fryer, 3 or 4 at a time, turning them frequently, for 7–8 minutes, until golden brown.

Serve hot, warm, or cold.

Nasi jaha
Manadonese sticky rice cakes

Rice cooked this way is excellent for any barbecue party. You can make nasi jaha well in advance and reheat them on the barbecue for 10 minutes or so, turning them a few times so they heat evenly all round.

These rice cakes are flavoured with lemon grass, shallots, ginger and pandanus leaf. The recipe comes from Manado, where they are cooked in bamboo segments. The uncooked rice and other ingredients are put into sawn-off lengths of green bamboo, in the proportion of half rice and half liquid. A number of these bamboo containers are placed, upright, around a wood fire, usually out of doors. Cooking takes about an hour, the bamboo being rotated several times so that the contents cook evenly.

Here, I suggest cooking the rice first in a steamer, then rolling the cakes in greaseproof paper or parchment, wrapping them in aluminium foil, and then roasting them in the oven. A more Indonesian way is to roll the rice cakes in banana leaf squares and then steam them. In West Sumatra we have a rice cake called lemang, which is similar to this but without any additional ingredients except coconut milk and a little salt.

For 10–12 people as an accompaniment

---

450 g/1 lb/2 cups glutinous rice, soaked in cold water for 2 hours, then drained
1 tsp very finely chopped lemon grass (the soft inner part only)
1 tsp very finely chopped ginger
4 shallots, very finely sliced

1 tsp salt
1 small pandanus leaf, cut with scissors into 2 or 4 pieces (optional)
450 ml/16 fl oz/2 cups very thick coconut milk

Mix all the ingredients, except the coconut milk, in a large bowl. In a saucepan, bring the coconut milk almost to boiling point. Pour the rice and other ingredients into the saucepan. Stir with a wooden spoon, level the top, and leave the whole thing to simmer, stirring once or twice, for about 10 minutes. All the liquid will then have been absorbed by the rice.

Cover the pan, take it off the heat, and let it stand for 10 minutes. By this time the rice will be almost cooked and cool enough to handle. Divide it into 2 or 4 portions, discarding the pandanus leaves if used.

Roll each portion in banana leaves or paper parchment. Banana leaf rolls can be fastened at both ends with wooden cocktail sticks. Parchment rolls need to be wrapped again with aluminium foil; twist both ends to make them watertight.

Steam the rolls for 10 minutes, or put them in a pre-heated oven at 160°C/320°F/Gas Mark 3 for 20 minutes. If you are going to cook the banana leaf rolls in the oven, it is advisable to wrap them first in aluminium foil. For steaming, and for reheating near the edge of the barbecue, the banana leaf by itself is adequate.

Serve hot, warm, or cold, unwrapped and cut into thick slices.

Lalampa
Glutinous rice cakes stuffed with tuna fish

Lemper are Javanese glutinous rice cakes filled with savoury chicken meat; other fillings are sometimes used, for example on feast days in Wonokromo, a village outside Yogyakarta (see page 164). Lalampa are very similar rice cakes from Minahasa; they are made in exactly the same way as lemper, but the filling is the one used for panada. The quantity used in the panada recipe on page 95 will be ample for the amount of rice shown here.

Makes about 20 lalampa

For the filling:
As for panada filling (page 95)

For the rice:
675 g/1¹/₂ lb/3 cups white glutinous rice, soaked in cold water for at least 1 hour, then drained

675 ml/24 fl oz/3 cups thick coconut milk
1 pandanus leaf, cut across into 3 (optional)
¹/₄ tsp salt

Heat the coconut milk in a large saucepan until it is just on the point of boiling. Remove from heat and add the salt and pandanus leaf. Stir, add the rice, and stir again with a wooden spoon. Cover the pan and leave undisturbed for 10 minutes. By that time all the coconut milk has been absorbed by the rice. Now transfer the rice to a steamer, placing it over a bottom pan which already has very hot water in it. Bring the water quickly to the boil and let it steam the rice for 10 minutes.

Turn off the heat, and transfer the rice to a large tray. Leave to cool a little, and discard the pandanus leaf, if used. When the rice is cool enough to handle, divide it into 20 equal portions. Put 1 portion on to a square of greaseproof paper or aluminium foil, flatten the rice, and put a tablespoon of filling on to it. Roll the rice, with the filling inside, to make a sausage shape. Then unroll the paper or foil so you can use it for the next one. Repeat the process until you have 20 lalampa.

In Indonesia each lalampa would be wrapped in a banana leaf; then, in batches, they would be grilled over charcoal. They would be turned once or twice, to prevent the banana leaf wrappers from charring too quickly, then unwrapped and served straight away. In England, I just arrange them (unwrapped) on a flameproof dish and put them under a hot grill for about 2 minutes each side, turning them only once. (You can, of course, wrap each lalampa in a banana leaf before grilling, if you wish; the leaf will give the rice a pleasant tinge of green and a subtle extra flavour. Discard the leaf before serving.) Serve hot or cold, as snacks at tea-time or with drinks a bit later on.

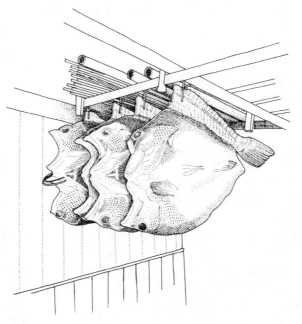

Pallu mara ikan
Hot and sour fish from Ujung Pandang

This is a delicious cold fish for a picnic, served with a good summer salad. It is also excellent as a sandwich filling if you mix a little mayonnaise into it to moisten it. Indonesians of course still eat pallu mara with rice, either plain boiled rice or compressed rice, but now that I have made a lot of un-Indonesian rice salads, I really think that a rice salad is the right accompaniment for this fish.

The taste is much better if the fish is cooked a day in advance. We normally use cakalang (skipjack), or tongkol or ambu-ambu (mackerel tuna or little tunny), with lots of lemon grass stalks to line the cooking pan. Make sure that the water for poaching the fish is sufficient to submerge it completely.

For 6–8 people

About 1.5 kg/3 lb 6 oz fish (3–4 mackerel tuna or 1 little tunny)	5–10 large red chillies, de-seeded and sliced
1 tsp salt	4 cloves garlic, sliced
1/4 tsp ground turmeric	5-cm/2-inch piece of ginger, peeled and thinly sliced
2 tbsp lime juice	225 ml/8 fl oz/1 cup tamarind water
450 g/1 lb lemon grass, washed	570 ml/1 pint/2 1/2 cups (or more) cold water
10 shallots or 2 large onions, sliced	1 1/2 tbsp coarse sea salt

Clean the fish well and rub all over with salt, ground turmeric and lime juice. Keep in a cool place for 1 hour before cooking.

Line the bottom of the saucepan with the lemon grass, and sprinkle about half a tablespoonful of sea salt over it. Spread half of the sliced shallots or onions on top of the lemon grass, followed by half of the chillies, garlic and ginger. Sprinkle on another half-tablespoonful of coarse salt. Lay the fish on top of this in one layer, then spread on top the rest of the onions, garlic, chillies and ginger, and the rest of the salt. Pour in the tamarind water and add water to submerge the fish.

Cover the pan and cook on a low heat for 40–50 minutes. The lemon grass may get a little burned but this will only give a nice smoky taste to the fish. Leave the fish to get cold in the pan, unless the lemon grass is too burnt, in which case transfer the fish with the rest of the solids, (except the lemon grass, which you can now discard) to a glass container to cool. When cold, store in the fridge. Just before you serve the fish the next day, discard all the solids and serve as suggested in the introduction above.

MALUKU

Spiced Islands

These are the Spice Islands. Cloves from Ternate and Tidore, nutmegs from the Bandas, were the triggers that released so much violence and jealousy in the hearts and minds of overseas traders, especially Europeans. Curiously, there is not much evidence that the locals ever cared very much about their spices. Wherever you live in South-East Asia, there are plenty of pungent, aromatic flavourings to be had from local resources. Why were the foreigners so insistent that they must have nutmeg and cloves, when they could have got lemon grass, turmeric and galingale in profusion? (Not, of course, chillies, which were brought to us by the discoverers of Central and South America.) The usual explanation is that spices masked the taste of salted or rotten meat at the end of winter, but food historians now think that this was not so. People simply liked the taste. (I have a suspicion that one of the chemical constituents of nutmeg may be mildly addictive.) They also used nutmeg and clove as medicines. More important perhaps, rare spices were a good way of forcing down your guests' throats how rich you were.

Maluku is the name of the Indonesian province which the English have long called the Moluccas, an area that includes Ambon (still called Amboina in some European history books), its much larger neighbours Seram (Ceram in old atlases) and Buru, then Halmahera and its tiny neighbours Ternate and Tidore, the minute Banda Islands, and so on and on – the Tanimbars, the Aru Islands, the Kei, Bacan, Morotai... nearly a thousand of them, some so tiny and remote that even imagination can scarcely reach so far. If you have weeks to spare, it must be an unforgettable experience to cruise these waters in a comfortable ship. The sea is deep and intensely blue; inshore water is translucent emerald, clear and unpolluted. But it is the sky and clouds and the light that put on the most memorable shows, especially around dawn and sunset, as if the sea was a stage for some extraordinary performance, to be played out by water and air and distance.

These islands are too far east to catch the full impact of the monsoon rain clouds, and many are too small either to make the clouds release their moisture or to catch whatever rain does fall. They are rocky, mountainous, dry, covered for the most part by jungle or scrub. They grow little or no rice, and the original staples were taro, sago and yams, with sweet potatoes and cassava arriving here in the early Portuguese ships. Coconuts of course grow everywhere (the eruption of Gunung Api in 1988 destroyed 120,000 coconut palms, but there seem to be lots left) and there are bananas, breadfruit and excellent durian. There are pockets of fertile soil in many places which are used for maize/corn, beans, squashes and various leaf vegetables, but you are obviously not going to grow aubergines/eggplants and fancy salads in these tropical conditions. For variety and excitement at table, the one food you should be able to depend on here is fish.

I admit that I found Maluku a disappointment gastronomically, though there are some good things which can be further improved. We went first to Ambon, where we stayed in a family hotel whose management and chef had all graduated from hotel school; it was therefore well run and the dining room was good enough to attract not only the hotel's guests but people from the town as well. Several of the recipes in this section were given me by the chef, Stefanie Wairisal, who also went to a lot of trouble to cook a complete Ambon banquet for us. It contained, as I expected, some excellent fish and seafood dishes and some very good local cooked salads. When I asked her what her Indonesian customers ordered, she said, 'Mostly steak.'

In general, however, the fish in these parts lack the variety I had hoped for. The fishermen here catch a great deal of tuna, but most of the more interesting fish, the anchovies and shrimps particularly, seem to be harvested by Japanese and Korean trawlers and exported, under complex agreements about aid and war reparations.

Andre, one of the family who owned the hotel, took us to his mother's house a few kilometres out of town, in a sequestered spot near the shore, well shaded by trees in a delightful garden. We talked about the soil and what will grow in it, and I asked him why there seemed to be no rice fields on Ambon, though the ground was obviously fertile. He said the people have never learned the technique of growing rice, which is very laborious, and they see no need for it. A single sago palm, between eight and twelve years old, will produce enough sago to feed a family for four months, with much less work than rice demands. With the sago they eat kenari nuts, kangkung or water spinach, a few vegetables that they grow for themselves, and a great deal of seafood. If they want rice they buy it in the market; it is imported from Java, and from Seram, the island that you constantly see from the north coast of Ambon. Seram is far larger than Ambon, and looks rather sinister on the near horizon; its forest-clad hills are obviously difficult to penetrate, and it is almost unknown to outsiders, or at least to the tourist trade.

On the day after Easter we flew to Banda, in a noisy little box-with-wings just about able to get on to and off the tilted runway that cuts across the whole width of Bandaneira. As soon as the engines are switched off, you are aware of the extraordinary silence of small islands in the middle of the ocean. There are very few motor vehicles. The clock on the Dutch church has stopped – it is said, at the moment the Japanese landed in 1942. The mosques broadcast their calls to prayer on loudspeakers less strident than elsewhere. The schoolchildren whose families live next door, on Gunung Api, commute to school on Bandaneira not in a motor boat but in little canoes; only their cheerful shouted conversations are heard briefly across the glassy water. The shoals of two-wheeled Hondas and Suzukis that fill the streets of every Indonesian town dwindle here to a gentle put-puttering along roads not much wider than footpaths. There is a curious atmosphere of time standing still, yet of tropical vegetation running riot on any patch of ground where it is not quickly suppressed.

You see this in the perkenier houses that form the old centre of Bandaneira town. These grandiose bungalows, with their deeply arcaded, massive-pillared streetfronts, were the homes of planters and merchants in colonial days. Some are still beautifully maintained, tiled floors polished, walls whitewashed; such places often make very comfortable homestays, where a room for the night in elegant surroundings (though perhaps without air-conditioning) costs little. But most of the perkenier houses are well on their way to ruin, their high cool rooms roofless and choked with weeds.

It is a strange sensation to stand on the Bandaneira quayside, or better still on the towers of Fort Belgica above the town, and try to imagine the explorers, traders, merchantmen and warships that have thronged this little harbour over the past five or six centuries. Today, all is silent and deserted. A Japanese pearl farm on Banda Besar, a few nutmeg plantations still recognizable from afar by the canopies of their sheltering kenari trees, a single surviving Dutch perkenier selling his nutmeg and mace at fixed prices to government buyers: economic activity in the Banda islands has declined sadly since the great days.

So has the local seafood. We got very tired of watching the same overcooked pieces of tuna reappear on the table at meal after meal. An Indonesian guest at the hotel went out for a day's sea fishing and came home with a splendid barracuda. When it had been weighed (17 kg, almost 40 lb) and photographed, he wanted to barbecue it and share it with the crew of his boat. But they whisked it from under his nose and took it to the market and sold it, saying it wasn't good to eat.

Next day we accomplished the return journey to Jakarta in three hops. While we waited five hours at Ambon for our flight to Ujung Pandang, I got talking to the man who had caught the big barracuda.

He was a retired banker, whose wife had given him permission to take a fishing holiday. The barracuda was the only big fish he had caught, but he seemed perfectly happy. 'Of course, I had to buy these for my wife,' he said, and showed me a beautiful pair of pearl earrings, which had no doubt come from the Japanese pearl farm on Lontar island. I was impressed, and I hope she was too. It is a universal custom in Indonesia, if you have been on a journey, to take presents back with you for your spouse, parents, children, relations, friends ... but from Banda, there is not very much you can take, except nutmeg, and pearls.

Terung goreng dengan saus santan
Fried aubergines/eggplants with coconut milk sauce

Stefanie Wairisal of the Mutiara Hotel in Ambon cooked this for me using long, thin, purple aubergines, which have a soft skin. You may be able to get these, or white aubergines; if these are not available, use the large, fat, purple ones, but cut them lengthwise into quarters instead of halves.

Farther east, in the Banda Islands, the sauce is often made with kenari nuts instead of coconut milk. The kenari must be blanched first. If you are making this in the West, I suggest you use blanched almonds instead. Put them in a blender with 112 ml/4 fl oz/1/2 cup water, and blend to a thick, smooth paste. Shrimp paste is used in Banda, but not in Ambon; so in my recipe it is optional.

For 4 people

---

4 long thin aubergines/eggplants, cut in half lengthways (or 2 large fat ones, cut in quarters)

2 tbsp salt
Vegetable oil for frying

For the sauce:
2 tbsp peanut oil or olive oil
4 shallots or 1 onion, finely sliced
1–3 red chillies, de-seeded and finely sliced
168 ml/6 fl oz/3/4 cup very thick coconut milk
3 cloves garlic, finely sliced

Salt and pepper
1 tbsp mild vinegar
1 tbsp dark soy sauce (optional)
1 tsp crumbled shrimp paste (optional)

Rub the aubergines/eggplants well with salt and put them in a colander. Keep aside for 2–3 hours, to allow a quantity of brownish-coloured water to come out. Then rinse them thoroughly to get rid of all the salt. Dry them with kitchen paper, and deep-fry them in a wok in two batches for about 3–4 minutes each time. Drain on absorbent paper to get rid of the excess oil.

Now heat the 2 tablespoonfuls of oil in a saucepan or wok, and stir-fry the shallots, chillies and garlic for 2 minutes. Add the thick coconut milk, salt and pepper. Simmer this for 10 minutes, then add the vinegar and soy sauce, if used. Continue to simmer for another 5 minutes until the sauce is quite thick. Adjust the seasoning. Put the fried aubergines/eggplants on a plate and pour the sauce over them. Serve straight away.

Ikan asam pedis
Hot and sour fish

This is another Ambonese dish from Stefanie – pedis is the Ambonese spelling of pedas, chilli-hot. The people there usually make this with tuna fish, but any fish steak that does not break up too easily will do very well. The secret of this recipe is the kalamansi juice, which gives the dish that subtle sourness. Lemon or lime juice (or even a mild vinegar), mixed with an equal quantity of orange juice, makes a reasonable substitute, but the taste, though good, will be different.

This is quite a soupy dish and in Ambon is usually served as a main course with pepeda (sago porridge), which is the staple food there.

For 4–6 people

450–675 g/1–1¹/2 lb fish steak, cubed, then rubbed with 1 tsp lime juice, ¹/2 tsp salt and a

little freshly grated pepper; keep aside for not more than 1 hour before cooking

For the paste:
2 cloves garlic, chopped
4 shallots, chopped
1 tsp chopped ginger
¹/2 tsp chopped galingale
2 red chillies, de-seeded and chopped

¹/2 tsp chopped fresh turmeric or powdered turmeric
2 tbsp vegetable oil
2–3 tbsp water

Other ingredients:

*1 stem lemon grass, cut across
into 3 lengths and slightly
bruised*

1 daun salam or kaffir lime leaf

*A handful of basil, or mint,
shredded*

*2 hard red tomatoes, peeled
and sliced*

*Juice of 3–4 kalamansi, or
1 tbsp each of lime juice and
orange juice*

Salt to taste

390 ml/14 fl oz/1³/4 cups water

Put all the ingredients for the paste in a blender and blend until smooth. Then put the paste into a saucepan or wok and heat, stirring frequently until the water evaporates and the oil begins to fry the paste. Add the lemon grass and daun salam or kaffir lime leaf and go on stirring until a pleasant aroma comes from the mixture. Add the water and salt, bring almost to the boil, and simmer for 15 minutes.

Then bring the liquid to a gentle boil and add the fish cubes. Lower the heat a little and cook for 2 minutes. Add the tomatoes, basil or mint, and kalamansi or lime and orange juice. Continue simmering for another 2 minutes. Adjust the seasoning and serve hot.

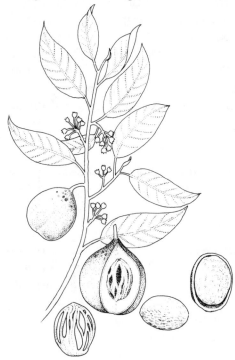

Dabu-dabu kenari
Raw vegetable salad from Ambon

Most Indonesians eat their vegetables raw and only cook them if cooking is really necessary. If there is not enough time to prepare them delicately, chopping and cutting them into fine julienne strips, you simply cut your carrots, cucumber, aubergines/eggplants, cabbage, and so on, into halves or quarters, shred them roughly if appropriate and put them on the table, just as you would do in the West with crudités served with a cheese or yogurt dip. In Indonesia the dip will be one of the sambals or chilli sauces or a peanut sauce.

Dabu-dabu kenari is typically Ambonese, as kenari nuts (page 265) are the commonest local nuts. Among the Minahasa people of North Sulawesi, dabu-dabu is nothing more than a chilli sauce (page 88), though it varies from district to district. Another well-known raw vegetable salad is the karedok of West Java (page 160). Here is my adaptation of a recipe given to me by Stefanie Wairisal.

For 4–6 people

The vegetables:

225 g/8 oz/2 cups yard-long beans or very young French beans

6 small round white or purple aubergines/eggplants (picture on page 101), or 1 large ordinary purple one

3 medium firm red tomatoes, skinned and seeded

112 g/4 oz/1 cup beansprouts, cleaned

1 medium cucumber

A handful of kemangi, or a mixture of basil and mint

For the dressing:

1–2 tsp sambal ulek (page 219)

1 shallot, very finely sliced

2 cloves garlic, very finely sliced (optional)

60–85 g/2–3 oz/^{1}/3–^{1}/2 cup blanched kenari nuts or almonds, finely chopped

1 tsp sugar

2.5-cm/1-inch piece of kencur, peeled and finely chopped, or ^{1}/2 tsp powder

Juice of 3–4 kalamansi or 2 tbsp lime and orange juice, mixed

1 tbsp finely chopped kemangi, or basil and mint

^{1}/2 tsp salt

Wash the beans and cut them into thin rounds, as if you were cutting spring onions/scallions. If you are using small round aubergines/eggplants, wash them, then cut them into quarters. Wash or peel the cucumber, cut into halves lengthways and discard the soft seeds, then slice across thinly. Slice the tomatoes. Put all these prepared vegetables in a large bowl together with the beansprouts and kemangi.

In another, smaller bowl, mix well all the ingredients for the dressing. Adjust the seasoning. Just before serving, mix the dressing into the vegetable bowl, toss the salad well, and serve as a starter or as a vegetable dish to accompany the main course.

Daun kasbi gudangan
Cooked green salad with coconut dressing

Daun kasbi is the Ambonese name for cassava leaves, a favourite green vegetable all over Indonesia. I am hoping that before too long they will be available in the West, but until that time comes it is worth making this cooked salad with curly kale. Alternatively, if you like vegetables with a bitter taste, make it with bitter gourd (also called bitter cucumber), or a combination of both vegetables, as described here.

For 4–6 people

---

225 g/8 oz/2 cups curly kale
2 medium-size bitter gourds

For the dressing:
1–2 tsp sambal ulek (page 219)
1 shallot, finely chopped

1 tbsp salt

225 g/8 oz/1 cup freshly grated
  coconut, or desiccated coconut
  softened with 112 ml/4 fl oz/
1/2 cup tamarind water

Wash the curly kale well. Trim off and discard the hard ribs, and shred the leaves finely. Keep aside. Cut the bitter gourds in half lengthways, and scoop out and discard the seeds. Slice the gourd halves across thinly, and put these thin slices into a colander. Add the salt to them, mixing well so that they are all coated with salt. Put the colander on a plate, because water will drip out of the salted gourd. Leave in a cool place for

40–50 minutes, then rinse well to get rid of all the salt.

Mix all the ingredients for the dressing in a bowl. Then wrap this mixture in a banana leaf, or aluminium foil, to make a small packet. Bake this packet in a frying pan or a skillet for about 5–7 minutes. Boil the vegetables separately in slightly salted water for 5–7 minutes. Drain thoroughly and mix the cooked vegetables in a serving bowl. Unwrap the dressing and toss it with the vegetables. Serve hot or cold.

Kohu-kohu
Salad of smoked fish and beansprouts

To make this salad exactly as it is served in the restaurant of the Mutiara Hotel in Ambon, you need first-class smoked tuna, which is a speciality of Ambon as well as of the Minahasa region in North Sulawesi. Very expensive smoked tuna is available in specialized delicatessens in the West, and it is, of course, perfectly suitable. However, smoked salmon is an excellent substitute, is easier to find, and gives a much more attractive colour. If the smoked salmon has already been sliced thin, cut each slice into narrow ribbons, like pasta. Another alternative is smoked rainbow trout. The best beansprouts for this dish are soya beansprouts, which are short; but the long mung beansprouts will do very well.

For 4 people

---

225 g/8 oz smoked fish, cut into small pieces
112 g/4 oz/1 cup beansprouts, blanched with hot water for 1 minute only and drained

56 g/2 oz/^{1}/2 cup cos lettuce or rocket, finely shredded

For the dressing:
4 tbsp grated fresh coconut
^{1}/2 tsp sambal ulek (page 219)
1 shallot, finely sliced

1 clove garlic, very finely sliced
2–4 tbsp lime or lemon juice
Salt to taste

Mix all the ingredients for the dressing in a glass bowl. Add and mix the fish, beansprouts, and lettuce or rocket just before serving.

Ikan pindang kenari
Central Maluku fish dish cooked with kenari nuts

The people of Maluku make this with tuna fish. In London I use mackerel, cooked whole, and serve it hot or cold. Blanched almonds can be substituted for kenari nuts. You can use kalamansi juice, or a mild vinegar, to give the necessary sourness to the dish, although in Java a fish pindang is usually cooked in tamarind water. The choice is yours.

For 4 or 8 people

---

4 medium-sized mackerel, about 225–336 g/8–12 oz each, cleaned, with the heads intact; — rub the fish inside and outside with some salt, and keep aside for 1–2 hours before cooking

For the paste:
2 cloves garlic, chopped
4 shallots, chopped
56 g/2 oz/^{1}/$_3$ cup blanched kenari nuts or almonds, chopped
1 tsp chopped ginger
^{1}/$_2$ tsp chopped galingale

2 red chillies, de-seeded and chopped
1 tsp chopped fresh turmeric or powdered turmeric
2 tbsp vegetable oil
3 tbsp water

Other ingredients:
1 stem of lemon grass, cut into 3 lengths and slightly bruised
1 daun salam or kaffir lime leaf
500 ml/14 fl oz/1^3/$_4$ cups water
2 tbsp mild vinegar or 3 tbsp tamarind water

A handful of basil and mint, shredded
2 hard red tomatoes, peeled and sliced (optional)
Salt to taste

Put all the ingredients for the paste in a blender and blend until smooth. Then put the paste into a saucepan or wok and heat, stirring frequently, until the water evaporates and the oil begins to fry the paste. Add the lemon grass and daun salam or kaffir lime leaf, and go on stirring until a pleasant aroma comes from the mixture. Add the water, vinegar or tamarind water, and salt, bring almost to the boil and simmer for 15 minutes.

Then bring the liquid to a gentle boil and add the fish. Lower the heat a little, cover the pan and simmer for 20 minutes. Uncover, and add the tomatoes, if used, then the basil and mint. Continue simmering for another 2 minutes. Adjust the seasoning and serve hot or cold, with some salad.

Sasate
Fish cake from Maluku

Until recently, the best fish cakes I had ever made were to a Thai recipe. But these Indonesian ones are as good. The recipe is from Mrs Nella Lesiwal of Nusa Laut, one of the islands in the Moluccas. The popular fish there are tuna, tenggiri and tongkol, and the nuts are kenari nuts. In London I make these fish cakes with fresh Spanish mackerel or fresh cod, replacing the kenari nuts with the same quantity of blanched almonds or brazil nuts.

For 4–6 as part of a main course

2 mackerel, skinned, boned and filleted; or 450 g / 1 lb boneless	*cod fillet, cut into small cubes*

For the spice mixture:

2 tsp coriander seeds, roasted	*2 tsp finely chopped lemon grass*
1 tsp cumin seeds, roasted	*112 g / 4 oz / 2/3 cup blanched*
1–2 small dried chillies (optional)	*kenari, almonds, or brazil*
3 shallots, finely sliced	*nuts, blended to a paste*
3 cloves garlic, finely sliced	*1 tsp salt*
1 tsp chopped ginger	*2 tbsp tamarind water or*
1 tsp chopped fresh galingale	*kalamansi juice or lime juice*

To be added during blending:
The white of 1 egg, lightly beaten

Mix all the ingredients for the spice mixture in a glass bowl and mix in the fish cubes. Leave to marinate for 3–4 hours or overnight in the fridge. Just before you are ready to serve the fish cake, put everything from the glass bowl plus the egg white into a blender or food processor, and blend for a few seconds. Fry a teaspoonful of the mixture to taste the salt, and, if necessary, add more salt or light soya sauce to taste. Form the fish mixture into 6 or 8 round cakes and shallow-fry them for about 3 minutes on one side. Turn them over and fry for 3–4 more minutes. Serve hot with potatoes or rice and some salad.

Variation: The original Indonesian way of frying these fish cakes is to deep-fry them in a wok. Usually they are formed into cakes the size of small fritters.

Bumbu hijau ayam
Banda style chicken, stir-fried with green chillies

Tanya Alwi from Bandaneira gave me this recipe. Again, I don't think the way I cook this resembles very closely what you would get in restaurants on the island. I use all the ingredients that are used there, but my chicken is limited to tender slices of chicken breast, without the skin.

For 4 people

4 chicken breasts, without skin	*1 green chilli/green pepper,*
1 tbsp lime juice	*de-seeded*
1/4 tsp salt	*1 tbsp peanut oil*
10-cm/4-inch stem of lemon grass, outer leaves discarded	*3–4 tbsp hot water (if necessary)*

For the paste:

3–5 large green chillies, or 1 green sweet bell pepper, de-seeded and chopped	*30 g/1 oz/2 tbsp kenari nuts or blanched almonds*
5 shallots, chopped	*2 tbsp peanut oil*
4 cloves garlic, chopped	*2 tbsp tamarind water or lime juice*
1 tsp chopped ginger	*1/4 tsp salt*

Slice each of the chicken breasts diagonally into 5 or 6 thin slices. Put these into a glass bowl and rub them all over with the lime juice and salt. Keep aside while you prepare the rest of the ingredients. Slice the inner part of the stem of lemon grass very finely, and keep aside. Do the same with the green chillies or green pepper.

Put all the ingredients for the paste into a blender or food processor, and blend until smooth. Transfer the smooth paste to a wok or a shallow saucepan. Simmer the paste on a low heat for 4–6 minutes, stirring often. Now add the extra 1 tablespoonful of oil. Then add the sliced lemon grass and green chillies or pepper, stir-fry for 1 minute, and add the chicken slices. Continue to cook, now on a higher heat, stirring often, for 6–8 minutes. Add 3 or 4 tablespoonfuls of hot water halfway through cooking, if necessary. Adjust the seasoning, and when the chicken is cooked serve at once.

BALI AND NUSATENGGARA

An Unexpected Pleasure

'The south-eastern islands' – it sounds less romantic in English than it does in Indonesian. It even suggests that there must be something a bit miscellaneous about them. And indeed they do not have very much in common. The largest, and the most south-easterly, is Timor. Another big island, south of the main group, is Sumba, a great place for weavers. But most of the islands lie strung out across the ocean like the eroded vertebrae of some long-dead sea monster. Between Flores and Sumbawa lies a tiny island that everyone knows about: Komodo, famous for dragons. At the western end of the sea monster's spine you will find Lombok, just beginning to penetrate the sun-seeking tourist's consciousness, and between Lombok and Java perhaps the most celebrated, least understood island in the world – Bali.

I had better not pretend to understand the soul of Bali; I am not a Balinese. Still, one of my grandparents came from Central Java, which was the birthplace of the Hindu culture we now regard as the essence of Balinese life, so I can regard the Balinese as distant cousins. Much more important, modern Bali is Indonesian. The Indonesian language, way of life, administration, attitudes – these are firmly in place, overlying the traditional life of ritual and craftsmanship (still expressed in the Balinese language), and underpinning the surface gloss of international travel and commerce (expressed, with increasing confidence, in English).

The Balinese have always had, even more than other Indonesians, a genius for absorbing and then changing ideas and knowledge from other countries. Hinduism came to Bali over 1,000 years ago. Later, when the last Hindu kingdom in Java fell to the forces of Islam, its traditions, regalia and many of its people crossed the narrow straits and took refuge in Bali, where they continued pretty well undisturbed for another 400 years. The Dutch left the Balinese more or less alone until 1900, though they knew the island well and were fascinated by its culture as well as shocked and titillated by the Hindu custom of widow-burning. So Bali developed for centuries in isolation, rather like a sort of miniature Japan, developing a style of its own which is instantly recognizable, and which nowadays therefore is spread like butter over airports, five-star hotels and other intrusive buildings.

Lombok, next door to the east, has a more prosaic history. Its people are mostly Muslim, with a Hindu minority descended from the Balinese who ruled the place in the days when its original Sasak inhabitants were primitive animists. Lombok is in the transition zone between tropical wet South-East Asia and tropical dry Australasia; it has suffered from recurrent drought and famine. At the moment, it is a fertile, friendly and altogether delightful spot, more relaxed than Bali and definitely one of my favourite islands. About its future, I am not so sure.

Everyone tells you Bali has been spoilt by tourism. Even the Balinese, if pressed, will look gloomy and say, 'Yes, of course, Bali is ruined.' I don't think they believe this themselves. We first went to Bali on honeymoon in 1962, and I find that in many ways those thirty years have greatly improved it. It depends on what you want, or expect, to see. Bali was never a happy, innocent tropical paradise of artists who did a bit of rice farming on the side. It was a complex, inflexible society of clever and sensitive people who had to work enormously hard to get a living from a hostile landscape. Most of western Bali and much of the north is still infertile and sparsely populated; tourists don't go there much. The Bali the world knows about is the eastern half, especially the south-east corner, where rushing rivers cut long, narrow valleys through the foothills of Gunung Agung. Agung, the volcano, has made this part of Bali fertile but has often destroyed it. The terraced fields that climb the hillsides create some of the most beautiful landscapes in the world, but their building and maintenance demand many skills and continual labour.

Bali is a place where the tensions of tropical life are focused and intensified. Every middle-aged Balinese today has lived through two terrible experiences: the eruption of Gunung Agung in 1963, and the anti-Communist massacre two and a half years later. Older people remember the Japanese occupation and the revolution. In the 1960s there were people still living who could recall the final Dutch takeover of the island in 1906 and 1908, marked by ritual mass suicide and the burning or bombardment of temples and palaces.

Against such a background, my complaint in 1962 that you couldn't get a decent meal in Bali unless you knew some very influential people will sound trivial and unworthy. Still, the lack of good food was a facet of Balinese poverty and a result of Balinese suffering. I have no time for tropical paradises that depend on the local population being kept poor and exploitable. Mass tourism has put many areas of the world under stress. The Balinese have accepted this and are responding to it. Their new way of life is very different from the old one, but the old survives within it.

I have to say, though, that Balinese food is still a little hard to find. On a previous visit I had had babi guling, a sucking pig roasted whole on a spit (page 10) in the seafront gardens of my hotel, and I had eaten bebek betutu (page 126) cooked by monks in a trench full of glowing embers. Probably you can still find both of these, but the hotels and restaurants we visited on our latest trip were serving almost nothing that could be regarded as specifically Balinese. I asked François Waller, the food and beverage manager of the Nusa Indah Resort, about his menu for the Brasserie La Lagune, which was full of intriguing combinations of Eastern and Western food. François told us that the menu had been compiled by his predecessor, an Austrian called Otto King, who now runs his own restaurant a few kilometres away. He also suggested we should eat at a seafood restaurant nearby which he thought represented contemporary Balinese food; he said it was very successful, government ministers always went there when they were on official trips.

This seafood restaurant was the first of three places that we ate at and that seemed to me to typify the present state of tourist and public eating in Bali. It had an enjoyably laid-back atmosphere and the food was not bad, but the menu and cooking were unimaginative and rather expensive. Against my better judgement, I was persuaded to order a seafood platter, which looked like a low-tide massacre, served in a dish too small for it. The fish and shellfish had been severely overcooked, and of course they were served the Indonesian way, with all their bones, shells and claws more or less intact.

The second, Otto King's Bali Edelweiss restaurant, is a small square building with perhaps a dozen tables. The place is run by Otto and his Indonesian wife as a kind of missionary outpost of gastronomy. Otto, who is still a freelance consultant to several international hotels, turned out to be much younger than we had expected, a thin, intense man with lank hair and side whiskers, evidently burning up calories to provide limitless energy and fuel a constant stream of ideas and talk. His menu is eclectic but there is no feeling of straining for effect. He likes and admires Indonesian food but sees no reason to compete with local warung-keepers who are specialists and have total control of their product from start to finish – something that hotel chefs, as he pointed out, do not have. He uses spices and chillies sparingly. I ordered the seafood platter because I wanted to compare it with the one I had had the night before; it arrived in a huge and very beautiful earthenware bowl, which Otto said was from Lombok, and everything was lightly cooked and tender, done in the Indonesian way but dressed and served Western-style with a tartar sauce.

Otto told us that we should have a look at the Amanda Food Center, and on our last night in Bali we ate there. It is on the main road to the airport, a brash new white-painted building, about the size and shape of a large chapel. The nave is lined on both sides with food stalls, about thirty of them altogether, like those you might see in a street market, but sparkling clean and very new. Behind them we could see cooking and washing facilities, also spotless. In fact, the place had only been open about six weeks when we went there. You can look around at what the stalls are selling, order what you want and eat it at any vacant table. The stalls are let to individual traders, and the proprietors hope that many regions of Indonesia will be represented. Significantly perhaps, there was no stall selling Balinese food. We had soto Madura, ayam goreng Kalasan, gado-gado and bakwan tahu (pages 157, 149, 183, and 153 respectively) – quite a gastronomic tour, and all good.

Of course, these experiences left the heart of Bali unvisited. Undoubtedly the most all-round satisfying meal that we had was in a lovely old Balinese family home, at the top of the hill in Ubud, sitting in an open-sided pavilion and enjoying a midday breeze lightly perfumed with the scent of rice ripening in the fields around us. Minced pork cooked in little banana-leaf packets; satay; shredded chicken; several dishes of lightly cooked, lightly spiced vegetables; these were personal versions of dishes found all over Indonesia, cooked by someone who had travelled all over the world but remained completely Balinese. This is the great gift that Bali gives to its people, the ability to know the world and do well in it, and to retain the character of their upbringing.

Some people say Lombok is like Bali was thirty years ago. It certainly has a distinct personality of its own, but it is less vivid than Bali's, more passive and I think less able to defend itself against the outside world. In the twenty-two months that had elapsed since my previous visit, the island had been assaulted by hotel mania; large areas on the west and south coasts, including many of the best beaches, had vanished behind high fences, brightly painted with the names of international hotel chains. I wonder if there will be enough visitors to fill all the bedrooms that are planned; and if there are, whether the necessary infrastructure – air services, food supplies, transport – can be provided without ruining the rather fragile charm of this small green place.

The oldest among the first-class hotels, and the one which has perhaps the best location of all, is the Senggigi Beach, set astride a little sandy peninsula, facing west across the strait to Bali, Gunung Agung and amazing sunsets. Comfortably appointed bungalows stand about under the coconut palms, and when we went outside on our first morning we found the ground covered with huge coconut-palm flowers, each with a dozen or twenty embryonic coconuts inside its hard, split sheath. Tales of coconuts dropping on people's heads are perfectly well founded, and can have fatal endings, so a local expert comes round at regular intervals to lop off the flowers and protect the hotel's reputation.

Lombok food, it has to be said, is unremarkable. The most unusual dish we found, in a restaurant in town, was sate sumsum, a satay made of bone marrow. The best was probably in the hotel restaurant, whose chef, Yularso Winduharjono, took me shopping with him one morning to the pasar in Mataram town. The market is not for anyone with claustrophobia. Its narrow, uneven alleys are jammed with people, stalls packed close together, ceilings or tented coverings often very low. But there is no public place where you can be closer to the heart of Indonesian life than in a market. There are few places where you can be farther from that heart than in a big tourist hotel. It was encouraging to see that on Lombok at least there is still a direct link between the pasar and the hotel kitchen. When all those new hotels are built, can the link hold?

Bebek betutu
Traditional long-cooked Balinese duck

I was hoping very much that during my trip around Bali in 1993 I would find this delicious duck on restaurant menus. But no, it was nowhere to be found. Back in 1987, I had bebek betutu at the Bali Beach Hotel, not cooked by the hotel chefs but brought in by the general manager and his wife; it had been specially made for me by his mother in Bangli, in the traditional manner, the duck stuffed with cassava leaves and spiced with the full Balinese spice mixture. The wrapping, which consisted of layers of banana leaves and seludang mayang (the hard outer sheath of the coconut flower; picture on page 255) opened to reveal a mass of black and tender meat. The colour of the stuffing had become black as well. Not very appetizing to look at, maybe, but the taste was exquisite.

Here is the recipe for preparing and cooking the duck in the oven.

For 4–6 people

1 duck, weighing about
  1.5–2 kg/3¹/₂–4 lb, cleaned
  and ready for roasting
170–225 g/6–8 oz/1¹/₂–2 cups

curly kale, vine or courgette/
  zucchini leaves, or spinach,
  blanched, squeezed dry and
  shredded

For the paste:

5 shallots or 2 medium onions,
  chopped
4 cloves garlic, chopped
5 red chillies, de-seeded and
  chopped, or 1 tsp chilli powder
2 candlenuts or macadamia nuts
  (optional)
2 tsp coriander seeds
1 tsp cumin seeds
2 cloves
2 green cardamoms
2.5-cm/1-inch stick of
  cinnamon

¹/₄ tsp ground or grated nutmeg
¹/₂ tsp ground turmeric
¹/₄ tsp galingale powder
¹/₄ tsp ground white pepper
5-cm/2-inch stem of lemon
  grass, outer leaf discarded,
  chopped, or ¹/₄ tsp powder
1 tsp shrimp paste
3 tbsp tamarind water or lime
  juice
2 tbsp peanut oil
2 tbsp water
1 tsp salt

Blend all the ingredients for the paste together until smooth. Transfer the mixture to a saucepan and simmer for 6–8 minutes, stirring often. Then remove it to a bowl and leave it to get cold. Adjust the seasoning.

When the paste is cold, mix half of it in a bowl with the shredded leaves. Then rub the remaining paste on the duck, inside as well as outside. Stuff the shredded leaves into the duck. Wrap the duck, first with some banana leaves, then with two or three layers of aluminium foil, quite loosely, but sealing the top well. Everything up to this point can be done the day before, and the parcel can be left in the fridge overnight so that the duck marinates thoroughly.

To cook, pre-heat oven to 160°C/320°F/Gas Mark 3, and put the parcel on a baking tray in the middle of the oven. Cook for 2 hours, then reduce the heat to 120°C/250°F/Gas Mark 1/2 and continue cooking for a further 3–4 hours.

To serve, unwrap the parcel and transfer the duck to a large dish. Separate and discard the oil from the cooking juices. Put the cooking juices in a small saucepan, add to this all the stuffing, which has now become a dark-coloured purée (but tastes delicious), heat, and serve it as a thick sauce. The duck has become very tender, and the meat will come off the bones very easily. With a fork, transfer the meat to a well-heated serving platter. Serve straight away with plenty of hot boiled white rice, with the sauce poured over the duck meat or in a sauceboat for everybody to help themselves.

Bebek dengan bumbu betutu
Breasts of duck cooked in Balinese spices

This is a variation of the traditional bebek betutu (page 126). When I demonstrated it at one of my Indonesian evenings at the Gas Cooking School in Sydney in 1991, everyone in the audience liked it; one of them, Genevieve Harris, was inspired to go to Bali, where she became the founding executive chef of the Amankila Resort. She duly placed this on her menu, accompanied by urap (page 170), a Javanese vegetable salad with coconut dressing.

Here, I use the same marinade or spice mixture as for the traditional bebek betutu on page 126. You can then either long-cook the duck breasts, or cook them for a short time so that they are rare or medium-rare. They can then be served with the urap or some other salad, such as a combination of watercress, celery, oranges and fresh garden peas dressed in your favourite vinaigrette. In my home in Wimbledon, I often serve this as a first course at my dinner parties. As a main course, the duck can be served with a spinach sauce, and accompanied by rice, potatoes, or pasta.

For 6–8 people

---

6 or 8 duck breasts
450 g/1 lb/4 cups spinach
(stalks removed), well washed
and finely shredded

420 ml/15 fl oz/2 cups coconut
milk or chicken stock or water

For the marinade and sauce:
See bebek betutu on page 126

Make two deep scores through the skin of each duck breast. Put the breasts into the cold marinade, and turn each one once or twice to make sure it is well coated on all sides. Put them in the fridge to marinate overnight.

To long-cook the duck breasts, wrap them with half of the marinade, in three layers of aluminium foil, and cook in a pre-heated oven at 160°C/320°F/Gas Mark 3 for 3 hours, turning the heat down to 120°C/250°F/Gas Mark 1/2 after the first hour.

To short-cook the duck breasts, take them out of the marinade, and with a knife or the side of a fork scrape off all the marinade from the skin side of the breasts. Then put the duck breasts on a wire rack and roast in a pre-heated oven at 200°C/400°F/Gas Mark 6, for 20–30 minutes.

While the duck is cooking, put 2–4 tablespoonfuls of the marinade or the remaining half (depending on how strong you like it) into a saucepan. Add the coconut milk, stock, or water. Bring to the boil and simmer for 10 minutes. Add the spinach and continue to cook for 4–5 minutes more. Adjust the seasoning. Keep aside this sauce until ready to use. It can be reheated. (If you long-cooked the breasts, separate and discard the oil from the cooking juices, and mix the cooking juices into the sauce.)

Cut each duck breast diagonally into several slices, and serve hot as suggested above. The spinach sauce can be served separately.

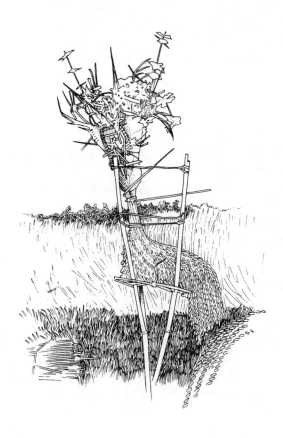

Pelecing kangkung
Water spinach in a hot and sour dressing

Kangkung is a kind of water spinach, and the kangkung of Lombok is reckoned to be the best in Nusatenggara. It is vital that water where the kangkung is grown should be clean and free from pollution of any kind. Whatever the real situation is now, I am fond of kangkung, so much so that I buy it in London at a very inflated price. Use only the best-looking leaves, discarding the rest as well as the thick part of the stalk, which is hollow and can carry dirt inside. Wash every part that you are going to cook very carefully, rinsing it in several changes of water in a large bowl. You will see that every time you transfer the leaves to a colander there is sand and soil at the bottom of the bowl.

Pelecing is the name given to a dish cooked with a lot of shrimp paste, bird chillies and lime juice. There are many different kinds of pelecing, but in Lombok and the neighbouring islands, if you order a pelecing in a restaurant, you will be given pelecing kangkung, and if you want some other kind, you have to name it: for instance, pelecing paria, made with bitter gourd, pelecing ayam, made with chicken, and so on.

For 4 people

450 g/1 lb/4 cups trimmed and cleaned kangkung	*1 heaped tsp crumbled shrimp paste*
2–6 bird chillies, or dried small red chillies	*1/2 tsp salt*
3 candlenuts, chopped (optional)	*2 tbsp peanut oil*
2 cloves garlic, chopped	*Juice of 1 lime*

If dried chillies are used, soak them first in hot water for 10 minutes, so that they become soft. Put the chillies, candlenuts, garlic and shrimp paste in a mortar and crush them with a pestle until smooth. Heat the oil in a wok and stir-fry the paste from the mortar for 2 minutes. Add the kangkung, and continue stir-frying for 5–8 minutes until the kangkung is tender. Add the lime juice and adjust the seasoning. Serve straight away as an accompaniment to rice and meat or a fish dish for the main course.

Note: For pelecing ayam, use the meat only from the breast of chicken, cut into small cubes. Stir-fry the chicken cubes with the paste for 2 minutes, then add 112 ml/4 fl oz/½ cup hot water. Simmer for 10 minutes only. Add the lime juice last, and serve. The combination of pelecing ayam and kangkung on top of piping hot boiled white rice makes a very good one-dish meal for lunch or supper.

On the menu of the Senggigi Beach Hotel in Lombok, this is called kangkung lingsar. The chicken is replaced by fillet of beef, and the chef garnishes the dish with several peeled boiled quail eggs. The rice only comes with the kangkung lingsar if you ask for them to be served together.

Jukut murab
Balinese black-eye bean salad

This is one of the many mixed vegetable salads with coconut dressing that are found all over Indonesia. In Central Java you will find teran-cam, where the black-eye beans are replaced with tempeh and beansprouts are added to the salad, and another version called megono. In West Sumatra, people are very fond of anyang, where the tradi-tional and favourite 'vegetables' are papaya leaves and flowers. But the name that everybody knows, all over Java, is urap (page 170). This is not surprising, because coconuts grow everywhere, and you can always get nuts at different stages of ripeness for different purposes. For a coconut dressing you need one that is hard enough to grate on an old-fashioned hand grater, but young enough to be juicy and sweet and not fibrous. More information about coconuts can be found on pages 245–253. As the Balinese version is the only one that uses black-eye beans, I include the recipe here.

For 6–8 people

---

*450 g/1 lb/2²/3 cups black-eye
    beans, soaked in cold water
    overnight*
*1 large cucumber, peeled and
    thinly sliced*

*4 spring onions/scallions,
    cleaned and cut into thin rounds*
2–3 tbsp chopped mint or basil
1 tsp salt

For the dressing:

1 tsp crumbled shrimp paste
(optional)

225 g/8 oz/1 cup freshly grated
coconut

1 large red chilli, de-seeded and
finely chopped

$^1/_2$ tsp chilli powder

2 cloves garlic, finely chopped

Juice of 1 lime

1 tsp soft brown sugar

1 tsp salt

Drain and rinse the black-eye beans and put them in a saucepan. Cover them with cold water and boil for 40–50 minutes. Add 1 teaspoonful of salt about 5 minutes before cooking is finished. Drain the beans in a colander and leave them to get cold.

Put the shrimp paste, if used, in a large glass bowl, and mash it further with a wooden spoon or a pestle. Add the remaining ingredients for the dressing, and mix them well. Adjust the seasoning, and, just before serving, mix the black-eye beans, the cucumber and the rest of the ingredients into the coconut dressing. Toss well and serve.

Sate pusut
Minced beef satay

When I was in Lombok early in 1993, this satay was to be found in only a few restaurants on the tourist track. As a rule, it is served with rice and pelecing kangkung (page 130). In the neighbouring island of Bali, minced meat satay is usually called sate pentul, though they recognize the name sate pusut as well. The sate pentul of Bali is made with minced pork, and you can find it almost anywhere, especially on holy days, when there are Balinese religious ceremonies in the major temples. The road or path, usually steep, that leads to the temple will be lined on both sides with vendors of all sorts of food, including a great variety of satays. Each has his or her small charcoal stove, some quite modern-looking, not dissimilar to Japanese hibachi, others very primitive, made from thin sheet aluminium, often stained and battered; but as long as the fire is really hot, you will get good spicy minced satays. Ignore the vendors who are still working hard to fan their stoves, because they will put paraffin on the fire to get it going faster and this will affect the smell and taste of the satay.

Made at home, sate pusut can be as hot and spicy as in the recipe below, or as mild as a hamburger. If you want it mild, leave out the sambal ulek.

For 4–6 people

---

500 g / 1 lb 2 oz rump steak, minced

1 tsp salt
2 tsp lime juice

For the spice mixture:
1–2 tsp coriander seeds, roasted
2 tbsp desiccated coconut, roasted (optional)
1–2 tsp sambal ulek (see introduction)
2 shallots, very finely chopped
2 cloves garlic, very finely chopped

1 tsp finely chopped ginger
1 tsp soft brown sugar
1 tbsp light soya sauce or 1 tsp crumbled terasi
6 tbsp thick coconut milk or plain yogurt

In a bowl, rub the salt and lime juice into the minced beef. Keep aside. Put the roasted coriander seeds and desiccated coconut into a mortar and crush them with a pestle. Mix these with the other ingredients for the paste, then mix this well into the meat. Knead it for a while with your hand, then divide the meat and shape it into small balls the size of a walnut. Put 4 meat balls on to a bamboo or metal skewer just before you are ready to grill. You can prepare the mixture up to 24 hours before, but don't mould it or put it on to skewers until the last possible moment; if you do, the balls will tend to split and fall off. Grill slowly, turning carefully from time to time. After 4 or 5 minutes, when the satays should be half cooked and pretty firm, brush the balls with some oil, and continue cooking for 2–3 minutes longer. Serve hot, as canapés with drinks, or as a separate course, or with rice and salad.

Note: Brushing oil on to hot meat with a nylon brush can result in melted nylon. I suggest you use a lemon grass brush, as explained on page 266.

Tom
Spiced minced pork Balinese style

This is a recipe that my friend Murni gave me when I visited her in Ubud. She says it is pronounced *toom*. It is very similar to what in Java is called pais or pepes, which consists of meat or fish or vegetables, chopped up and cooked with a mixture of spices, all wrapped in banana leaves. Alternatively, as here, you can wrap it in foil, make it into a large sausage shape, and roast it in the oven. I have found black pudding quite a satisfactory substitute for the fresh blood, or failing that I use the same quantity of pig's liver.

For 4–6 people

450 g/1 lb boneless pork chops	peeled and chopped
168 g/6 oz/1¹/2 cups papaya	285 ml/¹/2 pint/1¹/4 cups
or cassava leaves, or young	coconut milk or cold water
vine leaves or curly kale	85–110 g/3–4 oz/¹/2 cup black
A 10-cm/4-inch stem of	pudding or pig's liver
rhubarb or 1 green apple,	Salt and pepper

For the paste:

5 shallots or 1 onion, chopped	2 tsp coriander seed
5 cloves garlic, chopped	2 tsp chopped ginger

3–6 red chillies, de-seeded and chopped	1/2 tsp kencur powder (optional)

3–6 red chillies, de-seeded and
chopped
2.5-cm/1-inch piece of
galingale, chopped
1 tsp turmeric powder

1/2 tsp kencur powder
(optional)
1 tsp shrimp paste
1 tsp salt
5 tbsp coconut milk or peanut oil

With a cleaver chop the pork chops, or mince them in a mincer. Keep aside. Shred the leaves finely, and chop the black pudding, discarding the skin. If liver is used, chop this also. Put all the ingredients for the paste in a blender or food processor and blend until smooth. Then transfer to a small saucepan and simmer for 6 minutes, stirring often. Add the shredded leaves and the chopped rhubarb or apple, stir well, then add the coconut milk. Continue to simmer for about 10 minutes. Adjust the seasoning and leave this to get cold.

Meanwhile, put the chopped or minced pork together with the chopped black pudding or liver in a large glass bowl. When the paste with the leaves is cold, mix this well into the meat. Divide the mixture into equal portions, wrap each portion in a banana leaf square, and steam for 35–40 minutes. Alternatively, place the meat mixture on a large piece of aluminium foil, roll it to make a sausage shape, and wrap it loosely in the foil, preferably with a second layer of foil around it. Put this parcel on a baking tray, and cook in a pre-heated oven at 160°C/320°F/Gas Mark 3 for 50–60 minutes. Serve hot or warm, with rice.

Sepat banang
A milkfish dish from Sumbawa

This dish makes a good starter, or a fish course in a four-course dinner. Banang is the Sumbawa name for milkfish, which in Indonesian is ban-deng. At the time of writing, only frozen milkfish are available in the West, so I recommend using fresh sea bass or red snapper instead. I also find that the unripe mangoes which Indonesians prefer are not as attractive as the ripe mangoes I have got into the habit of using with my fish dishes in London.

This is one of the Nusatenggara recipes that taste so delicious because the combination of ingredients is so good. The cooking is unsophisticated – everything is put together into one saucepan, deliciously spiced, but with the bones and the skin of the fish, chilli seeds and vegetables all mixed together and usually overdone. As part of my mission is to tempt Westerners to include Indonesian dishes in their elegant dinner parties as well as at family meals, I suggest a cooking method which is subtler but still quite simple.

For 4–8 people

---

1 sea bass or red snapper
weighing about 1 kg/2 lb,
cleaned and scaled, then
filleted, with the skin left on

For the paste:
3 candlenuts or macadamia nuts
3 shallots
1 large red chilli, de-seeded and
chopped

Other ingredients:
1 large aubergine/eggplant,
roasted in the oven or under a
grill until the skin is charred

For garnish:
1 medium-size ripe mango,
peeled and cut into julienne
strips

2 tsp lime juice
1/2 tsp salt
8 uncooked king prawns/jumbo
shrimp, peeled and de-veined

2 bird peppers
112 ml/4 fl oz/1/2 cup thick
coconut milk

2 medium tomatoes, skinned,
de-seeded and chopped
Salt to taste

A handful of basil leaves

Cut each fish fillet into 4 pieces and put them in a glass bowl together with the prawns. Mix in the lime juice and salt and keep the bowl in a cool place.

Blend all the ingredients for the paste, transfer it to a saucepan, and simmer, stirring often, for about 4 minutes or until it becomes thick. Meanwhile, skin the roasted aubergine/eggplant and chop or mash the flesh in a bowl with a fork. Set aside.

Leave the cooked paste to get cold, and when cold put half into the bowl with the fish fillets and prawns/shrimp. Make sure that every piece of the fish and prawns is coated with the paste.

Stir the mashed aubergines/eggplants into the remaining paste in the saucepan, and adjust the seasoning. Add the chopped tomatoes. Keep aside until you are ready to serve the sepat banang.

Arrange the fish and the prawns/shrimp on a baking dish, and cook under a very hot grill or in a pre-heated oven at 200°C/400°F/Gas Mark 6 for 4-5 minutes. To serve, heat the aubergine/eggplant mixture on a low heat, stirring all the time, for 2 minutes. Divide this equally among 4 or 8 plates, and arrange the fish and prawns/shrimp on top of the aubergine/eggplant. Top with the mango and basil garnish, and serve straight away.

Sepat ayam
A chicken dish from Sumbawa

Like the sepat banang (page 135), this easy-to-make chicken dish has mango as one of the ingredients. But here, an unripe mango is more suitable than a ripe one. You are looking for the sourness of the fruit. Unripe mangoes are available in Indian or Thai shops, and they are usually small. Replace the mango with a sour apple if need be.

When I don't feel like eating rice, I like to serve this dish with potatoes baked in their jackets or hot garlic bread and a green salad.

For 2 people

---

2 chicken breasts without skin
1 tsp lime juice
A large pinch of salt
570 ml/1 pint/2 1/2 cups cold
water
1–2 small unripe mangoes or
apples

2 tsp salt
285 ml/1/2 pint/1 1/4 cups thick
coconut milk
2 firm red tomatoes, skinned,
de-seeded and sliced
2 spring onions/scallions,
cut into thin rounds

For the paste:
3 candlenuts or 5 blanched
almonds, chopped
1 small red chilli, de-seeded

6–8 whole peppercorns
4 tbsp of the coconut milk
1 tsp salt

Rub the chicken breasts with the lime juice and a pinch of salt. Leave to stand for half an hour while you are preparing the rest of the ingredients.

Peel the mango or apple and cut into matchsticks. Put these in a bowl and rub the 2 teaspoonfuls of salt into them. Leave to stand for 10 minutes, then rinse well in cold water to get rid of all the salt. Keep aside.

Put all the ingredients for the paste in a blender and blend until smooth. Transfer to a saucepan and simmer, stirring often, for 4 minutes. Then add the remaining coconut milk, and continue cooking, stirring often, for another 5–6 minutes. Take off the heat, and add the mango or apple sticks and the spring onions/scallions. Leave this to cool.

In another saucepan, boil the water. When boiling, put in the chicken breast and simmer for 10–12 minutes. Leave to cool in the water. When it is cool enough to handle, either shred the chicken meat roughly (this is how people in Sumbawa serve the chicken), or, as I myself prefer, slice the chicken breast, on the slant, thinly into 5 or 6 slices. Just before serving, add the shredded chicken or chicken slices to the cool sauce with the mangoes. Divide the mango mixture between 2 large dinner plates, piling it in the middle of each. Arrange the sliced tomatoes around these piles. Adjust the seasoning, and serve at room temperature.

JAVA AND MADURA

Among the Volcanoes

It is hard not to think of Java as the centre of Indonesia – hard, especially, for the Javanese. They certainly have, from the point of view of geography, economics and politics, the best island. They would add that of the larger islands it is also the most beautiful, and the half of me that is Javanese agrees with them.

Madura, Java's companion on the north-east coast, is smaller, lower, emptier, poorer, altogether less glamorous. It still has much charm and interest. The two islands together inevitably share much of their history, though Madurese princes maintained their independence until the middle of the eighteenth century and often intervened quite effectively in Javanese dynastic wars. Today, when big cities are the magnets, Madura has lapsed into rural peace. But it is economically still active, and the building of a bridge to link it with Surabaya may have startling effects.

Java is full of contrasts. Being long and narrow, it has always tended to split into regions, corresponding very roughly with the modern provinces of West, Central and East Java. An equally important split has been geographic, between the areas north and south of the volcanic backbone. The north, by and large, is a wide coastal plain, liable to flooding, with large river-mouths and good harbours for shipping in the South China Sea. The south is a narrower, drier strip. Here you feel a mild evening chill in June and July from the Australian winter. There are few harbours. Dangerous currents are ruled by Nyai Loro Kidul, the Queen of the South Sea who has had an enigmatic relationship with so many Javanese rulers. Much of the romance, the strangeness of Java is gathered in the south, and comes to a sharp focus in the town of Yogyakarta.

Like Bali, Java has succeeded by being adaptable, by learning fast whatever the outside world wanted to teach it. Only two layers of its history seem to have been totally expunged from the memory, Japanese and communist. Both are associated with nightmares of the receding past, though in fact the Japanese have not only been given a second chance but are now welcomed as the bringers of consumer goods and even of Japanese food, which is becoming very popular in Jakarta and will no doubt make its way elsewhere.

Bandung, 'the Paris of Java' as someone once unhelpfully called it, has always had a reputation for good food, and it is still perhaps the best town in Indonesia for a gourmet to be stranded in, outside Jakarta. Three restaurants remain in my memory. We had lunch on our first day at Sindang Reret, whose name means 'Drop in and see us': a large room, cooled by many fans in the high ceiling, with a sensible menu that ranges quite widely over Indonesian and foreign food without forgetting that there are many good Sundanese dishes. On our last night in Bandung, we walked up the street to the Rasa Bakery and had a few simple things for supper, very well cooked and served, and bought snacks for our long journey the next day. A couple of small eating houses as good as these in every town in Indonesia would transform the food scene.

Saung Kabayan, in the north-west quarter of town, is a restaurant which seems to have outgrown its original indoor space and taken over its own front garden, where little pavilions are artfully constructed in bamboo with thatched roofs, each sheltering a table for anything up to a dozen people. This is a sensible arrangement in a tropical climate, and the food here is particularly good – explicitly and consciously Sundanese, and very well cooked. Naturally the menu included the unavoidable ikan bakar and fried chicken, but with the characteristic local sambal, neither too hot nor too sweet.

Bandung is also the home of the largest of the BPLP, the state-run hotel and tourism schools; there are others in Medan, Bali and Ujung Pandang. In addition there are about eighty private hotel schools, with about 100,000 students altogether. As a cookery teacher, I naturally wanted to make contact with the BPLP, and one morning we found ourselves being carried in a taxi up the steep hill to the school. Shortly afterwards I was in a lecture theatre, addressing sixty student chefs on the future of Indonesian food and restaurants, inside the country and abroad – the sort of opportunity that comes all too rarely. Will my audience, at a class reunion in thirty years' time, remember that afternoon as a seminal one in their careers? Possibly not, but at least they listened politely.

They also invited us to have lunch in the main dining hall. Each day a team of five or six students takes its turn at producing lunch and dinner from a cuisine it has researched in the rather modest resources of the school library; today it was the turn of the United States, the room was decorated with American flags and emblems, we had turkey and pumpkin pie, we sat on the top table with the principal and senior staff, and of course we had to make speeches afterwards – Indonesians love speeches, or at any rate feel that no occasion is complete without several.

From Bandung we went by road to Yogyakarta, which I shall say more about in due course, and Surabaya. Surabaya has a long history, but wears it extremely lightly. There is very little to show for all the triumph and disaster, and even the places we thought we remembered from our own youth had vanished. This town exists solely for business. It is of course the only practical gateway to East Java and Madura, unless you travel by road to Malang, but there is nothing here to detain the transient visitor, certainly not the food. Even the shopping malls look desolate and unkept, hectares of grey tiles swept only by the wind. The stalls at the open-air food centre in Taman Kayoon sell overpriced, unappetizing dishes, including one which made even me ill, though I thought I was proof against most food bugs.

The ferry crossing from Surabaya to Madura takes about forty minutes. There is a little fleet of these square-ended car ferries nipping back and forth all day and probably all night, always jammed with trucks, cars, Hondas, pushbikes, baggage and people. Sellers of mineral water, fruit, peanuts and newspapers push their way through, and as the ferry pulls away from the jetty throw themselves and their unsold stock across the widening gap. Bootblacks stay on the boat, so I suppose they find customers have less sales resistance here than on land.

Madura, when you get there, seems entirely peaceful and rural. We decided to look at the royal tombs at Arosbaya, which are hidden away down a very quiet side-road: you climb a flight of shallow stone steps, pass through a lych-gate with square brick pillars and a tiled roof, and find yourself in a little garden. Beyond a second gate are the tombs, crowded together under two pyramid roofs held up on tubby pillars, with some lesser tombs in the open air, weathered like Yorkshire stone. Riady, our guide, pointed to a feature in the formalized decoration of the upright stone slabs that made a kind of protective fence around the tombs: each one had a small parallelogram, filled with wavy lines or cross-hatching. 'It's fish skin,' he said. 'It's to remind the people here that they depend on fish for their living.' Maybe he was right, but I thought it could just as well be a field of rice.

Yogyakarta, the home of my youth and early married life, turned out to be so changed that within ten minutes of entering its familiar streets we were hopelessly adrift. After a day or two's culture shock, however, we found the old Yogya and many old friends still there behind the brash modern face of the city. The food scene, likewise, has remained fundamentally unchanged, though today it is far more varied. Street food still flourishes, especially at night; I have to admit that my years abroad have softened me and I no longer care to buy cooked food whose age and ingredients are doubtful. The successful fried chicken places, such as mBok Berek and Nyonya Suharti, which were just starting up in the 1960s, are still flourishing. A few of the Chinese restaurants we went to in our courting days are still in their old premises, and still offering much the same menus.

Indonesian restaurants, almost unknown in the old days and very rudimentary if you could find one, are becoming rather smart. Within the kraton area that surrounds the sultan's palace a few princely families have opened their houses to the public and offer lunch or dinner at around US$20 a head. My impression here was that the food was all right, but that only the surroundings are really special.

A new-found friend who looked after us most carefully in Yogya was Ibu Etty Soeliantoro. She introduced us to various people, arranged our trip to the gudeg factory (below) and other visits, and organized the meeting at which I addressed the university's alumni association on the future of Indonesian food. She also took us to one of the best warung soto in town, where for about 30p you can have a plate of really hot, nourishing soup with enough meaty chicken bones and vegetables to feed you for half a day. Why can't soto in hotel restaurants, where you pay five or ten times the price, be as good as this? This was the sort of question I tactfully hinted at in my address to the alumni, but I did not get any direct answer.

As for the gudeg factory – that was a real piece of Javanese culinary and social tradition. Gudeg is not necessarily a breakfast dish, you can eat it at any time of day, but from now on I shall always associate it with the hour of 5.30 a.m.

That was the time of our appointment to visit the premises of a gudeg producer, situated on the edge of the campus of Gajah Mada University, my own alma mater. The location was not a matter of chance; most of the gudeg went to nearby foodstalls which catered for students. The kitchen was high and dark, lit only by two or three dim bulbs and by the wood fires on which woks and saucepans were bubbling away. A dozen women were busy at these, tasting to ensure that the contents of each were seasoned and cooked just right, stirring the chicken joints as they fried, then taking them from the hot oil and piling them in baskets. Others assembled the portions of gudeg, placing a spoonful of rice on a banana leaf square, then a small leaf 'plate' to separate the rice from the meat and sauce that were placed on top; finally folding the ends of the packet and pinning them shut with long bamboo pins. Two women were engaged all the time in sweeping the floor, clearing up rubbish and chasing away chickens, which wandered unconcernedly about, unaware that they were next week's raw materials. Small children ran through the room with towels round their middles and toothbrushes grasped in their hands, or set off for school in smart uniforms with lunchpacks on their backs bearing Mickey Mouse logos.

At the centre of this activity sat Madam herself, or Ibu, 'Mother', as we all respectfully addressed her, the proprietor of this thriving business. She was a woman in her sixties, wearing faded Javanese dress and a knitted woollen cap in case the dawn air was chilly. She chatted to us in Javanese as she cut banana leaf squares with a large knife, from time to time tasting samples brought to her by her assistants. By 6.30 a.m. all the gudeg for breakfast and lunch had been delivered or collected, and the staff were preparing the ingredients for cooking for the mid-afternoon and evening sessions. We were each given large portions to eat on the spot, much more food than even I could manage to finish. Portions this big retail for Rp 1,000 (35 pence/US 50 cents); Ibu said that smaller portions, with less fine ingredients, could be had by students for as little as Rp 100. I found the flavours and textures of the gudeg complex and intriguing, a little too sweet for me but every bit as good as I recalled it from the old days.

Anyhow, I have no hesitation in starting my Javanese recipes at this point.

Gudeg
Traditional Yogya one-dish meal

This is the most satisfying and delicious of all meals for the Yogyanese, but too sweet (as a savoury dish) for everyone else. Most tourists regard it as an acquired taste, and one that they are not staying long enough to acquire. But once you have tried gudeg at the right place, you will realize how good it can be.

Here, then, is my version, which I have developed specially for cooking at home. Gudeg Yogya asli, real Yogya gudeg, is a collection of several dishes served on one plate. There are no set recipes for these, and the gudeg producers of Yogya will not tell you their secrets. But there is no doubt about the main components: a dish of jackfruit, nangka, served with opor ayam and sambal goreng krecek on top of a large pile of white boiled rice. The whole thing is topped with a large tablespoonful of very thick creamed coconut, or blondo (page 252). Krecek is a Javanese word for krupuk jangat or buffalo-skin crackling. As this is not easily available in the West, I suggest here that it should be replaced by sambal goreng tahu (page 154). Instead of fresh young jackfruit (only occasionally available in some Thai and Indian shops), you can use canned green jackfruit, available from almost any Oriental store.

If, however, you can get fresh young jackfruit, nangka muda, you need to cut off a thick layer of peel, as if peeling a pineapple. Then cut the flesh into small segments. (The sticky juice that comes out when you are peeling and cutting the nangka will stick to your hands and can only be removed by rubbing them with cooking oil and then washing them with soapy water or detergent. If the juice gets on to your clothes, it is almost impossible to remove, and will leave a dark stain.) The jack-fruit segments must be boiled in plenty of water, with a teaspoon of salt, for 50–60 minutes, then drained and left to cool before the next stage of cooking. Canned jackfruit need only be drained and rinsed.

For 6–8 people

---

900 g/2 lb parboiled jackfruit segments, or canned green jackfruit, drained and rinsed

6–8 hard-boiled eggs, peeled

1.1 litres/2 pints/5 cups thin coconut milk

850 ml/1 $\frac{1}{2}$ pints/3 $\frac{3}{4}$ cups thick coconut milk

3 salam leaves or bay leaves

5-cm/2-inch piece of galingale

For the paste:

5 shallots, chopped

4 cloves garlic, chopped

1 tsp chopped ginger

8 candlenuts or macadamia nuts, or 10 blanched almonds, chopped

2 tsp ground coriander

1 tsp crumbled shrimp paste

1 tsp ground white pepper

1 tsp sugar

8 tbsp of the thick coconut milk (see above)

1 tsp salt

Other ingredients, optional:

4–5 tbsp blondo (page 252)

1/4 tsp salt

1/4 tsp ground white pepper

1 tsp sugar

Blend all the ingredients for the paste until smooth and transfer it to a saucepan. Simmer, stirring often, for 6 minutes. Add the thin coconut milk, the salam or bay leaves, galingale, and jackfruit, and continue to simmer for 20 minutes. Now add the thick coconut milk, and adjust the seasoning. Continue to simmer, stirring often, for 30–40 minutes or until almost all the liquid has been absorbed by the jackfruit.

Add the boiled eggs, and continue cooking for another 4–5 minutes. Just before serving discard the leaves and galingale, and serve hot as explained above, with opor ayam and sambal goreng tahu, topped with the reheated blondo, if used. If you use the blondo, just before serving mix all the ingredients in a small saucepan, and heat for 1–2 minutes.

Ayam betutu
Chicken with Balinese spice mixture

If you are wondering why this chicken dish is not in the Nusatenggara section of the book, it is because the original ayam betutu was a West Javanese dish from the area around Banten. It was always a chicken dish, never duck, and the chicken was always cooked whole and stuffed, with or without cassava leaves, and with several hard-boiled eggs. I have had this ayam betutu many times in restaurants in Jakarta and elsewhere in West Java, and my impression each time was that they were not spiced enough. In any case, back in 1987 I had already developed the following recipe for ayam betutu, and it was included in *Indonesian and Thai Cookery*, the book I published the following year. The recipe has become quite well known in Britain, where people who cook or write about it call it Balinese Chicken, the name under which it appears there.

The recipe that follows is for a whole chicken, boned, or for breasts of chicken with their skins. The stuffing, without the eggs, is placed under the skin, and the cooking is as long as for the traditional betutu. The cassava leaves are replaced here by curly kale, or spinach.

For 6–8 people

1 oven-ready chicken, weighing about 1.5–2 kg/3^1/2–4 lb, boned; or 6–8 boneless chicken breasts with their skins on	*280 g/10 oz/2^1/2 cups curly kale or spinach (stalks removed), well washed, then blanched, squeezed dry and shredded*
	3 hard-boiled eggs, peeled

For the paste:

5 shallots or 2 medium onions,
   chopped

4 cloves garlic, chopped

5 red chillies, de-seeded and
   chopped; or 1 tsp chilli powder

2 candlenuts or macadamia nuts
   (optional)

2 tsp coriander seeds

1 tsp cumin seeds

2 cloves

2 green cardamoms

2.5-cm/1-inch stick of
   cinnamon

1/4 tsp ground or grated nutmeg

1/2 tsp ground turmeric

1/4 tsp galingale powder

1/4 tsp ground white pepper

5-cm/2-inch stem of lemon
   grass, outer leaf discarded,
   chopped, or 1/4 tsp lemon
   grass powder

1 tsp shrimp paste

3 tbsp tamarind water or lime
   juice

2 tbsp peanut oil

2 tbsp water

1 tsp salt

Blend all the ingredients for the paste together until smooth. Transfer the mixture to a saucepan and simmer for 6–8 minutes, stirring often. Then remove it to a bowl and leave it to get cold. Adjust the seasoning.

When the paste is cold, mix half of it in a bowl with the shredded leaves. Then rub the remaining paste all over the boned chicken or chicken breasts. Stuff the shredded leaves into the chicken with the hard-boiled eggs in the middle. If only chicken breasts are used, omit the eggs, divide the leaf filling equally, lift the skin up, spread the stuffing over the chicken breasts, and pull the skin back to cover the stuffing. If the chicken has been boned by cutting through the back of the bird, sew the cut with strong thread. Then wrap the chicken in two or three layers of aluminium foil, quite loosely, but well folded over to seal it at the join. Everything up to this point can be done the day before, and the parcel can be left in the fridge overnight so that the chicken marinates thoroughly.

To cook, pre-heat the oven to 160°C/320°F/Gas Mark 3, and put the parcel on a baking tray in the middle of the oven. Cook for 1 hour, then reduce the heat to 120°C/250°F/Gas Mark 1/2 and continue cooking for a further 2–3 hours.

To serve, unwrap the parcel and transfer the whole chicken or the breasts to a large dish. Separate and discard the oil from the cooking juices. Put the cooking juices in a small saucepan, to be reheated just before serving. If it is a whole chicken, remove the thread (if used) and cut the chicken into thick slices. Breasts of chicken can be served whole or cut into slices diagonally. Serve at once, with plenty of hot boiled white rice, and the sauce in a bowl or a sauceboat for everybody to help themselves.

Ayam mBok Berek
The original fried chicken of Kalasan

Every visitor to Yogyakarta goes to see the temple complex at Prambanan, about 15 kilometres out of town on the Solo road. In 1960, the scene was very different from what it is today; there were virtually no tourists, and very few Indonesians could afford to travel any distance to see their own historic monuments. Many of the smaller temples that now stand proudly on the site were heaps of rubble. The open-air Ramayana Theatre did not exist. There were several kilometres of green rice fields between Yogya and Prambanan, and the place was a favourite picnic spot for students from the town. We used to progress sedately from Yogya on our high Dutch bicycles, and if we felt particularly rich that day we might treat ourselves to fried chicken at a warung near the temples. 'Warung mBok Berek' (*mBok* means 'mother' in Javanese, but like the Indonesian word *ibu* it is used as a polite term of address for any lady over the age of about twenty-five), was rapidly becoming famous all over Yogya – soon, all over Java. Before long, so it was said, airline pilots were taking packages of mBok Berek's chicken to Indonesian expatriates in New York ...

Times have changed, but the original warung was still there when I visited Prambanan in April 1993, and indeed still getting bigger. But of course similar businesses have sprung up and expanded into other parts of the country. Already, in 1987, I ate this style of fried chicken, so tender inside and crisp outside, at a large restaurant called Ayam Goreng Nyonya Suharti, right next door to the Ambarrukmo Palace Hotel. Nyonya Suharti has now become a chain, with several restaurants in Jakarta, and others in large towns and cities all over Indonesia. There must be almost as many of them as there are Kentucky Frieds. Nyonya Suharti's chicken attracts the older generation with small children, while Kentucky Fried is a magnet for school and college students – the generation I belonged to when mBok Berek was just starting up.

What follows, of course, owes much to mBok Berek and Nyonya

Suharti and nothing to Colonel Saunders. The only ingredient that may present problems if you are in Europe is the coconut water, and this is absolutely essential. Water out of thick-shelled old coconuts from the supermarket will do well enough, but you need 850 ml/1^1/2 pints/3^3/4 cups of it – the contents of several nuts. In Indonesia, of course, the water is from kelapa muda, the young coconuts that grow profusely everywhere and are full of water because their flesh has not begun to form.

At mBok Berek's and Nyonya Suharti's restaurants, this chicken is served hot, with plenty of white rice and the usual accompaniment of lalab, crudités, and sambal or hot chilli sauce. You can order more accompaniments, such as fried tempeh, krupuk, or emping, and, which are very popular indeed, the chicken's innards – liver, gizzard, intestine, all fried until quite crisp on the outside.

For 2 or 4 people

---

1 free-range chicken, cut in half or into quarters	1/4 tsp ground turmeric
850 ml/1^1/2 pints/3^3/4 cups coconut water	2 salam leaves or bay leaves
5 shallots, finely chopped	1 tsp salt
2 tsp finely chopped ginger	2 tbsp plain/all-purpose flour
3.5-cm/1^1/2-inch piece of galingale	Salt and pepper
	Vegetable oil for deep-frying

Put the coconut water in a deep saucepan, and add to it the shallots, ginger, galingale, turmeric, salam or bay leaves and 1 teaspoonful of salt. Mix these well, then put in the chicken halves or quarters. Leave to marinate for 2–4 hours, then boil the chicken on a medium heat for 60–75 minutes. Leave to cool in the remaining cooking juices. When cold, take the chicken pieces out and dry them with kitchen paper.

On a large plate or a tray, season the flour with salt and pepper. Rub the flour all over the chicken pieces. Heat the oil in a deep-fryer or a wok to 165°C/325°F, and fry the chicken until golden brown. The pieces should be crisp outside and still soft and tender inside. Serve hot straight away, or cold for a picnic.

Bakwan tahu
Tofu and beansprout fritters

These are very easy and quick to prepare; they are similar to the many kinds of fritters which in Java are called pergedel and are often served as a side-dish or garnish to the traditional Central Javanese nasi tumpeng (page 173). The tofu here can be replaced by fish (bakwan ikan) or prawns/shrimp (bakwan udang).

Makes 12–16 fritters

---

5 shallots or 1 onion, chopped
4 cloves garlic, finely chopped
1 tsp ground coriander
450 g/1 lb/4 cups fresh firm tofu
3 tbsp finely chopped flat-leaf
    parsley
1 tsp salt
1/4 tsp chilli powder or freshly
    ground pepper

56 g/2 oz/1/2 cup beansprouts,
    cleaned
1 egg, lightly beaten
2–3 tbsp rice flour or plain/
    all-purpose flour
1 tsp baking powder
168–225 ml/6–8 fl oz/3/4–1
    cup peanut oil for frying

Heat 2 or 3 tablespoonfuls of the oil in a wok or frying pan, and fry the shallots or onion and garlic, stirring all the time, for 3 minutes, or until they are just turning light brown. Transfer the shallots and garlic, without the oil, into a glass bowl and leave to get cold. (Keep the oil in the pan.) When they are cold put the rest of the ingredients, except the oil, into the bowl and mash the tofu with a fork or wooden spoon, mixing everything well together. Adjust the seasoning: you may need to put in a little more salt to taste.

Put the rest of the oil into the wok or frying pan containing the little oil used for frying the shallots, and heat. When the oil is hot, drop a spoonful of the tofu mixture into it, then three or four more. Fry until golden brown. Take out the fritters with a slotted spoon and drain them on absorbent paper. Repeat this process until all the mixture has been fried. Serve the fritters warm or cold as explained above.

Gule kambing
An aromatic lamb stew

Restaurants with tourist menus will list this as a lamb curry. In fact, it is a goat stew, with a lot of sauce, and Indonesians still eat it today the way people used to at the street vendor's stall near my parents' house in Magelang: they put the white rice in a deep plate, and ladle the meat over it with plenty of sauce. Then the customer is offered some sambal in a bowl, so he can help himself. A teaspoonful of the sambal will be more than enough for a plateful of rice and gule. Other garnishes will be put on the gule – crisp-fried onions, chopped flat-leaf parsley. You can of course bring your own plate or bowl, take the gule away and eat it at home. It will still be quite hot, because the street vendor keeps his gule on a low fire all the time. The secret of getting one that is not already cooked to death is therefore to arrive when the vendor has just finished cooking a new batch.

Here are two methods of cooking gule at home. Both use the whole leg of lamb. However, when I was in Australia, early in 1993, teaching Indonesian cooking at several cookery schools there, I used the Australian cuts of shank and fillet of lamb, cut into evenly sized medallions. The fillet, I think, was from the best end of neck, or possibly the saddle.

For 6 or 8–10 people

1 leg of lamb, weighing about 2.5 kg/5–6 lb
4-cm/1¹/₂-inch stick of cinnamon
2 salam leaves or kaffir lime leaves or bay leaves

For the paste:
5 shallots or 1 onion, chopped
4 cloves garlic, chopped
6 candlenuts or macadamia nuts
2–4 large red chillies, de-seeded and chopped
¹/₄ tsp ground white pepper

1 stem of lemon grass, cut into 3
570 ml/1 pint/2¹/₂ cups hot water
225–335 ml/8–12 fl oz/1–1¹/₂ cups thick coconut milk

¹/₄ tsp cayenne pepper or paprika
2 tsp chopped ginger
1 tsp chopped galingale or ¹/₂ tsp powder
1 tsp turmeric powder
2 tsp ground coriander

| 2 cloves | 4 tbsp thick tamarind water |
| 1 tsp salt | 2 tbsp peanut or olive oil |

For the garnish:

2 tbsp crisp-fried onions	Some sambal terasi (page 220)
(page 230)	(optional)
A handful of flat-leaf parsley	

Method 1

Cut the lamb into 1-cm/$1/2$-inch cubes, removing and discarding the fat and sinews. Put all the ingredients for the paste into a blender or food processor, and blend until smooth. Transfer the paste to a large saucepan, and simmer, stirring often, for 6–8 minutes. Add the meat, and stir continuously for 2 minutes, then add the hot water, cinnamon stick, lemon grass and salam or the other leaves. Cover the pan and continue to simmer for 40 minutes. Uncover, and add the coconut milk and continue cooking on a low heat, stirring the stew often, for another 30–40 minutes, depending on how runny or thick you want the sauce to be. Adjust the seasoning. Take out and discard the cinnamon stick, the lemon grass and leaves, and serve piping hot as explained above.

Method 2

Bone the leg carefully, and with a cleaver cut the bones into several pieces. Keep aside. Cut as many medallion-sized pieces as you can from the best part of the leg fillet. Remove the fat, and cut the rest of the meat into small cubes. Put the medallions of lamb into a glass bowl, and rub them with a mixture of half a teaspoon of salt and some freshly ground pepper. Keep the meat aside, while you blend all the ingredients for the paste. Transfer the paste to a large saucepan and simmer, stirring often, for 6–8 minutes. Add the bones and the small cubes of meat, and stir these around for 2 minutes. Add the hot water, cinnamon stick, lemon grass, and salam or the other leaves. Cover the pan, and continue to simmer for 40 minutes. Uncover, add the coconut milk, and continue cooking on a low heat, stirring often, for another 30–40 minutes. Adjust the seasoning. Up to this point, this can be prepared well in advance.

Just before serving, heat the sauce in a saucepan until it is nearly boiling, then strain it into a smaller saucepan. Discard the bones. The smaller cubes of meat can be kept for other uses (if you chop them finely, they can be used as martabak filling – see page 56).

153

Pan-fry the medallions of lamb in olive oil for 3–5 minutes each side, turning them over once. To serve, arrange the medallions on heated dinner plates, reheat the sauce, and ladle it into the plates. Put the garnish on the meat, and serve straight away, with the rice served separately, and some cooked vegetable or salad.

Sambal goreng tahu
Fried tofu sambal goreng

This sambal goreng is good for vegetarians and vegans. It is included here principally, however, as an accompaniment to gudeg (page 145), in places where krecek and sambal goreng krecek are not available.

The tofu used here must be fried tofu, available in Chinese or other Oriental shops. You can, of course, fry fresh tofu yourself (see page 277).

For 4 people

---

420 ml/15 fl oz/2 cups hot water
5-cm/2-inch piece of fresh lemon grass
2 kaffir lime leaves or lemon or bay leaves
2 ripe tomatoes, peeled and
chopped
112 g/4 oz/1/2 cup creamed coconut, chopped
225–340 g/8–12 oz/2–3 cups fried tofu, cut into quarters

For the paste:
3 shallots or 1 small onion, chopped
2 cloves garlic
5-cm/2-inch piece of fresh ginger, peeled and sliced
3 large red chillies, de-seeded and chopped
1 tsp shrimp paste (optional)
2 candlenuts, chopped (optional)
1 tsp ground coriander
1 tsp paprika
1/2 tsp salt, or more to taste
1 tbsp tamarind water or lemon juice
2 tbsp olive or peanut oil
2 tbsp cold water

Blend all the ingredients for the paste until smooth. In a saucepan, bring this paste to the boil and cook it for 4 minutes, stirring continuously. Add the hot water, lemon grass, and kaffir lime, lemon or bay leaves.

Bring the mixture back to the boil and simmer gently for 20 minutes. Add the tomatoes and the creamed coconut; stir to dissolve the coconut. Simmer and stir for 2 more minutes. Adjust the seasoning. Up to this point, the sauce can be made up to 24 hours in advance and kept in the fridge (but it cannot be frozen).

When you are ready to serve, bring the sauce to a rolling boil, stir it, and put in the fried tofu. Continue to simmer for 4–5 minutes. Discard the lemon grass and leaves. Serve hot with rice, or as part of gudeg (page 145).

Besengek daging
Boiled silverside with spicy sauce

Besengek: it sounds Javanese, and it comes from Central Java. However, if you asked anybody there what it means, I am sure no-one could tell you. I have had this recipe for years, since I was a student in Yogya. The important thing is that the meat, after being boiled in one or two pieces, should be cut into quite large, but thin, steak-like slices. Silverside is what I make it with in London. There is also besengek ayam, more often called ayam bumbu besengek, which of course is made with chicken; for that, I would recommend the boned breast meat, or a small whole chicken cut in half, with some of the bones discarded. This is very suitable for a picnic, when you can prepare and pre-cook the chicken at home, carry it into the country in your cold box, and barbecue the chicken just to make it piping hot. I can't help remembering a splendid barbecue with Indonesian friends near Melbourne in March 1993 – it was strange to have kookaburras watching us while we fanned the flames. Beef besengek, of course, is just as good for a barbecue, as are other birds, such as guinea fowl and pheasant.

If you use chicken, guinea fowl, or pheasant, the initial boiling with water is not necessary, but you need to double the amount of coconut milk. Cook the spices with the coconut milk for 10 minutes, and while the coconut milk is still boiling, put in the fowl, and simmer, uncovered, until the sauce is thick and the meat is tender. Then leave it all to cool and marinate in the sauce until you barbecue it. While grilling, you can brush the remaining sauce over the meat, but do use a lemon grass brush (page 266), not a brush made of nylon.

---

*675 g/1¹/2 lb silverside, in one
  or two pieces*
¹/2 tsp salt
225 ml/8 fl oz/1 cup stock

For the spice mixture:
2 tbsp peanut oil
1 onion, finely chopped
*1–3 large red chillies, de-seeded
  and chopped, or 1 tsp sambal
  ulek*
1 tsp crumbled shrimp paste
2 tsp ground coriander

*568 ml/1 pint/2¹/2 cups coconut
  milk, or 1.1 litres/2 pints/
  5 cups for chicken, etc.
  (see introduction)*

¹/2 tsp ground turmeric
*1 tsp finely chopped lemon grass
  (the inner part only)*
*¹/2 tsp salt, or a little more to
  taste*
¹/2 tsp sugar
3 tbsp tamarind water

Boil the beef for 1¹/2 hours, adding only ¹/2 tsp of salt. Leave it to cool in the stock. When cool enough to handle, cut the meat into large pieces about 1 cm/¹/2 inch thick. Keep aside. Strain the stock, measure what you need, and keep this aside also.

Heat the oil in a saucepan, and fry the onions and chillies, stirring all the time, for 2–3 minutes. Add the crumbled shrimp paste, ground coriander, turmeric and lemon grass, and stir with a wooden spoon, crushing the shrimp paste further with the spoon. Add the salt, sugar and tamarind water, and simmer for 2 minutes. Add the meat slices, stir and mix, and then add the stock. Cover the pan and continue simmering for 5 minutes. Uncover the pan, and add the coconut milk. Cook on a low heat for 45–50 minutes, until the sauce is thick and the meat very tender. Adjust the seasoning. Serve hot straight away, or keep in the fridge for a barbecue as explained in the introduction above.

Note: If, for a barbecue, you want to use rump steak, you don't need to boil the steak first. Cook the coconut milk sauce until thick, and leave it to get cold. When cold, put it into a glass bowl, and marinate the rump steak in it for at least 2 hours, or overnight in the fridge. Let the steak return to room temperature before grilling.

Soto Madura
Spiced beef soup

Nowadays, soto Madura is made with chicken as often as with beef. When I was young it was always thought of as a beef dish, and I give the beef version here because I would like you to start by making this with brisket. After more than twenty years of making soto Madura and experimenting with different cuts, I find nothing else is quite so good. When you want to make chicken soto, the recipe is on page 193 – it is simply the chicken soup for the bubur ayam. Or you can use this recipe, and replace the brisket with a whole chicken so that you get good stock from the chicken bones.

The quantities below are for a one-dish meal for 6–8 people, depending on how much rice or rice noodles you are serving with the soup. I find, in London, that this is one of the best and most popular late supper dishes for any mid-winter celebration or party. Not only is it very warming, but it will go well with whatever canapés you serve beforehand, with almost any wine, and with any fruit or cheese you serve afterwards.

For 6–8 people

1–1.5 kg/2–3 lb brisket
2.5 litres/4 pints/10 cups water
1 tsp salt
2 tbsp peanut oil

4 shallots, finely sliced
2 tsp lemon juice
1 tbsp light soya sauce
Freshly ground black pepper

For the paste:
3 shallots, chopped
3 candlenuts, chopped
112 g/4 oz dried prawns or
*   shrimps, soaked in hot water*
*   for 5 minutes, then drained*
1 tsp chopped ginger root

1/2 tsp ground turmeric
1 large red chilli, de-seeded and
*   chopped*
1/2 tsp salt
2 tbsp peanut oil

For the garnish:
2 tbsp flat-leaf parsley
1 tbsp chopped spring onions/
*   scallions*

56–112 g/2–4 oz/1/2–1 cup
*   beansprouts, cleaned*
6–8 lemon slices

*450 g/1 lb/2 cups white
long grain rice, plain boiled,
or 225 g/8 oz biehun (rice
vermicelli), cooked for 3*

*minutes just before serving,
then drained and served
immediately*

Cut the beef into two, and boil it in the water with 1 tsp of salt over a low heat for 1–1½ hours. Strain off and reserve the stock, and cut the meat into small cubes, discarding all the fat.

Put all the ingredients for the paste into a blender and blend for a few seconds only to get a rough-textured mix. Transfer this into a small saucepan and simmer, stirring almost all the time, for 3 minutes. Add about 570 ml/1 pint/2½ cups of the reserved stock, and continue to simmer for 15 minutes. Now strain the stock into a bowl and discard the rough paste mixture.

In another, larger, saucepan, heat the 2 tablespoonfuls of oil and fry the sliced shallots for 2 minutes. Add the cubed beef, and continue stirring for 1 minute. Then add the strained stock from the bowl, and simmer for 10 minutes. Add the remaining stock and simmer for another 10 minutes. Adjust the seasoning with lemon juice, soya sauce and pepper.

To serve, put the soto, the rice or noodles, and the garnishes on the table in separate bowls or dishes. Then everybody helps themselves to rice or noodles, ladles the hot soup and beef on top, and takes whatever garnishes they wish.

Rawon
An East Java beef dish in a black sauce

Like gule on page 152, rawon is halfway between a meat dish and a soup – so do not thicken the sauce. Unlike gule, rawon does not have a warm golden colour but is very nearly black, as if the sauce had been made with Bovril. This colour comes from the kluwek nuts which are a small but important part of the dish. At the time of writing, this nut (page 265) is not yet obtainable in Britain, but dried kluwek can be bought in Holland. They usually break up into small pieces in the packet, so two kluwek can mean four or five good-sized pieces. Dried kluwek must be soaked in cold water for an hour or so and then boiled for about 10 minutes so that they become soft.

Rawon was originally a street food in East Java, just as gule was in Central Java (the famous one, during my student days in Yogya, was gule babat, the tripe gule of Klaten, a little town situated halfway between Yogya and Solo). Today, many big international hotels in Indonesia put rawon on their menus and serve it as a soup, perhaps because the black sauce is considered rather sophisticated. But traditionally rawon is always served with rice, garnished with raw beansprouts and accompanied by sambal terasi (page 220) and krupuk (page 226).

I prefer serving rawon as a lunch dish, not with plain rice, but with lontong.

For 4 as a lunch or supper dish; or for 6–8 people as a soup

680 g/1¹/2 lb beef, brisket or silverside, in 1 or 2 pieces	*1 tsp salt*
1.1–1.7 litres/2–3 pints/5–7¹/2 cups water	*1 stem of lemon grass, cut across into 2 or 3*

For the paste:

1–3 red chillies, de-seeded and chopped	*2 tsp ground coriander*
6 shallots or small red onions, chopped	*¹/2 tsp ground turmeric*
2 fresh kluwek, chopped; or 4–5 pieces of dried kluwek, soaked for 1 hour, then boiled for 10 minutes and drained	*1 tsp chopped fresh galingale or ¹/2 tsp powder*
	1 tsp salt
	3 tbsp tamarind water
	2 tbsp peanut oil

For the accompaniments:

84–112 g/3–4 oz/1 cup beansprouts, cleaned	*Sambal terasi*
2 tbsp chopped flat-leaf parsley	*Krupuk (optional)*
	Boiled rice or lontong (page 241)

First, put the beef, water and salt in a large saucepan, bring to the boil, then simmer for 60–75 minutes, skimming the froth frequently. Leave the beef to cool in the stock while you prepare the rest of the ingredients. When it is cool enough to handle, cut the beef into small cubes, and strain the stock into a bowl.

Put all the ingredients for the paste in a blender, and blend until smooth. Then transfer this to a saucepan, and simmer, stirring often, for 5–6 minutes. Add the stock, the lemon grass and the meat, and continue to simmer for 40–50 minutes. Take out and discard the lemon grass and serve hot as suggested above. The sambal terasi should be served in a small bowl for everybody to help themselves, spooning it into the soup. The beansprouts and parsley are to be scattered on the individual helpings, and the krupuk eaten as bread with the soup. The rice or lontong can be served separately, or put into the soup.

Karedok
A Sundanese raw vegetable salad

The Sundanese, the people of West Java, are very proud of their karedok. They will tell you that nowhere else in Indonesia can you find a salad as crisp in texture and as refreshing in aroma and taste as this. As the daughter of a Sundanese mother, naturally I am very partial to this salad, which I used to make often when I had a kencur plant growing in a pot on my kitchen windowsill. Kencur, known in English as 'lesser galingale' (page 265), is an important ingredient of karedok, and unfortunately has no substitute. Sometimes you can get small jars of kencur powder in specialized delicatessens in the West, but the powder doesn't have the aroma of the fresh rhizome.

Another characteristic ingredient of karedok is kemangi, and most Sundanese cooks use plenty of it. Indonesian kemangi is very similar to the purplish Thai basil which is now available in Thai and other Oriental shops in Western cities. If you can't get it, the best alternative would be a combination of sweet basil and mint. The small round aubergine/eggplant, *Solanum melongena*, is available in Thai or Indian shops. The ones you buy in the West are greenish white in colour, but in the East these aubergines/eggplants come in different colours, white, greenish, yellow, slightly purple and magenta purple. There is one variety that actually is egg-shaped and white.

For 4–6 people

---

112 g/4 oz/1 cup yard-long
   beans (page 278), cut into
   thin rounds
112 g/4 oz/1 cup beansprouts,
   cleaned
4 small round aubergines/
   eggplants, quartered
1 small (about 112 g/4 oz)
   sweet potato, peeled

112 g/4 oz/1 cup yam
   bean/jicama, peeled
112 g/4 oz/1 cup white cabbage,
   finely shredded
1/2 cucumber, peeled, cut into
   halves lengthways, de-seeded
   and thinly sliced
84 g/3 oz/3/4 cup kemangi, or
   mint and basil, roughly
   chopped

For the dressing:

112 g/4 oz/2/3 cup roasted
   peanuts
1–2 cloves garlic, very finely
   chopped
1 tsp crumbled shrimp paste
1 tsp chopped kencur or 1/4 tsp
   powder

2–4 bird chillies
1 tsp soft brown sugar
Juice of 1 lime
1 tsp salt or more to taste
110–170 ml/4–6 fl oz/1/2–3/4
   cup boiling water

When preparing the vegetables, do the sweet potato last. Cut into small matchsticks and immediately immerse in slightly salted water to prevent discoloration. Cut the yam bean/jicama also into matchsticks. Transfer all the prepared vegetables, except the sweet potato, into a large salad bowl.

Grind the roasted peanuts in a mortar, coffee grinder, or blender until fine. Finely chop the chillies, put these with the shrimp paste into a mortar or bowl, and crush them with a pestle. Then add all the ingredients for the dressing, except the water, and mix them well in the bowl. Add the boiling water a little at a time, stirring vigorously with a wooden spoon until you have a smooth thick sauce. Adjust the seasoning and leave this sauce to get cold. Just before serving, drain the sweet potato, add to the bowl of vegetables, then pour the dressing over the prepared vegetables. Mix and toss the salad well, and serve at room temperature.

Pais ikan dengan udang
Fish and prawn/shrimp parcels

Pais in Sundanese, pepes in Javanese and Indonesian, or palai in the Minangkabau area, are all names for this concoction of fish and prawns/shrimp, together or separately, wrapped in banana leaves. The spice mixture varies slightly from region to region, since good cooking is a matter of using the freshest ingredients from the garden around your house. My Sumatran grandmother would use limau, very similar to lime, that grew on her patch of land, while my West Javanese aunt in Tasikmalaya always used belimbing wuluh (page 258) because she had her own tree. People elsewhere use whatever ingredients are easily available to give sourness to the pepes: kedondong and their leaves, asam Jawa (tamarind), or asam kandis (page 275).

The recipe below is my own variation as I make it in Wimbledon. I use banana leaves to wrap the pais, as these are widely available now. If you can't get them, use greaseproof paper or aluminium foil.

For 4 people

---

4 fillets of salmon or cod,
  weighing about 100–115 g/
  3¹/2 –4 oz each
225 g/8 oz peeled prawns/shrimp
1 tsp lime juice
1/2 tsp salt
1 tbsp thick tamarind water,
  or 28 g/1 oz rhubarb, finely
  sliced, or 28 g/1 oz young
  vine leaves, shredded

1–2 large red chillies, de-seeded
  and finely sliced
5-cm/2-inch stem of lemon
  grass, outer leaves discarded,
  finely chopped
2 kaffir lime leaves, finely
  shredded
112 ml/4 fl oz/1/2 cup coconut
  milk

For the paste:
1 tsp sambal ulek
3 candlenuts or macadamia
  nuts, chopped
3 shallots, finely chopped
2 cloves garlic, finely chopped

1 tsp chopped ginger
1 tsp crumbled shrimp paste
5 tbsp coconut milk
1/2 tsp salt

Rub the fish fillets with the lime juice and salt. Keep aside.

Put all the ingredients for the paste in a blender and blend until smooth. Transfer the paste to a wok or frying pan, and simmer, stirring often, for 4 minutes. Now add the rest of the ingredients, except the fish and the prawns/shrimp. Continue to simmer until the mixture has no more liquid but is still moist. Add the prawns/shrimp, remove from the heat, and stir to coat them with the spice mixture.

Now put each fish fillet on a square of banana leaf or greaseproof paper or foil, and top the fish with an equal amount of spiced prawns/shrimp. Wrap neatly, and bake in a pre-heated oven at 200°C/400°F/Gas Mark 6 for 8–10 minutes. Serve straight away, either as a first course on some lettuce leaves, or with rice in the main course.

Lemper
Javanese stuffed rice rolls

These little rolls, about as big as a croquette or sausage roll, are made to an old Yogyakarta recipe and are immensely popular, as they deserve to be. The traditional stuffing, of shredded chicken very mildly spiced, perfectly complements the glutinous rice cooked in coconut milk. Nowadays, however, they may be stuffed with minced beef, abon (page 229), roasted grated coconut, fish, or shellfish; whatever the filling, it is usually pounded, minced, or shredded. Strictly speaking, lemper should be cooked in banana leaves, but here I make them in a Swiss roll tin.

During my student days in Yogya I was more interested in literature than food, so, although I ate a great many lemper, I didn't enquire about their folklore. It was only on my last visit to Yogya that I was told an interesting story. For at least the past hundred years, the people of Wonokromo, a few kilometres outside Yogya, have been celebrating Lemper Day once a year, when a certain day in the Javanese lunar calendar falls on a Wednesday, hari Rebo. The Javanese call this day 'Rebo Wekasan', and during it the whole village will cook and eat only lemper, nothing else. This quite makes me want to introduce the idea to England; but better still, during the festival everybody is encouraged to shout the strongest and maddest swear words, to say whatever they want to utter, just to get rid of any ill-feeling and frustration they have within themselves. This, too, is something I often very much want to do, but I can appreciate the common sense of setting aside a special day for it.

For the rest of the year, people make their lemper with the usual chicken filling. But on this one day they use all sorts of fillings, savoury and sweet, because after all this is their only food for the day. They form the sticky rice into the shapes of parts of the human body, so there are lemper paha, meaning thigh lemper, a lemper in the shape of your thigh, or lemper kelingking, as small as your little finger, and so on. No part of the human body (I was assured) is forgotten.

Perhaps the lemper wrapped in omelette and called Semar mendem, 'drunken Semar' (page 166), has some connection with this custom. Anyway, here is how to make lemper. You will need a Swiss roll tin about 22.5 by 32.5 cm/9 by 13 inches, and some greaseproof paper.

450 g/1 lb/2 cups glutinous rice,
  soaked in cold water for
  40–60 minutes, and drained

For the stuffing:
2 chicken breasts
4 shallots, chopped
3 cloves garlic, chopped
3 candlenuts or macadamia nuts
  or blanched almonds, chopped
1 tsp ground coriander
1/2 tsp ground cumin

450 ml/16 fl oz/2 cups coconut
  milk
1/4 tsp salt

1/2 tsp brown sugar
1 kaffir lime leaf (optional)
1/2 tsp salt
1/4 tsp ground white pepper
2 tbsp peanut oil or olive oil
140 ml/5 fl oz/generous 1/2 cup
  thick coconut milk

Boil the rice in the coconut milk with a quarter of a teaspoonful of salt until all the liquid has been absorbed by the rice. Transfer the rice to a steamer or double saucepan and steam it for 15 minutes. Turn off the heat, but leave the rice in the steamer until you are ready with the stuffing.

Boil the chicken breasts in water with a large pinch of salt for about 40 minutes. Take them out, and let them cool on a plate. When they are cool, shred them finely.

Blend the rest of the ingredients for the stuffing with half of the coconut milk until smooth. Put the liquid into a small saucepan, bring it to the boil and simmer for 8 minutes. Add the shredded chicken meat and the rest of the coconut milk and continue simmering until all the coconut milk has been absorbed by the meat but the mixture is still moist. Adjust the seasoning, and leave to cool.

Line the Swiss roll tin with a sheet of greaseproof paper and spread the rice on this, pressing it down (with another piece of greaseproof paper) to fill the tin evenly. Spread the cool spiced chicken evenly over the rice. Then roll it up as if you were making a Swiss roll. Cut it into slices with a large knife that has been wetted in hot water. Serve warm or cold as a tea-time snack, or with drinks.

Semar mendem
'Drunken Semar'

Semar is one of the famous quartet of clowns who appear in every wayang play in the traditional Javanese theatre. But he is also a god in disguise, and in some sense is the guardian spirit of all Java; and though he may say outrageous things I have never seen him anything but sober. Semar is an important person both in wayang orang, which is played by human actors, and in wayang kulit, where the characters are intricately pierced shadow puppets, made of leather. Along with his three sons, he is a licensed Fool, permitted to make rude jokes about authority, not only in the world of the play but also in the real world outside.

For Semar mendem, start by making the lemper as described above. When the rice is ready, put it on a sheet of non-stick paper or banana leaf, and pat it out into a layer about 1 cm/½ inch thick. Cut it into oblongs about 10 by 6 cm/4 by 3 inches. Divide the filling among the pieces, and then roll each one, starting on one of the shorter sides. Seal the ends by patting them together so that each lemper has the shape of a croquette. Now, instead of wrapping each lemper in banana leaf, wrap each one in a wide strip of thin omelette, and serve warm or cold.

Opor ayam
Chicken in white coconut-milk sauce

You will find this recipe all over Java. In Yogyakarta, it is the chicken traditionally served with gudeg (page 145). The sauce is white, because it does not use any chillies or turmeric, as do the sauces of many Indonesian dishes cooked in coconut milk. One thing it should contain is belimbing wuluh (page 258), but this particular belimbing is getting more difficult to find, even in many parts of Indonesia, and as far as I know is never available in the West. I always use rhubarb to take its place.

For 4 people

---

1 medium-size roasting chicken,
   or 4 chicken breasts with the
   skin
1 tsp lemon juice
$1/2$ tsp salt
2 kaffir lime leaves or bay leaves

For the paste:
5 shallots or 1 onion, chopped
4 cloves garlic, chopped
5 candlenuts or macadamia nuts,
   or 8 blanched almonds,
   chopped
1 tsp ground coriander

3 belimbing wuluh, or an 8-cm/
   3-inch stick of rhubarb, finely
   chopped
570 ml/1 pint/$2^{1}/2$ cups thick
   coconut milk
More salt and pepper if necessary

$1/2$ tsp ground cumin
$1/2$ tsp ground white pepper
1 tsp chopped fresh galingale
   or $1/4$ tsp ground galingale
5 tbsp of the coconut milk
1 tsp salt

Cut the chicken into 4 pieces, and rub them all over with a teaspoonful of lemon juice and half a teaspoon of salt. Do the same to the chicken breasts if you are using these. Then roast the chicken in a medium oven at 160°C/320°F/Gas Mark 5 for 40–45 minutes. Alternatively, deep-fry the chicken in coconut or peanut oil for 10–15 minutes, or until the chicken is just slightly coloured. Keep aside.

Blend all the ingredients for the paste until smooth, and transfer the paste to a saucepan. Simmer for 5 minutes, stirring often, then add the rest of the coconut milk. Bring almost to boiling point, then add the chicken pieces and the rest of the ingredients, except the extra salt and pepper. Bring almost to the boil again, then simmer for 40–50 minutes. Adjust the seasoning, take out the kaffir lime or bay leaves, and serve hot with rice and some cooked vegetables, or with gudeg (page 145).

Botok tempe
Spiced tempeh from Central Java

I must not forget to include this recipe, even though most Indonesians would, I fear, apologize for serving tempeh to guests, instead of being proud of it, as they should be. I tried very hard, during my recent trip around Indonesia, to convince chefs in some international hotels that they should have more confidence in their Indonesian food. Of course, not all tourists are curious to taste everything that is different from what they eat at home. But I have no doubt at all that if Indonesian food is made with the best and freshest ingredients, talented Indonesian chefs will fill their restaurants with foreign visitors in no time.

Tempeh is high in protein, it has a nutty flavour, and is an excellent food for vegetarians. For me, botok tempe, made with peté beans (page 270) and coconut milk, is one of the taste combinations that I miss most every time I leave Indonesia. A number of hotel restaurants in Yogya make this with tofu, but for the tempeh variety you need to go to the market or have it made at home by friends. Botok is wrapped in banana leaves and steamed, but like many such dishes it can be cooked in ramekins, then steamed or cooked in a bain-marie in the oven.

I give below some alternative ingredients that may be more widely obtainable; with these, the dish will still taste good, but naturally it won't be quite the same.

For 6–8 people

---

336 g/12 oz/3 cups tempeh, diced very small
60–110 g/2–4 oz/¹/2–1 cup peté beans, diced very small, or yard-long beans or French beans, cut into thin rounds
28 g/1 oz/¹/4 cup daun melinjo (page 268), or sorrel, roughly shredded
168 ml/6 fl oz/³/4 cup very thick coconut milk

2–4 fresh green chillies, de-seeded and cut into thin rounds
1-cm/¹/2-inch piece of fresh galingale, very finely chopped
4–6 large prawns/shrimp, peeled, heads removed, and chopped (optional)
1–2 tsp sugar
2 fresh salam leaves or bay leaves, finely shredded
2 tbsp freshly grated coconut or desiccated coconut

For the paste:

3 shallots, chopped
3 cloves garlic, chopped
1–2 large red chillies, de-seeded
  and chopped
1 tsp chopped ginger

$^1/_2$ tsp ground turmeric
1 tsp salt
2 tbsp peanut oil
4 tbsp coconut milk

Put all the ingredients for the paste in a blender, and blend until smooth. Transfer to a wok or saucepan and simmer, stirring often, for 8 minutes. By this time the paste will be quite oily. Add the tempeh and stir for 2 minutes, then add the rest of the ingredients, except the prawns/shrimp (if used), and the grated or desiccated coconut. Stir once, and simmer for 15 minutes. Then add the prawns/shrimp and grated coconut. Stir for 2 minutes and adjust the seasoning.

Now you can either wrap the tempeh mixture in banana leaves, or divide it among 6–8 ramekins. Cover the ramekins with foil and steam them for 15 minutes, or put them in a bain-marie in a pre-heated oven at 160°C/320°F/Gas Mark 3 for 15–20 minutes. Serve hot, warm, or cold, either as an accompaniment to rice, or just as it is, with plenty of salad.

Notes: Botok can be made with many other ingredients. For example, there are botok tahu (with tofu), botok hati ayam (with chicken liver), and botok made with mushrooms, minced beef, fish, prawns/shrimp, mussels, and so on. In short, botok is really the Central Javanese name for a variation of West Javanese pais or pepes. But botok is always wrapped in banana leaves. If the cooked mixture – the combination is a little different from the one described here – is wrapped in edible leaves, such as those of taro or cassava, the dish is called buntil.

Urap
Vegetable salad with coconut dressing

This is the basis of all vegetable salads with coconut dressing in this book. All the others are regional variants of urap, and naturally each has its own name. (See jukut murab on page 131.)

Urap can be made out of almost any combination of vegetables that you like, and these may be either cooked or raw. So the recipe here is divided into three parts: first, a section on cooked vegetables; second, an alternative section on raw vegetables; and third, the ingredients for the dressing or bumbu, and the instructions which apply to it.

Whether you use cooked or raw vegetables, it is advisable to use fresh coconut, freshly grated. See the chapter on coconut on pages 245–253, and the note below on using desiccated coconut.

For 4–6 people

For the cooked vegetables:

112 g/4 oz/1 cup of each of the following: cabbage or spring greens, shredded but not too finely; French or runner beans, cut into pieces 1 cm/¹/₂ inch long; carrots, peeled and cut into sticks the same length as the beans; cauliflower florets

---

Boil each vegetable separately for not more than 5 minutes, or steam them, putting the vegetables on top of each other, carrots at the bottom, then cabbage, then beans, then cauliflower on top. Serve them hot or warm as explained in the final part of the recipe.

For the raw vegetables:

1 bunch watercress, trimmed and washed, then drained

112 g/4 oz/1 cup carrots, peeled and roughly grated or cut into fine julienne strips

6 small red radishes, or 112 g/ 4 oz/1 cup white radish/ mooli, cut into matchsticks

¹/₂ cucumber, peeled, cut in halves lengthways, de-seeded and thinly sliced

112 g/4 oz/1 cup beansprouts, cleaned

3 tbsp chopped spring onions/ scallions

3 tbsp chopped mint and basil or, in Indonesia, kemangi

170

For the dressing:

1/2 coconut

1 tsp crumbled shrimp paste

1/2–1 tsp chilli powder

1 clove garlic, finely chopped

1/2 tsp soft brown sugar

Juice of 1/2 lime, or 1 tbsp
thick tamarind water

Salt to taste

Break open the coconut and remove the flesh. Peel the brown rind from it with a potato peeler, so that you have pure white coconut. Grate this with a hand grater, or put it a little at a time into a food processor and process it until you get fine coconut granules. Put the shrimp paste into a large bowl, and crush it further with the back of a spoon or with a pestle. Add the grated coconut and the rest of the ingredients for the dressing, and mix well. Adjust the seasoning.

Just before serving, mix all the vegetables in a large bowl, and mix in the dressing, tossing the vegetables well. Serve as a salad for a first course, for example with the long-cooked duck breasts on page 128, or as an accompaniment to a main course of rice and meat.

Note on using desiccated coconut

Desiccated coconut can be used for the bumbu, although it does not taste quite as good as fresh coconut. If you do use desiccated, then you will need to *boil* the mixture of coconut, shrimp paste, garlic, chilli, salt and sugar in a cupful of water for 5 minutes. Stir continuously while it boils. Then, if you are using cooked vegetables, put them into the pan also, and stir well for a minute or two to let them heat up again. If you are using raw vegetables, you must let the bumbu get cold before you mix it with the vegetables.

Nasi rames
Rice with a selection of dishes

If you want to eat quickly, and don't want to go out and look for a nasi Padang, then you won't go wrong if you choose nasi rames. This is indeed a meal in itself, a plate of plain boiled or steamed white rice – nasi putih – with four or five different dishes. In Java, the choice for the meat dish would normally be sambal goreng, made of chicken or beef, or chicken with hard-boiled eggs. For the vegetables, it could be a tumis, for instance tumis buncis, French beans sautéed with some spices;

171

or goreng terong (fried aubergines/eggplants), or maybe some stir-fried tofu and tempeh with a hot relish such as sambal bajak. Depending on the price, there will probably be some krupuk or emping or serundeng. A good nasi rames will have a good balance of tastes – some sweet and sour, some hot and spicy, and not too much sauce because this will drown other flavours.

In the old days, you would be given fish as well as meat, all on one plate; but nowadays, you will be asked whether you want fish or shell-fish, or meat or poultry, and usually you will only be given one kind of vegetable at a time.

I suggest that if you are a foreign visitor in Indonesia, and want to eat in a warung or a small restaurant, you should order nasi rames only if you know that you like Indonesian food as it is cooked and served to Indonesians. These small eating places, if they are any good, cook in the traditional way, without making any concession to visitors' tastes. If you're going to eat nasi rames, it should be authentic!

Nasi tumpeng
Rice and accompanying dishes for a selamatan

This is not a recipe, but an account of a traditional ritual feast, a selamatan in a Central Javanese household. At its centre, of course, is rice,
and around the rice are many side-dishes, all chosen and made in careful accordance with the event that the family is celebrating or com-
memorating. The selamatan is always related to a landmark in the life
of a member of the family. In Solo and Yogya, the two remaining
small sultanates of Central Java, they will tell you that there are only
three true and original occasions for a selamatan: birth, marriage and
death.

The word *selamatan* expresses the notions of thanksgiving, blessing,
grace. At the same time, a selamatan is not really a religious feast.
Although prayers may be said and a passage read or chanted from the
Qur'an, this is something that goes back a long time before the arrival
of Islam. The people who are most observant in giving and attending
selamatan are not santri, the educated middle-class pious Muslims, but
abangan, the poorer and less educated people who are closest to the
ancient Javanese ways of life and thought. For them, the selamatan is
partly a way of expressing family and neighbourhood solidarity – very
important in Indonesia – and partly a way of seeking or keeping the
protection of unseen powers. When times are good, other selamatan
are held, as a form of thanksgiving for a good harvest safely gathered
in, the passing of an exam, a birthday, or the completion of a new
house. Before a major undertaking, a selamatan will help family members to prosper, to go safely on a long journey for study or business, to
return successfully. For similar reasons, you will find offerings of food
left under a big waringin tree, or even by the traffic lights at a cross-
roads, since these are places where spirits dwell.

But our concern here is the food. Tumpeng refers to a quantity of
cooked rice that is shaped like an upside-down kukusan, the woven
bamboo basket for steaming rice on the traditional dandang; in other
words, like a cone. The tumpeng may be large or small, depending on
the purpose of the selamatan. For example, the Javanese hold a special
selamatan called miton or mitoni when a woman is in the seventh
month of pregnancy. The name derives from *pitu*, the Javanese word
for seven, and the centrepiece of the feast will be a large tumpeng sur-
rounded by six smaller ones. In Javanese tradition, seven is a magic

173

number, and it is also believed that in the seventh month the baby can be born, premature but sufficiently grown to continue life as would a normal baby carried in the womb for the full nine months. Even if the family cannot afford to give a large-scale selamatan at the time the baby is born, as long as they have held the mitoni they can feel that they have done their duty and can expect spiritual benefits and protection.

The rice for a selamatan may be either white or yellow. White rice is cooked in coconut milk and is called nasi gurih or nasi uduk (page 242). Yellow rice, coloured with turmeric, is nasi kuning. The rice is displayed and served on a large round tray made from woven bamboo strips, called a tampah. This is lined with banana leaf. The accompaniments differ according to the function of the selamatan. For mitoni, apart from the seven nasi tumpeng, there should also be seven hard-boiled eggs. There should be urap, made with the prescribed vegetables – kacang panjang (yard-long beans), kangkung (water spinach), taoge (beansprouts), and, a little surprisingly perhaps considering its foreign origins, kol (cabbage). The bumbu or coconut dressing should not be pedes or chilli-hot because a pregnant woman must not eat hot food. There should also be a steamed coconut relish, similar to the urap dressing, but mixed with some minced beef and wrapped in seven banana-leaf packets.

To show that this is a selamatan for mitoni, a satay skewer is stuck upright in the centre of the tampah arrangement, bearing a peeled hard-boiled egg, then a small red onion or shallot, and finally, on top, a red chilli. There should also be another tampah full of fresh fruit from the market. Then, on a third tampah, a bowl of rujak, made of seven different kinds of fruit; some cendol (page 214), and es kelapa muda, the water of a young coconut, mixed with ice. Then a bowl of rice-flour porridge, made with palm sugar, so that it is brown in colour. On top of this porridge is laid one perfect banana, as a sign that the birth will be smooth and without a hitch.

In addition to all this, a couple from Solo would also put, on the third tampah or tray, two whole young coconuts, each with a picture engraved on it. The pictures are of Janaka and Sembadra, figures from the cycle of wayang stories. If the baby is a boy, he will be as handsome as Janaka (Janaka is the Javanese name for Arjuna), and if a girl, she will be as beautiful as Sembadra, Arjuna's wife and sister of Lord Krishna.

Finally, there should be seven banana-leaf containers filled with little balls of food, the size of walnuts, in seven colours: white, red, green, yellow, blue, orange and *coklat*, i.e. brown. The first six are sticky rice, but the chocolate-coloured one is grated coconut cooked with palm sugar, to provide something sweet to go with the coloured rice. Even in these arcane rituals, the Javanese remember that they have a sweet tooth.

Not all the rice for the selamatan needs to be in the form of a tumpeng. It can be moulded in any other shape, with the accompanying dishes – chicken, urap, goat meat satay or gule – arranged round it on the tampah. Some of the food will already have been neatly packed in small oblong boxes called besek, also made of bamboo. The guests, who are all near neighbours or family members, will each take a besek home with them.

The preparation and cooking for a selamatan is a party in itself. Everybody in the village will volunteer to help, and many of them will contribute raw materials and ingredients for the food as well, following the tradition of gotong royong, mutual help. Preparations and clearing up can last for days before and days afterwards. On my last visit to Yogyakarta, I was invited to watch the preparations for a selamatan in a village just outside the town. Ibu Etty and I stayed for two hours, watching people cook, gossip, drink cups and cups of tea and eat a great many little sticky rice cakes. The place was full of young men, waiting to be sent to fetch things or deliver messages, and older people ready to give advice.

The atmosphere was festive enough – it was, after all, a selamatan for a dead man, exactly 1,000 days after he was buried. But the entire village had come to a complete halt; nobody seemed to be in their place of work, whether that was the rice fields or the local garage. We could not imagine that events like this can continue much longer, even in the countryside. This is not just because people have less spare time and are under pressure to earn money to raise their material standard of living. It is because the thread of continuity in village life is being snapped, in village after village, with the spread of education, travel, rapid communication, the departure of sons and daughters to other islands and to the cities. The selamatan, at least in its traditional form, has no reason for its continued existence. On the other hand, the sense of community is by no means dead in the towns and may survive strongly in the country. What new forms of communal feasting may develop, and how those feasts may be supplied and cooked, we have yet to see.

JAKARTA

New Waves

And so, finally, to Jakarta. Riding along Jalan Thamrin in a rare moment of traffic flow, we are discussing some question of Indonesian food. 'I wonder what Detlef would think,' I say, 'pity he went to Singapore.' Our host reaches for the carphone, and a few seconds later passes it back to me. 'Here he is,' he says. 'Ask him.'

Detlef Skrobanek was executive chef, later resident manager, at the Jakarta Hilton. He was a major contributor to a book called *The New Art of Indonesian Cooking*, which tackled some of the problems I have been working on in London and in this book, though from a rather different point of view. He describes the work that he and his team of twelve Indonesian chefs did as 'applying modern cooking methods to what is essentially a village cuisine'. We were to meet, eventually; but on an early visit I found to my delight that Prahasto Soebroto, the food and beverage manager at the Hilton, had laid on a banquet for us, with a *menu de dégustation* based on the work done by Detlef and his team.

The list included Duck Breast in Peanut Sauce; Clear Prawn Soup with Lemon Grass; Yellow Tail Fish in Sour Turmeric Sauce; Lamb with Spicy Veal Stuffing; Roast Javanese Beef Fillet; and Tropical Fruit and Fermented Rice, gratinated with Cinnamon Sabayon and Coconut Ice Cream. It was a memorable meal. But it was a very special occasion, because few of these dishes have gained permanent places on the menu. They are European dishes with an Indonesian flavour, but they have not established themselves with the wealthy Indonesians who eat here. To my mind, Detlef has gone a little too far in internationalizing this food. For example, he cooks all his meat very rare, which is quite alien to Indonesian tastes, and all his sauces are passed through a fine sieve, so that they lose the rough texture that Indonesians expect in a sauce. But these are matters of taste. The food was by any standards extremely good as well as original.

Another guest present at the dinner was William Wongso, on whose carphone I had earlier talked to Detlef in Singapore. William, always addressed and referred to by everyone as Pak William, Father William, is one of the most impressive people we met on the Indonesian food scene, as well as one of the most hospitable. He gave a dinner party at his house at which we ate dishes from Java, Sulawesi and Maluku, some flown in specially, some cooked in his own kitchen, while yet others were made by Tanya Alwi, daughter of the celebrated Des, of the family that own much of Bandaneira. Father and daughter were both present, and that is where we laid our plans for the trip to Banda.

Pak William also gave me a long interview in his office above the bakery and pastrycook's shop that he runs; he invited us to a dinner of the Jakarta Chaine des Rotisseurs, of which he is president; at his Italian restaurant we had food that would have been regarded as outstandingly good in a smart restaurant in Milan; he introduced us to Dr and Ibu Ratulangi in Manado; and he told us all about his newest venture, the Sarinah Food Court, in the heart of Jakarta.

Sarinah is one of the city's big department stores. In the 1980s street food vendors were allowed to set up their stalls in Sarinah's car park every evening, when the building was closed. Pak William, with some influential backing, has now leased a large part of the Sarinah basement, which was still being fitted out as a food court at the time we returned to London. It has since opened for business. Like the Amanda Food Center in Bali, but on a bigger scale, it provides facilities for regional food to be cooked, sold and eaten in hygienic conditions. Some food is cooked on the spot, some is flown in from distant parts of the country – where, we must assume, cooks are as pernickety as Pak William is about hygiene.

On a grey New Year's morning Pak William took us on a drive into the empty streets of Glodok. This is the area near the waterfront, where the Dutch established themselves in the seventeenth century and a few colonial buildings survive. Not far away the fishing boats and trading ships from other islands tie up at the quayside. The descendants of Chinese immigrants from Dutch times still live and do business here. Glodok therefore is, and has always been, the place to find the best Chinese food, though nowadays I don't think I would go and look for it unless I had someone with me who knew the area well. In alleys we found open-sided restaurants whose customers lifted the lids of aluminium cooking pots to help themselves from the contents – mostly seafood and offal. A man with a barrow was selling kue pancung, which are doughy cakes of glutinous rice flour, smothered in shredded young coconut flesh and sugar. They were freshly cooked and we all burned our tongues on them.

Chinese influence on Indonesian cooking is deep and wide: fried rice and noodles are only its more obvious traces. Indian influences have been assimilated so completely that you might hardly notice them at first. Indonesians, for example, use the word *kare*, curry, but the resulting dish is quite different from any Indian curry that I know of. The Dutch legacy is mostly in sweets and cakes. The American fast food chains and their imitators flourish, and the Japanese are now entering the market strongly at several levels. In most shopping malls, you will find branches of Kurumaya, which serve popular versions of standard Japanese dishes in cheap and cheerful surroundings. But there is also good, expensive Japanese food. The best meal we had in the Hotel Indonesia was in the exquisite surroundings of its Japanese restaurant, where our lunch was cooked in front of us by an Indonesian chef who had trained in Tokyo. Entrepreneurial Thais are opening up small, unassuming but good restaurants, selling food that is in some ways so similar to Indonesian food, and in others so different.

One big difference, which is not directly a matter of cooking, is that Thais approach the whole business of running a restaurant quite differently from Indonesians. I don't think Thais are necessarily better business people, but they are, as William Wongso said, 'fifteen years ahead of us' in the food trade. Whatever the reason, a wealthy Indonesian very rarely decides to open a restaurant as an investment. He can get a surer return on his capital elsewhere, and knows that even a good restaurant would give him none of the prestige that he might get in a big Western city. At the same time, there is no tradition of restaurant-going in Indonesian small towns. People eat out only when they have to. A cook, on the other hand, who wants to start a restaurant finds it hard to get training or financial backing. Cooks have always had low status and low pay. Kitchen and front-of-house staff don't have the tradition of training that would motivate them to think creatively about what they are doing. And there is the old problem of lack of confidence in the real worth of their culinary tradition.

But things are starting, gradually, to change. There has been for some time a serious monthly food magazine, *Selera* (Taste). There is an Indonesian Chefs' Association, IJUMPI, and a lot of the chefs I talked to said that they thought their status had improved and would continue to do so. Most important, the market for good food is developing as people become better off, travel more and work in offices. Good medium-price restaurants are often located close to office complexes; shopping centres tend to attract fast food franchisees. Fish restaurants do particularly well, because Indonesians have always eaten more fish than meat. There is no real excellence yet, by international standards, but in ten years there has been a huge improvement in the quality of the average upmarket eating house.

We went to Soekarno-Hatta Airport to spend a day on the premises of Aerowisata Catering, a subsidiary of the national airline, Garuda, and a sister company of the one that owns hotels like Pusako, Senggigi Beach and Preanger. The catering operation has a large modern building on the edge of the airport, one of four centres that prepare over 20,000 airline meals each day. The company supplies not only Garuda but all airlines using the country's four 'gateways'. On international flights, you are offered a choice between Indonesian and European food, and I was pleased to hear that demand for the Indonesian menu is always high, even among non-Indonesian passengers.

Even if food on aeroplanes is improving, it remains true that Indonesians eat better at home than anywhere else. At the start and finish of our journey of more than four months, we spent a day at the house of relatives in a Jakarta suburb. On the way there, the first time, we stopped at a street vendor's stall and spent a long time choosing six perfect durian as a present for our hostess. Lunch was rice, vegetables and half-a-dozen fish dishes cooked in the styles of West Sumatra and West Kalimantan. Our dessert was nasi ketan, black glutinous rice, with coconut milk delicately flavoured with the flesh of slightly overripe durian. This of course is in a household where food is highly valued, and there is enough money and leisure for the family to eat well.

Like many fast-growing capital cities, Jakarta has very few dishes it can claim as its own regional specialities. People come to the city from the provinces, bringing their cooking with them. The selection of recipes in this section, therefore, represents the common property of these incomers rather than a local tradition. A bus ride through the town will show you what the popular dishes are at the street food stalls and small cafés: soto, nasi rames, bakso, pecel, sate. The recipes that follow include most of the 'clichés' that my Australian friends complained about, but I am glad to include them because they can all be made well (or badly), and most give scope for variation and experiment.

The population of Greater Jakarta today is estimated at somewhere round 12 million people, and the city is growing fast, its commuter belt spreading outwards into West Java. Jakarta is so far the only 'world city' that Indonesia possesses. At the moment, it is hard to see any other town reaching the same levels of size, complexity and energy. I am forced to realize that if I were ever to settle again in my native country, I would go to Jakarta, however reluctantly I was drawn to it. But the small towns, the villages and the countryside – especially the mountains – will be the real Indonesia, and Jakarta will look to them for its ideas and its inspiration, in food and cooking and hospitality as in everything else that makes life enjoyable.

Gado-gado
Cooked mixed vegetables with peanut sauce

The best gado-gado, and I still remember it well, used to be sold at a warung in Yogyakarta, in a small alley not far from the main street, Malioboro. This was in 1960. For my fellow-students and me, it was the main meal of the day. At 2 or 3 o'clock in the afternoon, after attending lectures in the decayed nobleman's house that in those days was the Faculty of Arts and Letters, we would set off on our bicycles to return to our lodgings on the other side of town. The late lunch break at the warung gado-gado was the turning-point of the day, when we could gossip, relax, enjoy the passing street scene, and eat fresh crisp vegetables with a stinging hot peanut sauce, a gourmet dish for a few rupiah. This bumbu, or sauce, was made to our individual orders while we watched. We each chose our vegetables, and the whole gado-gado was served with lontong, hard-boiled eggs, fried tempeh and tofu, and krupuk or emping. We were not hungry again until 9 o'clock in the evening.

In 1993, in Jakarta, I found the gado-gado in many small restaurants very disappointing. It was, alas, the same in many hotel restaurants, which were supposed to be promoting this as one of our national dishes. The reason is simple: everything now is mass-produced. The vegetables are cooked, and usually overcooked, early in the morning. The sauce is made from something in a packet, the krupuk is already stale, there is no yolk in the sliced egg (and where could it have gone?). In short, a classic dish, well worth any chef's attention, has been spoiled because it takes a little extra time and money to make it really well.

At home, you can make it as it deserves to be made. Gado-gado is excellent for lunch or supper, or as one of the dishes in a buffet party. It will be highly appreciated by your vegetarian guests, but not only by them.

For 4–6 people

The sauce:
Sambal kacang, as on page 222

The vegetables:
*112 g/4 oz/1 cup cabbage or
 spring greens, shredded
225 g/8 oz/2 cups French
 beans, cut into 1-cm/
 1/2-inch lengths*

*4 medium carrots, peeled
 and sliced thinly
112 g/4 oz/1 cup cauliflower
 florets
112 g/4 oz/1 cup beansprouts,
 washed*

For the garnish:
*Some lettuce leaves and
 watercress
2 hard-boiled eggs, quartered
1 medium-size potato, boiled
 in its skin, then peeled
 and sliced; or 225 g/8 oz
 of slices of lontong
 (page 241) (optional)*

*1/2 cucumber, thinly sliced
1 tbsp crisp-fried onions
 (page 230)
2 large krupuk, or a handful
 of fried emping, broken
 up into small pieces
 (optional)*

Boil the vegetables separately in slightly salted water, for 3–4 minutes, except the beansprouts which only need 2 minutes. Drain each vegetable separately in a colander.

To serve, arrange the lettuce and watercress around the edge of a serving dish. Then pile the vegetables in the middle of the dish. Arrange the eggs, sliced potatoes or lontong, and sliced cucumber on top.

Heat the peanut sauce in a small saucepan until hot; add more water if it is too thick. Adjust the seasoning, and pour the sauce over the vegetables. Sprinkle the fried onions on top. Serve warm or cold. If you want to serve hot gado-gado, it can be reheated in a microwave oven. When reheating, however, do not include the lettuce and watercress, cucumber slices, fried onions, krupuk or emping. Add these garnishes immediately before serving.

Sate daging
Meat satays

In Indonesia, if you ask for sate daging, you will be given beef satay. Here I am putting all three meat satays under one heading, because the marinade is the same and so is the sauce. So here are sate daging, with beef; sate ayam, which is chicken satay; and sate kambing, or lamb satay. I am putting the satay recipe here, in the Jakarta chapter, because this is one dish that you can get almost anywhere in Indonesia; it has become a national dish, and one that tourists from every corner of the globe will immediately like. Having said all this, however, I must add that you can get bad satays. The meat can be tough and gristly, and the marinade either tasteless or with too much of everything, and the sauce may be too hot, too sweet, or of the wrong texture, because it has been thickened with too much flour when no flour at all is needed.

The recipe here will give you a marinade with a combination of tastes that is guaranteed to be liked by everybody. This is a marinade I developed during the time I had an Indonesian delicatessen in Wimbledon, when I sold uncooked marinated satay to hundreds of satisfied customers. (The same is true of the peanut sauce or sambal kacang on page 222.)

The marinade below gives quantities for each kind of meat, not for all the meats together. In any case you need to marinate the different meats in separate bowls.

For 8–10 people

450 g/1 lb rump steak
450 g/1 lb lean meat from leg or shoulder of lamb

3 skinless chicken breasts
3 boned and skinned chicken thighs

For the marinade
(for each kind of meat):
2 shallots, finely chopped
2 cloves garlic, finely chopped
1 tsp finely chopped ginger
1 tsp ground coriander
1/2 tsp chilli powder

3 tsp malt vinegar or lime juice
1 tbsp light soya sauce
1/4 tsp salt
1 tsp sugar (optional)
2 tbsp peanut or olive oil

Mix all the ingredients for the marinade in a glass bowl. Keep aside.

Cut the meat into 2-cm/3/4-inch cubes, mix them well into the marinade, and keep in a cool place for 2 hours, or in the fridge overnight.

When you are ready to grill the satays, put the meat on bamboo or metal skewers, about 5–6 cubes per skewer. Grill on charcoal, or under a gas or electric grill, for about 2–3 minutes on each side, turning them over once. Or you can cook the satays on a rack in a pre-heated oven at 160°C/320°F/Gas Mark 3, for 6–10 minutes.

Serve straight away, with the peanut sauce (page 222) either poured over the meat or served separately for everybody to help themselves.

Sambal goreng daging
Diced beef in rich coconut sauce

Like rendang (page 40), this has become a national dish, and in fact is well known all over South-East Asia. I include it in all my books. Sambal goreng is really a kind of all-purpose recipe, or more accurately a general name for a whole class of dishes in which you can cook many kinds of meat. With chicken, it becomes sambal goreng ayam. If you use hard-boiled eggs as well, it becomes sambal goreng ayam dan telur. With prawns/shrimp, it is sambal goreng udang, and with fish, sambal goreng ikan. The recipe below, however, is for meat that needs much longer cooking than fish and shellfish. For sea- or river-food, start with the sambal goreng sauce (page 225), because the prawns/shrimp or fish are put into the sauce only for the last few minutes of cooking.

In Java, sambal goreng daging is the traditional dish for Lebaran when it is served with ketupat (page 278) or lontong (page 241).

---

450 g/1 lb topside or silverside, cut into 1-cm/ 1/2-inch cubes
112 g/4 oz/1 cup mangetout or sugar peas
56 g/2 oz/1/2 cup fresh peté beans (page 270), cut into halves (optional)
420 ml/15 fl oz/2 cups hot water

5-cm/2-inch piece of fresh lemon grass
2 kaffir lime leaves, or lemon or bay leaves
2 ripe tomatoes, peeled and chopped
112 g/4 oz/1 cup creamed coconut, chopped

For the paste:

3 shallots or 1 small onion,
    chopped
2 cloves garlic
5-cm/2-inch piece of
    ginger, peeled and sliced
1/2–1 tsp sambal ulek
1 tsp shrimp paste (optional)
2 candlenuts, chopped
    (optional)

1 tsp ground coriander
1 tsp paprika
1/2 tsp salt, or more to taste
1 tbsp tamarind water or
    lemon juice
2 tbsp olive or peanut oil
2 tbsp cold water

Blend all the ingredients for the paste until smooth. In a saucepan, bring this paste to the boil and cook it for 4 minutes, stirring continuously. Add the meat and stir until all the pieces are coated with the paste. Cover the pan and simmer for 4–5 minutes. Then add the hot water, lemon grass, and kaffir lime, lemon or bay leaves. Bring the mixture back to the boil, cover the pan again, and simmer gently for 30–40 minutes. Uncover the pan again and add the fresh peté, if used, the tomatoes and the creamed coconut; stir to dissolve the coconut. Simmer and stir for 2 more minutes, then add the mangetout. Continue to simmer for 2 more minutes. Adjust the seasoning. Serve hot with rice, ketupat, or lontong.

Nasi goreng
Fried rice

Like satay, this is one of the better-known Indonesian dishes, although it originated in China and, within Indonesia, has always been associated with the Dutch and the rijsttafel. There are right and wrong ways of making nasi goreng. A bad one is oily, and comes to the table cold or lukewarm, garnished only with a leathery fried egg. This is the kind of thing that gets Indonesian food a bad name. A good nasi goreng is light, hot, the grains moist but separate and quite fluffy, the garnish fresh and attractive to look at, its textures contrasting with the texture of the rice. Such a nasi goreng is not hard to make, but it needs to be prepared and cooked in accordance with a few basic principles.

The rice should be cooked 2–3 hours before it is to be fried, so that it has time to get cold. (There are some guidelines for different ways of cooking plain rice on page 237.) Freshly cooked, still-hot rice will go soggy and oily if you fry it. Rice that has been left overnight is too stale to make first-rate nasi goreng. Next, the cold rice must be mixed in with the other ingredients when those ingredients are already cooked and still hot. From then on, the mixing and stir-frying must be done on a low heat and must continue until the rice is hot but not burnt.

If you are going to use seafood or meat, it is best to stir-fry this separately. You can use the same spice mixture as is given here for the fried rice, if you wish. Then mix the meat or seafood into the rice in the final 2 minutes before serving; or simply spread it on top of the rice on the serving dish.

---

450 g/1 lb/2 cups long grain
    rice, cooked by the
    absorption method
    (page 238), and allowed
    to get cold
2 tbsp peanut oil
1 tbsp butter
3 shallots or 1 small onion,
    very finely chopped
1 tsp sambal bajak (page 221)
    or 1/2 tsp chilli powder

1 tsp paprika
2 tsp tomato purée or tomato
    ketchup
2 tbsp light soya sauce
3 medium-size carrots, diced
    very small
112 g/4 oz/1 cup button
    mushrooms, cleaned and
    quartered
2 tbsp hot water (optional)
Salt to taste

Heat the oil and butter in a wok or large frying pan. Stir-fry the shallots for 1–2 minutes, then add the other ingredients, including the hot water (if used) but *not* the rice. Then continue stir-frying for about 6 minutes or until the vegetables are cooked. Add the rice, and mix it thoroughly with the vegetables so that it becomes hot and takes on the reddish tinge of the paprika and tomato. Adjust the seasoning. Serve hot on a heated serving dish, either by itself as an accompaniment to the main course; or garnished with sliced cucumber, sliced tomatoes, watercress and bawang goreng (page 230); or topped with seafood or meat as described above.

Bakmie goreng
Fried noodles

Most of what I said above concerning nasi goreng applies equally to bakmie goreng. The ingredients for the spice mixture are identical. I recommend that you use dried Chinese egg noodles, which are easily available, or fresh egg noodles, which can be bought in Chinese shops. I find other kinds of dried egg noodles are a bit stodgy when cooked. I am told that the Chinese have a secret method of making their noodles so that they have just the right elasticity and are not brittle or stodgy.

Noodles must never be overcooked, or cooked too long before they are fried. (In this, at least, bakmie goreng is different from nasi goreng.) Boil the noodles just a few minutes before you stir-fry them with the rest of the ingredients.

For 4–6 people

450 g/1 lb dried egg noodles	*2.3 litres/4 pints/10 cups*
1 tsp salt	*water*

Boil the water in a large saucepan with the salt, and when it is boiling add the noodles. If you are using fresh noodles, boil them for 1–1½ minutes; if using dried noodles, boil them for 3 minutes. While they are boiling, tease them apart with a large fork or a wooden spoon so that they do not stick together. Put them in a colander under cold running water until they are cold, to stop them overcooking. Let the noodles drain in the colander, turning them several times so that all the water can drain off. Then proceed immediately, as described in the nasi goreng recipe on page 187.

Asinan Jakarta
A Jakarta fruit and vegetable salad

A more elaborate mixture of freshly sliced crunchy fruit and vegetables is made in Bogor, a hill town some distance south of Jakarta. Asinan Bogor, however, is available from only one or two small shops, where they pack the fruit, vegetables, dressing and garnishes in separate plastic bags for you to take away and mix at home. When I bought some in Bogor recently, I found the asinan very tasty and refreshing, though I could not interest my English husband in it. When I make asinan Jakarta at home in London, however, he eats it as cheerfully as any other mixed salad. So here is the recipe for asinan Jakarta, with suggestions for alternative fruit.

For 4–6 people

---

1 cucumber, peeled
2–3 medium carrots, peeled
2 kedondong or hard apples
2 small yam beans/jicama or unripe pears
1 small pineapple, peeled and cored (optional)

112 g/4 oz/1 cup beansprouts, cleaned
112 g/4 oz/1 cup white cabbage, finely shredded
56 g/2 oz/^{1}/2 cup Chinese cabbage, finely shredded

For the dressing:
56 g/2 oz/^{1}/4 cup brown sugar
4 tbsp water
1 tbsp castor sugar
1 tsp fried or grilled shrimp paste
2 tbsp dried shrimps (page 262)

3–5 bird peppers, or 2 small dried red chillies
1 large red chilli, de-seeded and chopped
225 ml/8 fl oz/1 cup distilled malt vinegar
2 tsp salt

For the garnish:
84 g/3 oz/^{2}/3 cup peanuts, fried or roasted

3 or 4 prawn/shrimp crackers
Some mixed lettuce leaves

Cut the cucumber and carrots into matchsticks, taking care not to make them too small. Slice the apples and pears, not too thinly, and cut the pineapple, if used, into small pieces. (If kedondong and yam beans/jicama are used, peel them first.)

To make the dressing, melt the brown sugar and the water in a small saucepan. Transfer this straight away into a large glass bowl. Keep aside. Put the rest of the ingredients for the dressing into a blender and blend, but not too smoothly. Transfer this into the bowl with the already melted brown sugar. Stir this dressing to mix well, and adjust the seasoning. Now mix all the salad ingredients in the dressing, and leave to stand for a few hours or overnight, in the fridge or a cool place, to let the juices penetrate.

Just before serving, transfer the salad mixture to a large platter, garnish with the peanuts and crackers, and arrange the lettuce leaves around the edge of the platter.

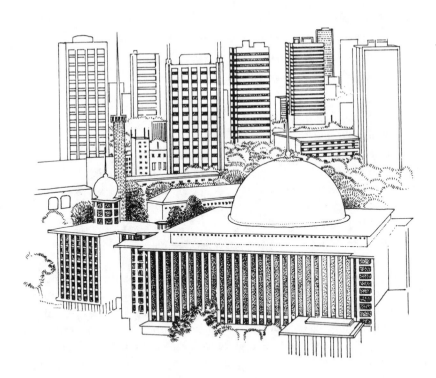

Kepiting pedas
Chilli crab

This dish is as much a popular Indonesian dish as a Chinese one. But on my most recent trip to Indonesia, I swore I would never again order chilli crab anywhere. The way it is cooked and served, however attractive it may look on the plate, is invariably disappointing. Even if you eat as local people do, by hand, there is very little meat inside the cracked shells. Maybe the cook has used the meat for something else, and leaves his customers licking their fingers, enjoying (or not) the taste of the chilli sauce. Yet somehow it is not a real chilli crab, if it is served elegantly with all the white meat piled on the body shell, and the rest of the shell debris discarded.

I am very fond of crab, and in any case the recipe must be recorded. So here is how I suggest you serve the crab, still with its shell but with all the meat easily accessible. This recipe is for hard-shelled crabs.

For 2–4 people

---

2 hard-shelled crabs, weighing about 400 g/14 oz each

4 tbsp peanut oil

For the bumbu:

8 red chillies, de-seeded, or 2 tsp sambal ulek

6 shallots or 1 large onion, finely sliced

4 cloves garlic, finely sliced

2-cm/3/4-inch piece of ginger, peeled

1 tsp ground coriander

3 tbsp water

2 tsp light soya sauce

1 tbsp thick tamarind water, or 3 tsp lime juice

Salt to taste

As with the lobster on page 76, rinse the live crabs well before plunging them into boiling water and leaving them simmering for 18–20 minutes. If you have bought crabs already boiled but still unopened, plunge them into boiling water but leave them to simmer for only 5 minutes. Take them out of the water, and leave to cool on a tray. Slice the chillies slantwise very finely. Slice the ginger thinly, then cut the pieces into tiny shreds.

Heat the oil in a wok or frying pan and stir-fry the shallot or onion for 3 minutes. Turn off the heat and spoon out and discard half of the oil. Now heat the remaining oil again, and add the sliced chillies or sambal ulek, garlic and ginger. Continue stir-frying for another minute, then add the coriander, water, soya sauce, and tamarind water or lime juice. Stir, and let it simmer for 2 minutes. Adjust the seasoning and turn off the heat while you finish preparing the crabs.

When the crabs are cool enough to handle, pull off the hood, which is actually the underside of the crab, and discard. Cut off the claws, break the shell open, and remove the meat on to a plate, separating the white and the brown meat. Take out and discard also the intestines and inedible parts from the body of the crab.

Cut the shell into 4 pieces, and put these, together with the larger fragments of the claw-shells, in a large bowl. Wash them in warm water, dry them with kitchen paper, and put them on a baking tray in the oven at 100°C/210°F/Gas Mark 1/4 until you are ready to serve.

I myself prefer to use the brown meat of the crab for something else, an omelette for instance, but you can if you wish mix it in with the white meat. Heat the wok or pan with the chilli, onion, and so on, and stir-fry for 1 minute, then stir in the crab meat and continue stir-frying for 2 more minutes or until the crab meat is hot. Add the lime juice, and stir again. Spread the pieces of shell from the oven on a serving platter, and spoon some chillied crab meat on each fragment of shell. Serve straight away.

Bubur ayam
Rice porridge with spicy chicken soup

This has become much more popular in the last ten years in many restaurants, especially in Jakarta. In big international hotels, bubur ayam has become one of the most sought-after dishes in a late supper menu. If the hotel has a coffee shop that is open 24 hours, the usual hour for bubur ayam is after 11 o'clock at night.

Many hotels also serve bubur ayam for breakfast, and I was told that in Jakarta, Bali and Medan there is great demand for it from visitors from Japan and other Asian countries – almost as great as the demand for nasi goreng at breakfast-time. I certainly would sooner have a choice of these two dishes than a basket of soggy microwaved croissants. Bread for toast is even less impressive. Here is a recipe for bubur ayam so you can try it first at home.

For 6–8 people

For the porridge:

225 g/8 oz/1 cup long grain rice, soaked in cold water for 2–4 hours, or overnight, then drained

670 ml/24 fl oz/3 cups cold water or chicken stock
1 tsp salt

For the chicken soup:

1 small chicken, cleaned and quartered, or 3–4 chicken breasts on the bone

1.7–2.3 litres/3–4 pints/ 7½–10 cups cold water
1 tsp salt

For the paste:

3 shallots, chopped
2 cloves garlic, chopped
1 tsp chopped ginger
3 candlenuts, chopped
½ tsp ground turmeric

¼ tsp chilli powder
1 tbsp light soya sauce
2 tbsp peanut oil
2 tbsp hot water
Salt and pepper to taste

For the garnish:

112 g/4 oz/1 cup beansprouts, cleaned
2–3 tbsp chopped flat-leaf parsley
2–3 tbsp chopped spring onions/scallions
2 lemons, quartered

Sambal kecap (page 221) or Tabasco sauce
3 tbsp crisp-fried onions (page 230)
3–4 tbsp sambal kacang kedele (page 223)

Make the porridge first, because this is to be served cold. It can be made quite a long time in advance. When the porridge is cooked, transfer it into a nice deep-sided platter. Leave to get cold, and refrigerate until needed.

Boil the chicken pieces in the water with the salt for 40 minutes over a low heat. Leave to cool, and when cool enough to handle, shred or slice the chicken meat into small pieces. Put the skin and the bones back into the stock, and continue cooking it for 10–15 more minutes. Then strain the stock and keep aside.

Put all the ingredients for the paste, except the salt and pepper, into a blender and blend until smooth. Transfer the paste into a large saucepan, and simmer, stirring often, for 5–6 minutes. Add the chicken pieces, stir around and season with salt and pepper. Add the stock, bring back to the boil, and simmer for 10 minutes. Adjust the seasoning.

To serve the bubur ayam, arrange all the garnishes separately in small dishes. Keep the chicken soup piping hot on the stove or hot plate. Ask everybody to help themselves. First, put a large spoonful or two of the porridge in a bowl or deep soup plate. Next, put some of the garnishes (except the fried onions and the sambal kecap or Tabasco sauce) on top of the porridge. Then ladle the hot soup with the chicken pieces over them. Last, sprinkle the fried onions over all, and add some sambal kecap or Tabasco sauce if you like your bubur ayam hotter and spicier.

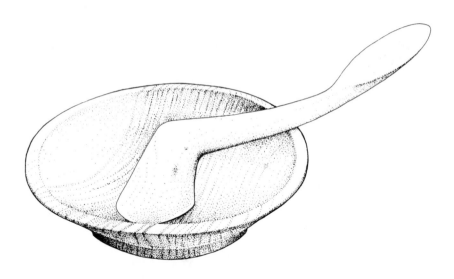

SWEET DISHES

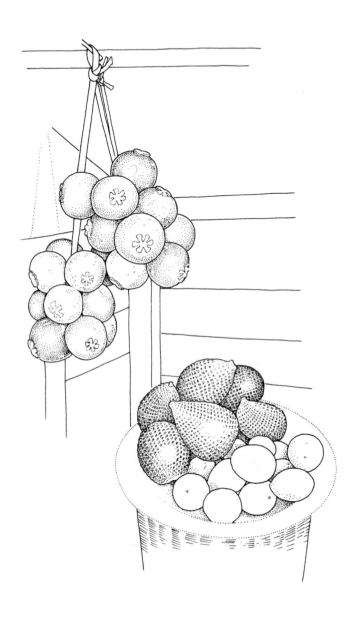

These are recipes for what Indonesians call jajanan, snacks you buy from street vendors or shops. Jajanan usually include savoury dishes as well, but here I am only concerned with sweetmeats, sticky cakes and snacks made of plain or glutinous rice flour and wheat flour, cassava and sweet potatoes. There are literally thousands of these, but most of them are variations of each other. Every region and family has its own favourite versions of the same kue or kueh (biscuits and cakes) and bubur (porridge). In my trip around Indonesia in 1993, I saw more jajanan than I ever saw before. Looking at what was on sale in local markets in Bukittinggi, Tomohon, Madura, or Yogyakarta, I didn't recall ever eating half of these 'small eats' when I was at school or university. Even now, I was not able to taste all I saw, not because they didn't tempt me, but because, after thirty years in London, I have become wary of eating anything that has been exposed to flies and dust.

However, in Jakarta, Bandung, Yogya, Surabaya and other big cities, there are delicatessens that sell their own selections of these Indonesian snacks alongside Western-style biscuits and cakes. The food halls of department stores often sell Indonesian cakes in miniature, each one literally a single mouthful. One of my sisters told me that these cakes are so popular that boxes and boxes of them are bought by well-off middle-class families for their private parties. It is encouraging that traditional sweets are still in demand, but sad that most cooks and domestic helps in middle-class households no longer know how to make them.

I would need a whole book devoted to this subject if I were to do it justice: I would have to put in at least a hundred recipes. Here I can only include a dozen or so, and I am forced to choose. I am therefore only putting in recipes that can easily be made in the West, using ingredients that are available everywhere, for dishes that do not need to be described as 'an acquired taste'. I shall leave to my fellow cookery writers in Indonesia the privilege of recording and rescuing from oblivion the traditional street food recipes of all the regions of their country, in their own regional languages and in Bahasa Indonesia, so that future generations can still make and enjoy all these delicious things.

Serabi
Breakfast pancakes

I called these 'breakfast pancakes' simply because, in my early youth, when we were living in a very small village on the border of West and Central Java, south of Cirebon, this was our family breakfast on at least three days of the week. The serabi were not made at home, but bought from a lonely street vendor, an elderly woman who set up her tray and cooking pot not very far from our house, and I was always the one who would go and buy the serabi at 6 o'clock in the morning. We would have two each of these pancakes, which we ate with red sugar syrup called tengguli in Sumatra, but in Java air gula, sugar water, or sirop gula merah, red sugar syrup.

Serabi-makers in Central Java and East Java still cook in small round-bottomed earthenware pots, shaped like little woks, with domed lids to match. These are placed on a charcoal stove, called anglo in Javanese, and the vendors fan the charcoal from time to time with a kipas, a fan woven from thin strips of bamboo.

In Wimbledon, I make my serabi in a blini pan (page 215), or a thick-bottomed frying pan or skillet. If I served them for breakfast, I would eat them with fresh fruit and some pouring cream, but they are equally good with savoury things, such as bacon or ham. If they are made in a blini pan, the thin serabi can be used as blini, topped with smoked fish of your choice and served as canapés or a first course. For canapés you can sandwich the filling between two of these small round pancakes and cut each pair into quarters.

Makes 30–35 small serabi

---

112 g/4 oz/1 cup plain/ all-purpose flour	1 egg
56 g/2 oz/¹/2 cup rice powder	500 ml/18 fl oz/2¹/4 cups thick coconut milk, slightly
¹/4 tsp salt	heated
¹/2 tsp sugar	Butter

Sift the two kinds of flour and the salt into a bowl. Make a well in the middle, and break the egg into it. Stir the sugar in a small bowl with 4 tablespoonfuls of the coconut milk, add this to the bowl, and with a wooden spoon gradually mix the flour in. Knead this dough by hand for about 10 minutes, until none of it sticks to your fingers. Now slowly and gradually pour in the rest of the coconut milk, while whisking the dough with a wire whisk or a wooden spoon until you get a smooth, thick batter, but still pourable.

Slowly heat a blini pan or skillet and brush it with butter. Pour the batter into the holes of the blini pan, or, for a skillet, use a tablespoon to pour on spoonfuls of batter in round shapes about 6 cm/2 1/2 inches across. Cook gently for about 2 minutes, then turn the pancakes over with a palette knife and cook them on the other side for a further 2 minutes. Serve hot, warm, or cold, as suggested above.

Buah jingah
Sweet potato fritters

I think the best sweet potato fritters we ever had were the ones Ibu Ratulangi made for us in Tomohon. She filled them with sugar for breakfast, and with cheese as tea-time snacks. Her name for them, the local name in Tomohon and elsewhere in North Sulawesi, is tai kuda, which literally means 'horse droppings'. In Ambon they have something very similar, slightly different in shape, and shallow-fried instead of deep-fried, called uli patatas. Buah jingah is the name given to these fritters by the Banjar people in South Kalimantan. The real Indonesian kind are always filled with sugar. The cheese filling was Ibu Ratulangi's own variation, because she thought I would prefer it to sugar and I would be able to experiment with different kinds of cheeses in London. She was right on both points; I like the fritters with cheese, though not, ideally, the processed cheese which is available in Tomohon, because it is rather tasteless. In the West you can have Stilton, or Gorgonzola, or any other strong-tasting cheese, to make a contrast with the sweet potatoes.

Makes about 12–14 fritters, or more smaller ones

---

450 g/1 lb/4 cups (peeled weight) sweet potatoes	*112–225 g/4–8 oz/1/2–1 cup palm sugar (or cheese),*
1 tsp salt	*chopped*

170 g/6 oz/1¹/2 cups rice flour
112 ml/4 fl oz/¹/2 cup cold
  water
¹/2 tsp salt
Limewater (page 266) made

by dissolving ¹/2 tsp kapur
sirih in 2 tbsp warm water
(optional)
Peanut oil for shallow- or
deep-frying

Boil the sweet potatoes in plenty of water with 1 teaspoonful of salt. When cooked, mash them until smooth. Keep aside to get cold. Mix the rice flour with the water, ¹/2 teaspoonful of salt and the air kapur or limewater (page 266), if used, until you have a smooth batter.

When you are ready to fry the fritters, divide the mashed sweet potatoes into as many portions as you want. Take a portion and press it flat on a plate or on the palm of your hand. Put ¹/2 teaspoonful of sugar or cheese, or a little more, on to the portion of sweet potato, close the potato round this filling, and form the fritter into a ball or the shape of a croquette. Repeat the process until all the ingredients are used up. Dip each fritter into the rice-flour batter before frying them in several batches until golden brown. Serve hot, warm, or cold.

Kue Bugis
Sticky rice-flour cakes with coconut filling

---

225 g/8 oz/2 cups glutinous
   rice flour
A pinch of salt

For the filling:
112 g/4 oz/1 cup freshly
   grated or desiccated coconut
168 ml/6 fl oz/³/4 cup water

For the cream:
568 ml/1 pint/2¹/2 cups very
   thick coconut milk

280 ml/10 fl oz/1¹/4 cups
   coconut milk

84 g/3 oz/scant ¹/2 cup brown
   sugar
1 tbsp glutinous rice flour

A pinch of salt

Put the rice flour in a saucepan and pour in the coconut milk carefully, stirring continuously. Add a pinch of salt. Cook this mixture, stirring occasionally at first but then, as it thickens, stirring continuously. It will begin to look very much like porridge. Continue cooking for 5 minutes longer.

Now make the filling. Heat the sugar in the water until it dissolves, then stir in the coconut and let it simmer until all the water has been absorbed into the coconut. Put in the 1 tablespoonful of glutinous rice flour, mix well, and continue cooking for another 2 minutes, stirring all the time.

In another saucepan, boil the thick coconut milk with a pinch of salt. You can boil this vigorously until it is well reduced in volume and the coconut milk has separated into sediment and oil. Transfer into a bowl, and stir vigorously so that the two separate parts mix together.

In Indonesia, kue Bugis are always wrapped in banana leaves for cooking, but here I use individual small pots, ramekins, or cups without handles. Put a teaspoonful of the cream into each cup, then a table-spoonful of the thick 'porridge'. Smooth this with a spoon and put on top of it a heaped teaspoonful of the filling, then another tablespoonful of the porridge, and top it off with a teaspoonful of the 'cream'. Put the cups or pots side by side in a large, wide saucepan. Cover each cup with foil. Pour hot water into the saucepan to come halfway up the outside of the cups or pots. Bring the water to the boil, then simmer for 10 minutes.

Kue Bugis, whether warm or cold, are best eaten with a spoon straight from whatever they have been cooked in.

Kue putu
Steamed coconut cup cakes

These are Central Javanese tea-time cakes. They are usually green because of the pandanus leaf juice (page 261) used in the batter. I prefer my kue putu white, and moulded in small ring moulds or rum baba moulds, so that when I take them out each one has a hole in the middle. But you can also use small Chinese teacups without handles, or small ramekins.

For kue putu, it is advisable to use freshly grated coconut. One coconut will be sufficient for the quantities shown here. Peel the brown skin from half of the coconut flesh, then grate it; or cut it into small pieces, put these into a food processor, and process until you get fine coconut granules. These go straight into the cakes. The rest of the flesh doesn't need to have its brown skin peeled off; just grate or blend it as you did with the other, then blend it with hot water to make coconut milk.

Makes 10–12 small cup cakes

---

5 eggs	*A pinch of salt*
4 tbsp castor sugar	*2 tbsp pandanus leaf juice*
112 g/4 oz/1 cup rice flour	*(optional)*
56 g/2 oz/¹/2 cup plain flour	*112 g/4 oz/1 cup freshly*
140 ml/¹/4 pint/generous	*grated coconut*
¹/2 cup thick coconut milk	

Beat the eggs and sugar until thick and pale in colour. Add the two kinds of flour, and continue beating while you slowly add the coconut milk, salt, and pandanus leaf juice, if used. Beat this batter for about 3 more minutes.

Heat some water in the bottom part of a steamer, and put 10–12 moulds or cups in the steamer to warm for 2–3 minutes.

Divide the grated coconut equally among the cups, pressing it in with a spoon. Then pour in the batter, the same amount for each cup or mould. Steam for 10 minutes. Turn out the cakes as soon as the cups or moulds are cool enough to handle. Serve warm or cold.

Lapis Surabaya
Layered chocolate cake

I am not quite sure why this delicious chocolate cake is called by the name of Surabaya, a coastal city in East Java. This recipe was given to me by an Indonesian friend in London, under that name. Since most Indonesian cake and bread recipes originated from the Dutch, my guess is that a bakery in Surabaya was once famous for this particular cake. We use cocoa for the chocolate layer, but in England I use cooking chocolate.

308 g/11 oz/scant 1^1/2 cups castor sugar	*180 g/6^1/2 oz/generous ^{3}/4 cup plain/all-purpose flour*
308 g/11 oz/scant 1^1/2 cups butter	*100 g/3^1/2 oz/3^1/2 squares dark cooking chocolate,*
16 egg yolks	*or 3 tbsp cocoa*
8 egg whites	*3 tbsp apricot jam*
A pinch of salt	

Beat the butter and sugar until creamy and white. Add the egg yolks one at a time while continuing to beat until you have a very creamy mixture. Sift and fold in the flour. Beat the egg whites with the salt until stiff and fold these as well into the cake mixture.

Melt the chocolate in a bowl over hot water, and mix it into one-third of the mixture. If cocoa powder is used, just sift it into the mixture and fold in. Put this chocolate mixture in a well-oiled cake tin, and put the rest of the creamy mixture, in equal measure, into two other well-oiled cake tins of the same size. Cook in a pre-heated oven at 190°C/375°F/Gas Mark 5 for 30–40 minutes.

When the layers are cooked let them cool slightly on wire racks. Then stack the layers on top of each other, with the chocolate one in the middle, the layers being held together by the apricot jam.

This is the easiest way to make this layered cake. You could, of course, make it the way Lapis legit (page 206) is made, in which case the apricot jam will be unnecessary.

Lapis legit
Indonesian spiced layered cake

Like the Lapis Surabaya on page 205, this is a Dutch recipe that has been popular in Indonesia for a long time – so popular that we now regard it as our own, and serve it as a treat for Lebaran as well as at Christmas. The Dutch call it spekkoek, a name that is also still used in Indonesia. Cooks of my mother's generation used to bake their spekkoek in a very simple oven, just a tin box on legs with a tray of glowing charcoal at the bottom and perhaps another at the top as a grill.

This cake is very rich, so it needs to be served in small pieces, usually thin slices about 5 cm/2 inches long. These are easier to cut if you make the cake in a square tin.

Makes one 20–25 cm (8–9 inch) cake

450 g/1 lb/2 cups unsalted butter	*A pinch of salt*
A drop of vanilla extract	*8 egg whites*
225 g/8 oz/1 cup castor sugar	*2 tsp ground nutmeg*
18 egg yolks (size 2)	*4 tsp ground cinnamon*
3 tbsp top of milk	*1 tsp ground cloves*
140 g/5 oz/1¼ cups plain/ all-purpose flour	*1 tsp ground mace*
	A pinch of ground white pepper (optional)

Beat the butter, vanilla and half of the sugar until creamy. In another bowl, beat the egg yolks with the rest of the sugar until creamy and thick. Beat these mixtures together and add the milk. Sift the flour into the bowl, and fold it in carefully. Beat the egg whites with the pinch of salt until stiff and fold in. Now stir in all the spices and mix well, but gently.

Butter the cake tin, preferably a square one with a loose bottom. Heat the grill to its maximum temperature; if you are using a grill inside an oven, heat the oven to 150°C/300°F/Gas Mark 2, then turn it off before turning on the grill. Pour a layer of the batter about 3 mm/1/8 inch thick over the bottom of the tin. Grill this for 2 minutes, until the batter has set firm. Take it out from under the grill, brush the surface of the cake with melted butter, and press it flat with the bottom of a tumbler.

Then pour on the same amount of batter again, grill, and continue the same process until all the batter is used up. A good Lapis legit will consist of 12–14 layers, or more. The heat of the grill browns the top of each layer, giving the cut cake its neat horizontal stripes. Finish cooking the cake in the pre-heated oven at 150°C/300°F/Gas Mark 2 for 10 minutes.

Remove the cake from the tin and cool on a wire rack. Lapis legit will keep moist and fresh in a cake tin or in the fridge for a week, well wrapped in greaseproof paper and an outer layer of aluminium foil. It can also be frozen.

Kue barongko
Banana cake from Central Sulawesi

Sulawesi is so oddly shaped that it is difficult to pinpoint its centre on the map. This recipe, however, must come from somewhere near there, as it is one of those developed by the Dharma Wanita, the official Indonesian Women's Organization, in the province of Sulawesi Tengah. I can see immediately, from the ingredients used, that this is a middle-class family recipe. The only problem about making it in Western countries is that the special cooking bananas, pisang kepok, are not available. Fortunately, ripe plantains will do very well instead, and at a pinch the Gros Michel, the only type of banana imported into Europe, is also quite acceptable.

For 6–8 people

---

450 g/1 lb bananas or ripe plantains (peeled weight)	*450 ml/ 16 fl oz/2 cups thick coconut milk*
6 eggs (size 2)	*1/2 tsp vanilla essence*
168 g/6 oz/3/4 cup castor sugar	*84 g/3 oz/1/2 cup raisins (optional)*

Cut the bananas or plantains in halves lengthways. With a small spoon, scrape out the tiny black seeds in the centre. Put the bananas in a large bowl and mash them. Add the eggs, while beating the mixture with a hand or electric beater for about 5 minutes. Then add the sugar, and continue beating until the batter is quite thick and smooth. Then add the coconut milk and vanilla essence, mixing them well in.

Line the bottom of a 20-cm/8-inch cake tin with greaseproof paper, and grease the sides of the tin. Steam the cake for 40–45 minutes, but spread the raisins, if used, on top of the cake after 25 minutes' cooking. Alternatively, you can cook the cake in a pre-heated oven at 180C°/350°F/Gas Mark 4 for 30–40 minutes, putting on the raisins halfway through the cooking time. Leave the cake to cool a little before taking it out of the tin. Serve warm or cold.

Bubur ketan hitam
Black glutinous rice porridge

This porridge, which is not really black but a lovely deep purple, is the basis of the delicious black rice sorbet I developed several years ago. The porridge, served hot or warm, will not fail to attract people, whether it is served as breakfast or dessert. If you don't like my suggestion of thick coconut milk with a pinch of salt, then pour plenty of cream on your porridge.

For 4–6 people

---

84 g/3 oz/scant 1/2 cup black glutinous rice, soaked for 2–8 hours, then drained
1.7 litres/3 pints/71/2 cups coconut milk
1/2 tsp salt
1 small stick of cinnamon

3 tbsp granulated sugar
140 ml/1/4 pint/generous 1/2 cup very thick coconut milk and a large pinch of salt, or the same quantity of single cream

---

Put the 1.7 litres/3 pints/71/2 cups of coconut milk in the saucepan with the rice, add the salt and cinnamon stick and bring to the boil. Simmer slowly for 10 minutes, then add the sugar. Continue to simmer, stirring often, until the porridge is thick. The cooking time will be

60–70 minutes. Serve the porridge hot or warm as suggested above.

Warm the thick coconut milk with the salt in a saucepan for a few minutes only. Do not boil. Use this or the single cream as a pouring cream on the black rice porridge.

Pisang goreng
Fried bananas

Fried bananas are very easy to make, and Indonesia has many different bananas that are suitable for frying. Yet you can still get bad pisang goreng. The trouble, usually, is the oil. Some warung owners are not careful always to use fresh, good-quality oil – because, of course, it is expensive. Another reason for bad pisang goreng is that the bananas used are too ripe, or not ripe enough.

The bananas you get in the West are perfectly suitable for frying, as they are for making kue barongko (page 207); alternatively, use ripe plantains, which give a firmer and nicer texture when they are fried.

For 4–6 people

4 medium–sized bananas, fairly ripe, or 3 ripe plantains	*28 g/1 oz/2 tbsp melted butter*
84 g/3 oz/scant 1/2 cup rice flour	*170 ml/6 fl oz/3/4 cup coconut milk*
28 g/1 oz/2 tbsp plain/ all-purpose flour	*A pinch of salt*
	Peanut oil or clarified butter for frying

Mix the two sorts of flour, butter, coconut milk and salt in a bowl, making a smooth batter. Cut the bananas lengthways down the middle, then cut each piece across into two. If using plantains, cut the halves into three pieces. Coat well with the batter, and shallow- or deep-fry in the oil or clarified butter until golden brown. Serve hot or cold.

Sari rasa ketan
A Kalimantan variation of glutinous rice cake

This is one of those sweet sticky cakes that everybody looks forward to eating as soon as they hear the announcement on the radio saying that it is waktu buka, or time to break your fast during the month of Ramadhan. Like so many Indonesian steamed cakes, this can also be cooked in the oven as explained below.

For 8–10 people

---

112 g/4 oz/¹/2 cup glutinous rice, soaked in cold water for 2 hours, then drained

20–23 cm/8–9 inch clipped form cake tin

For the batter:
3 eggs
84 g/3 oz/scant ¹/2 cup castor sugar or soft brown sugar

168 g/6 fl oz/³/4 cup coconut milk
112 g/4 oz/1 cup rice powder
¹/2 tsp salt

Steam the drained glutinous rice in a rice steamer or a double saucepan for 15–20 minutes. Line the cake tin with bakewell or greaseproof paper, and grease the side with butter. When the steamed rice is ready, leave it to cool a little, then transfer it to the cake tin, and press the rice down, using a large spoon wetted with water, until you have an even surface.

Beat the eggs and the sugar until quite thick, then add the rice powder and salt, and mix them well. Continue beating while you pour in the coconut milk, a little at a time, until you have a smooth batter. Pour this on to the rice in the cake tin, and bake in a pre-heated oven at 180°C/350°F/Gas Mark 4 for 30–40 minutes. Cut the cake into 8 or 10 portions, and serve warm or cold.

Martabak Kubang
Sweet stuffed pancakes from West Sumatra

At most martabak stalls, whether on the alun-alun in Yogyakarta, or on a street corner in Padang, the savoury martabak vendor will also sell sweet martabak; or, if he has only one skillet and is limited to one sort, a colleague, friend, or relative next door is selling the other. The recipe below is based on notes I made when we ate this sweet martabak in Padang. There, they call it Martabak Kubang, because that particular group of martabak sellers is from a village of that name nearby. If you are also serving savoury martabak with a meat filling, this sweet one will be ample for 4 to 6 people.

There are several standard fillings for sweet martabak. One of them is a sort of coloured sugar, usually coated in chocolate and similar to what in England are called 'hundreds and thousands'. Indonesians use the Dutch name, muisjes.

Makes 2 sweet martabak

For the batter:

225 g/8 oz/2 cups plain/ all-purpose flour

450 ml/16 fl oz/2 cups warm water

1 tsp bicarbonate of soda/ baking soda, or baking powder

1/2 tsp salt

1 tsp sugar (optional)

For the filling:

4 tsp demerara sugar

2 tbsp muisjes

2 tbsp crushed roasted peanuts

2 tsp roasted sesame seeds

Mix the batter about 30 minutes before you are ready to make the pancake. Use peanut or olive oil, or clarified butter, to grease a skillet or a large (23-cm/9-inch) pancake pan. Heat the pan until quite hot, but over a low heat, and pour on to it half the batter, tilting the pan so that the batter spreads evenly. Leave to cook for 3 minutes, then spread half of the filling onto the still quite soft pancake. Fold the pancake in half with the filling inside. Turn the folded pancake over. The outside by this time will be quite nicely browned. Turn off the heat, and leave the filled pancake to rest on the hot pan for a minute or two. Transfer to a large platter. Repeat the process with the remaining ingredients. Serve hot, warm, or cold.

Note: My notes from Padang also mention a batter made with yeast. This takes longer to prepare, but produces what you may well think a most tasty result. Don't use too large a pan to make the pancakes – very big ones are hard to turn over.

Makes 4–6 pancakes, 18–20 cm/7–8 inches across

225 g/8 oz/2 cups plain/ all-purpose flour	*1/2 tsp salt*
1 tsp compressed yeast	*450 ml/16 fl oz/2 cups warm water*
1/2 tsp castor sugar	*1 tbsp oil for frying*

Sift the flour into a bowl. Put the bowl in a warm place. Put the yeast, sugar and salt into a measuring jug and add 100 ml/3½ fl oz/scant ½ cup of the warm water. Stir well, then add the rest of the water. Leave in a warm place for 10 minutes or until bubbles appear on the surface. Then gradually mix the liquid into the flour, avoiding lumps. The batter will be quite thick. Leave to stand in a warm place for about 30 minutes.

Heat the oil in a frying pan or skillet. Spoon in nearly enough batter to cover the base of the pan. Spread it with a spatula – it should be able to slide in the pan. Then proceed as above. Remember that the pancake becomes very spongy. Don't cook it on a high heat; if you do, the outside will harden before the inside is cooked. As each pancake is quite thick, I suggest you keep the cooked ones in a warm oven while you make the others. Spread the filling just before serving.

Rujak
Spiced fruit salad

Indonesians, especially women, love eating under-ripe fruit. It must be fruit that is still crunchy, and that doesn't make a mess when peeled and sliced. Their demands do not stop there: the crunchy, slightly sour-tasting fruit must be dipped into something hot and sweet. On a hot and steamy afternoon, on your open veranda anywhere in the tropics, a mixed fruit rujak can be very refreshing. If you are like me, you will soon become addicted to it as an appetizer; it is not really a dessert. However, serve it as an ordinary fruit salad by all means, if you find you like it that way; or, as we do at home, eat it at any time.

Like other kinds of sambal, rujak sauce can be made in a good quantity and kept in the fridge for up to a week. The best sugar to use is what we call gula Jawa or gula Melaka; in the West this is usually labelled 'palm sugar' (page 273). But soft brown sugar or demerara sugar will do very well as alternatives.

For 4–6 people, or for more as an appetizer; quantities for the sauce will be sufficient for up to a week's supply

---

The fruit:

1 jeruk Bali or pomelo	1 small yam bean/jicama
1/2 cucumber	1 small pineapple
2 small green mangoes	1–2 hard green apples or pears
	1 tsp salt

For the dip or sauce:

225 g/8 oz/1 cup gula Jawa, or 140 g/5 oz/generous 1/2 cup soft brown or demerara sugar	1/2 tsp crumbled shrimp paste (optional)
1–3 bird chillies	1/4 tsp salt
	1 tbsp very thick tamarind water or lime juice

Peel and segment the pomelo. Slice the cucumber, not too thinly; this may be peeled or not, as you prefer. Prepare the other fruit, washing and peeling as required, and cutting everything into small pieces. Put the pieces straight into a bowl of cold water with 1 teaspoonful of salt.

When you are ready to serve, drain off this water and pile all the fruit on a plate or in a bowl.

To make the sauce, chop up the gula Jawa and put it into a mixing bowl. Crush the chillies and the salt in a mortar, with the shrimp paste, if used; then add this mixture to the sugar, crushing and mixing with the back of a wooden spoon. Add the tamarind water or lime juice, and mix well. You may need to add a tablespoonful of warm water to make your sauce the right consistency; it should look like a fairly thick, sticky syrup. Put half of the sauce in a jar to be refrigerated until you need it, and the other half in a small bowl to be served as a dipping sauce. Alternatively, you can mix this sauce with the fruit in a large bowl, and serve it just as you would an ordinary fruit salad.

Cendol
A popular Indonesian coconut milk drink

This is more often called *es cendol*, because it is an iced drink enjoyed by children. Many tourists now seem to be attracted by it, and I have seen cendol being sold in a Food Court in Sydney, at stalls that do Indonesian and Malaysian food. Australians who have been to Bali often mention cendol to me as one of the drinks they rather enjoyed. So I must include the recipe here, even if it is only to satisfy your curiosity.

For 4 people

For the cendol:
112 g/4 oz/1 cup rice flour
1 tbsp cornflour/cornstarch
570 ml/1 pint/2¹/2 cups water
A pinch of salt

2 tsp sugar
1 tbsp pandanus leaf juice
(page 261–262)

For the coconut milk drink:
850 ml/1¹/2 pints/3³/4 cups
coconut milk

112 g/4 oz/¹/2 cup gula Jawa
or soft brown sugar
112 ml/4 fl oz/¹/2 cup water
Lots of ice cubes

To make the cendol, mix the two kinds of flour smoothly with the water in a saucepan. Add the other ingredients, and cook over a low heat, stirring often, until you have quite a stiff porridge. Get ready a large bowl, half filled with cold water. Then, using a sieve with fairly large holes, sieve the porridge into the water in the bowl. What you get through the sieve are cendol – short strands of thick porridge, which will become firmer if left in the cold water for a few minutes. Drain these, and keep aside.

Boil the brown sugar in the water for 2–3 minutes, and pour the syrup into a jug.

To serve the es cendol, divide the cendol among 4 tall glasses. Add equal amounts of the coconut milk, then of the sugar syrup, and top with ice cubes. Stir well before drinking. Cendol is often served with a long-handled spoon.

Kopi jahe (bandrek)
A hot ginger drink

This is the drink for somebody who likes to feel a warm inner glow after being out of doors on a wet and windy day. Sumatrans call this kopi jahe, though there is no coffee in it; the Javanese call it bandrek. I remember drinking piping-hot kopi jahe at a warung in North Sumatra. It was made with very little sugar, which is how I like it. However, my sister in Jakarta tells me that in Bandung the custom is to stir into it some of the flesh of kelapa muda, a young coconut, with a small amount of gula Jawa to improve the colour.

To make 1.1 litres/2 pints/5 cups

---

*1.3 litres/2¹/4 pints/5¹/2 cups
    water*
*56 g/2 oz/¹/2 cup fresh ginger,
    peeled and thinly sliced*
1 small pandanus leaf, cut into 3
*1 stem lemon grass, cut into 3
    and bruised*

*4–5 cm/1¹/2–2 inch
    cinnamon stick*
3–4 cloves
28 g/1 oz/2 tbsp gula Jawa
*2–4 tbsp granulated sugar
    (optional)*

Put the water in a saucepan with the other ingredients, except the sugar. Bring the water slowly to the boil, and leave it boiling for 2–3 minutes. Add the sugar, and continue to simmer, stirring several times, for another 2 minutes. Strain the 'kopi' into a jug and serve hot. Discard all the solids.

216

SAMBAL ACAR AND OTHER SIDE-DISHES

A sambal in Indonesia is any sauce or relish made with chillies. The chillies can be red or green, small or large. They are usually not de-seeded, because we want our sambal hot and the seed is the hottest part of a chilli. That is why, in this book, I usually suggest that you remove the seeds, on the assumption that you are not used to their excessive heat. For those who like their food chilli-hot, these sambals are useful: they make it possible for the main dish to be quite mild, without disappointing guests who expect Indonesian food to have a powerful kick. Different sambal recipes produce very different flavours. And many people who object to over-hot food still enjoy a little dab of sambal from the side of the plate.

Acar (pronounced *achar*) is a generic term for a mixed vegetable dish, raw or cooked, lightly pickled with vinegar, and mildly or very highly spiced. I have only included two acar recipes here, one cooked and the other raw, but from these you can make your own variations. As the purpose of most acar is to preserve the vegetables, it will keep for many days if stored in a jar in the fridge. It is nearly always served cold, so it is no trouble to have it always handy. You can serve acar instead of chutney, or as a relish to go with a rich meat or fish dish cooked in thick coconut milk.

Sambal ulek
Crushed red chillies with salt

This is the basis of all the sambals that Indonesians use, either as a hot relish or for spicing a cooked dish. You can buy it in jars, usually made in the Netherlands and labelled *sambal oelek*.

However, if you have a food processor this is quite an easy sambal to make at home, and of course it will be much better value. Make plenty, and you can pack it in plastic bags and freeze it, or keep it for up to 2 weeks in an airtight jar in the fridge. For small quantities, see below. If you want the sambal less hot, discard the seeds of the chillies.

Makes about 450 g/1 lb

---

450 g/1 lb red chillies, stalks removed	*1 tbsp mild vinegar*
	1 tsp sugar (optional)
570 ml/1 pint/2½ cups water	*2 tbsp peanut or soya oil*
1 tbsp salt	*6–8 tbsp boiled water*

Put the chillies in a saucepan and cover them with the water. Bring to the boil and simmer for 15 minutes. Drain, and put the chillies in the blender with salt, vinegar and sugar (if used). (You may need to do this in batches.) Add the peanut or soya oil and the boiled water, and blend until smooth.

Sambal terasi
Shrimp paste relish

You can make this with raw or cooked chillies. It is usually very hot, as most Javanese prefer to make it with cabe rawit, bird chilli, which I think is the hottest of the chillies. And it is usually made in small quantities – just enough for one meal. Make sure that the shrimp paste has already been grilled or fried. If you don't want to make it with raw chillies, then boil them first for 2–3 minutes.

Sambal terasi is particularly good as a dip for raw vegetables.

For 4–6 people

---

10 bird chillies	*1/4 tsp salt*
1 small shallot, chopped	*1/2 tsp brown sugar (optional)*
1 tsp crumbled shrimp paste	*Juice of 1/2 a small lime*
1 clove garlic	

If you have the Indonesian cobek and ulek-ulek (page 195), use them to crush these ingredients. Otherwise use a mortar and pestle. Put everything except the lime juice in the mortar, and crush them until you have a rough paste. Add the lime juice, mix well, and transfer the sambal to a small bowl for everybody to help themselves.

Sambal kecap
Soy sauce with chilli

This is excellent with satay, and is specially recommended to those who don't like, or want a change from, peanut sauce. It is also good with raw vegetables.

2–4 small chillies, de-seeded and finely chopped	Juice of 1 small lime or lemon
	1 tsp peanut oil (optional)
2 shallots, finely sliced	1 tbsp light soy sauce
1 clove garlic, finely chopped (optional)	1 tbsp dark soy sauce

Mix all the ingredients together in a bowl, and serve.

Sambal bajak
Chilli relish cooked with spices

Like sambal ulek, this can be bought in jars. In London, most sambals are imported from the Netherlands, still labelled with the old spelling, in this case *sambal badjak*.

Stored in an airtight jar, and in the fridge, it will stay good for 2–3 weeks. If you find you still have some left over, remember that this is one of the sambals suitable for making nasi goreng.

Makes about 340 g/12 oz of sambal bajak

225 ml/8 fl oz/1 cup thick coconut milk	1 tsp brown sugar
	2.5-cm/1-inch slice of galingale (optional)
1 tsp salt	

To be blended:

225 g/8 oz/2 cups large red chillies	1 tsp chopped ginger
	3 candlenuts
8 shallots or 1 large onion, chopped	1 tsp crumbled shrimp paste
	3 tbsp of the coconut milk
5 cloves garlic, chopped	2 tbsp peanut oil

De-seed the chillies, if you prefer them less hot, before chopping them roughly. Then blend all the ingredients that are to be blended to a smooth paste. Transfer this to a wok or saucepan and simmer, stirring often, for 6 minutes. Add the rest of the coconut milk and the other ingredients. Bring to the boil, and simmer for 30–40 minutes, until the coconut milk has been absorbed by the chillies. By this time some oil will be visible, so stir the sambal, as if you were stir frying, for 4–5 minutes. Adjust the seasoning: you may need a little more salt and sugar. Leave the sambal to get cold before storing it in a jar and in the fridge. Serve at room temperature.

Sambal kacang (bumbu sate)
Peanut sauce

This is the best-known, most popular sauce for satay. It is also used for gado-gado (page 183), and goes well with any grilled meat.

If you like your satay sauce chilli-hot, there are several quite passable powdered instant sauces on the market. For making it yourself, there are various so-called short cuts, most of them involving crunchy peanut butter. Avoid these; the method described below is as easy, cheaper and much nicer.

Makes about 280 ml/^{1}/2 pint/1^1/4 cups of sauce

112 ml/4 fl oz/^{1}/2 cup vegetable oil	*Salt to taste*
225 g/8 oz/1^1/3 cups raw peanuts	*^{1}/2 tsp chilli powder*
2 cloves garlic, chopped	*^{1}/2 tsp brown sugar*
4 shallots, chopped	*1 tbsp dark soy sauce*
A thin slice of shrimp paste (page 272) (optional)	*450 ml/16 fl oz/2 cups water*
	1 tbsp tamarind water (page 274) or juice of a lemon

Stir-fry the peanuts for 4 minutes. Remove with a slotted spoon to drain in a colander, and leave to cool. Then pound or grind the nuts into a fine powder, using a blender, coffee grinder, or pestle and mortar. Discard the oil, except for 1 tablespoonful.

Crush the garlic, shallots and shrimp paste in a mortar with a little salt, and fry in the remaining oil for 1 minute. Add the chilli powder, sugar, soy sauce and water. Bring this to the boil, then add the ground peanuts. Simmer, stirring occasionally, until the sauce becomes thick; this should take about 8–10 minutes. Add the tamarind water or lemon juice and more salt if needed.

When cool, keep in a jar in the fridge. Reheat as required for use with satay or as a dip for lalab (crudités) or savoury snacks. The sauce will keep in the fridge for up to 1 week.

Sambal kacang kedele
Soya bean relish

This is a lovely crunchy relish, used to garnish bubur ayam (page 193), or, for instance, on nasi goreng or nasi rames.

Makes about 225 g/8 oz

225 g/8 oz/1^{1}/3 cups dry soya beans, washed and drained	*2 cloves garlic, finely chopped*
	^{1}/2–1 tsp chilli powder
1.7 litres/3 pints/7^{1}/2 cups water	*Salt to taste*
3 shallots, finely chopped	*225 ml/8 fl oz/1 cup peanut oil*

Put the beans in the water and bring this to a rolling boil. Turn off the heat, skim off and discard the froth that comes to the surface, cover the pan and leave the beans to soak for 1 hour.

Now boil the beans again in the same water for 1 hour, by which time the beans should be tender. Then add 1 teaspoonful of salt and continue to simmer for 5–8 minutes. Drain the beans into a colander and leave them to get cold. When cold, pat them dry with kitchen paper.

Heat the oil in a wok or large frying pan, and fry the beans, stirring often, for 5–8 minutes, or until they are nicely browned. When cold, the beans should be crisp. Discard all the oil except 1 tablespoonful. Heat this and stir-fry the shallots for 3 minutes, then add the garlic. Continue stir-frying for 2 more minutes, and add the chilli powder. Stir and mix, and turn off the heat. Add the fried soya beans to the shallot mixture, and stir to mix them well in. Taste one, and add more salt if necessary. Leave the spiced beans to get really cold, before storing them in an airtight container, where they will stay crisp for at least a week. Serve cold as a relish or garnish.

Kacang goreng dengan teri
Fried peanuts with dried anchovies

This side-dish is not highly spiced, but it is savoury and crunchy and equally good either on the dinner table or as an appetizer to be served with drinks.

450 g/1 lb dried anchovies, heads removed	*112 ml/4 fl oz/^{1}/2 cup sunflower oil or peanut oil*
450 g/1 lb/2^2/3 cups peanuts	*^{1}/2 tsp chilli powder (optional)*

Stir-fry the peanuts in the oil in a wok or frying pan in three batches, for 4 minutes each time. Remove them with a slotted spoon and drain them in a colander or on absorbent paper. Use the same oil to stir-fry the dried anchovies in three batches, for 3–4 minutes each time. Drain these in the same way. Allow peanuts and anchovies to go cold, then mix them well together. Put them in an airtight container, add the chilli powder (if used) and shake well to mix the powder evenly. This relish keeps for up to 2 weeks.

Kuah sambal goreng
Sambal goreng sauce

This is a rich, creamy sauce, so it will taste nicer if you make it quite spicy.

Makes about 570 ml/1 pint/2^1/$_2$ cups of sauce

For the paste:

4 shallots, chopped

2 cloves garlic, chopped

3 large red chillies, de-seeded
  and chopped; or ^{1}/$_2$ tsp chilli
  powder + 1 tsp paprika

1 tsp shrimp paste

2 candlenuts (optional)

1 tsp chopped ginger

1 tsp ground coriander

A large pinch of galingale powder

^{1}/$_2$ tsp salt

2 tbsp peanut oil

2 tbsp tamarind water

2 tbsp of the coconut milk
  (see below)

Other ingredients:

850 ml/1^1/$_2$ pints/3^3/$_4$ cups
  coconut milk

5-cm/2-inch stem of lemon
  grass

2 kaffir lime leaves

2 large red tomatoes, skinned,
  de-seeded and chopped

Salt to taste

Blend all the ingredients for the paste until smooth, and transfer to a saucepan. Bring to the boil and simmer, stirring often, for 5 minutes. Add the coconut milk, lemon grass and kaffir lime leaves. Bring everything to the boil again, then simmer for 50 minutes, stirring occasionally.

Add the chopped tomatoes and some more salt. Go on simmering for another 10 minutes. Adjust the seasoning, and serve hot. Alternatively, let the sauce cool and refrigerate it until needed. The sauce will stay good in the fridge for 3–4 days. To serve, reheat the sauce gently almost to boiling point, then simmer for 15 minutes, stirring frequently.

If you are making sambal goreng udang or sambal goreng ikan, this is the time to add the prawns/shrimp or fish; then continue cooking for 4 minutes longer. Serve straight away. Once you put in the prawns/shrimp or fish, it is advisable not to reheat.

Krupuk udang
Prawn crackers

Indonesia has a wide range of different krupuk and keripik. As the names suggest, all of them are crisp, brittle and crunchy. All are made of some kind of flour – wheat, rice, cassava, or maize/corn – and all are dried in the sun and then fried. They all have different flavours, as potato crisps do, though a better comparison would be with Indian popadums. Flavour, appearance and colour differ from region to region. In any market place you will find raw and cooked krupuk displayed in baskets and large trays, and the sellers are usually very willing to tell you what ingredients have gone into them and to let you sample their wares.

The national flag-carrier for krupuk, if one can call it that – the export variety, anyway – is krupuk udang, of which the best and most famous type is krupuk Sidoarjo; this is what you will most often find in the West. Sidoarjo is a town in East Java, somewhat south of Surabaya. The krupuk are made with shrimps or prawns, which they taste of quite strongly. Their appearance is pinkish, and they come in different sizes, the smallest being similar to the prawn/shrimp crackers you get in Chinese restaurants, though the flavour is more interesting.

To cook krupuk, you need a wok and plenty of very hot oil. Raw krupuk are quite small, hard, and darker in colour than cooked ones. The largest are about as big as a shoe-horn, and you put them in the oil one at a time. As soon as the krupuk is in the hot oil it curls up, and as a well-fried krupuk must be flat, you press it down with a spatula against the bottom of the wok. Don't be afraid to do this; you won't break the krupuk, which remains pliable while it is in the oil. Fry the krupuk for 1 minute, then turn it over and fry the other side for a little less than a minute. It only becomes crisp after it is taken out of the oil and has cooled down a little. The smallest size, and the Chinese prawn/shrimp crackers, can be fried a handful at a time for a minute or two, then scooped out with a wire scoop and drained on absorbent paper. They will curl a little, but for the small ones this does not matter. In fact, it is an advantage, because you can use them like little cups, filling them with different kinds of savoury relish and serving them as canapés.

Raw krupuk will keep for a long time. Once they are cooked, they will stay fresh and crisp in an airtight container for up to 2 weeks. Serve them to be eaten with fingers as a side-dish, or break one or two into pieces and use the fragments to garnish dishes such as gado-gado (page 183) or nasi goreng (page 187).

Emping
Melinjo nut crackers

As far as I know, this is an exclusively Indonesian food product. I don't think any other Asian country makes emping. You can get them in Malaysia and the Philippines, but I am pretty sure they are imported from Indonesia, which certainly exports them to Europe and Australia.

Emping are made from melinjo nuts (page 268), crushed and dried in the sun. They look something like underdone potato crisps, but the flavour is quite different: dry, savoury but not salty, slightly nutty. To cook them, drop a few at a time into hot oil in a wok and let them sizzle for just a few seconds. They will become bigger, but not dramatically so. Take them out with a wire scoop, drain them on absorbent paper and sprinkle a little salt on them. Serve them just as they are with drinks, or use them, like krupuk, to garnish nasi goreng or gado-gado (pages 187, 183).

The original emping are small, just like the smallest krupuk, but nowadays you can also buy larger ones, and some that are slightly sweetened with sugar. Like krupuk, uncooked emping will keep for several months in an airtight container; cooked ones, in a really airtight jar, will stay crisp for 5 days or a week at most.

Rempeyek kacang
Savoury peanut brittle

During my most recent trip around Indonesia, rempeyek, usually just called 'peyek', frequently saved me from feeling very hungry. I have said elsewhere in this book that the remoter your location in Indonesia, the harder it becomes to find good food. People in small villages cook very simply, and the little warungs there don't cater for tourists, because usually there are none. But they have the inevitable large airtight jars, with big screw-on lids, in which they keep various dubious-looking cakes, sweets and biscuits. You pick what you want, and tell the warung keeper how many you have eaten when you pay your bill. At least in small places they always trust you!

If you are lucky, you can get really delicious rempeyek, with finely chopped chilli, garlic, chives, kencur (lesser galingale), or roughly crushed peppercorns. The coffee you must ask for in these small places is 'kopi tubruk', coarsely ground black coffee onto which hot water has just been poured. If you don't take sugar, announce this clearly before they make the coffee, otherwise they will put in several spoonfuls as a matter of course. Anyone who doesn't like sugar is regarded as a mild eccentric. I asked the man in one coffee shop for bitter coffee. 'Bitter coffee, of course,' he said. 'With sugar?'

Many Indonesians find rempeyek hard to make properly, or say they do. I have never found them difficult, but a little practice may be necessary before you get them quite perfect. Here is a rempeyek recipe that has never failed me, whether I make them in small or large quantities, in Wonosobo or in Wimbledon. I used to sell these by tens of kilos when I had my shop.

For best results, however time-consuming it is, it is worth cutting the peanuts in halves, unless you can find very tiny peanuts or ones that have been split. It is important to go to an Oriental shop and get really fine rice powder; the rice flour sold in most supermarkets is not fine enough.

Makes 50–60 rempeyek

140–170 g/5–6 oz/1 cup peanuts, cut in halves	*1 tsp salt*
2 candlenuts	*112 g/4 oz/1 cup rice powder*
1 clove garlic	*225 ml/8 fl oz/1 cup cold water*
2 tsp ground coriander	*Peanut oil or sunflower oil for frying*

Pound the candlenuts and garlic together, or put them in a blender with 56 ml/2 fl oz/¼ cup of the allocated water and blend until smooth. Transfer to a bowl, then add the coriander and salt. Mix in the rice powder, and add the remaining water, a little at a time, stirring and mixing thoroughly. Add the halved peanuts to this batter.

To fry rempeyek, you need a non-stick frying pan and a wok. Heat some oil in the pan, and enough in the wok to deep-fry the rempeyek. Take 1 tablespoon of batter, with some peanuts in it, and pour it into the frying pan so that it forms a single flat shape like a biscuit. Go on until the frying pan is full – you will probably be able to fry 6 or 7 at a time. When they have been frying for between 1 and 2 minutes, transfer them into the hot oil in the wok. Deep-fry them until crisp and golden – this will take a few minutes. Then put them to drain and cool on absorbent paper. Continue until the batter and peanuts are used up.

Leave them to get cold before storing in an airtight container. In the container, rempeyek will stay crisp for up to 2 weeks.

Abon
Savoury meat flakes

This is a great favourite among the people of Java as a side-dish, and is much loved by children, who will eat a lot of plain boiled rice if it is accompanied by abon. But I don't think many people make it at home nowadays, as the process is laborious and takes a long time. Factory-made abon is sold under many brand names; some are excellent, others not so good. It can be made from beef, chicken, fish or prawns/shrimp. The Chinese make it with pork. It can be soft in texture, or crisp. Most of the abon made for sale in Central Java is far too sweet for anyone except a Javanese. Below is a simple recipe for home-made abon ayam, crisp chicken flakes. These can be served hot or cold, as a side dish or a garnish. In an airtight jar, they will stay fresh for several weeks. Commercially produced abon contains preservative so that it can be kept for much longer.

Makes about 285–340 g/10–12 oz

4 chicken breasts	*1 tbsp tamarind water*
1.1 litres/2 pints/5 cups water	*2 tsp brown sugar*
1/2 tsp salt	*4 tbsp peanut or soya oil, and*
2 cloves garlic, crushed	*more later*
1 tsp ground coriander	

Boil the chicken breasts in the water with the salt, garlic and ground coriander, for 45–50 minutes. Leave to cool. When they are cool enough to handle, drain off the cooking liquid and keep it aside for

229

other uses. Discard the skin. Beat the chicken breast lightly for a few minutes with the flat of a large knife or a pestle. Then shred the meat finely. Season the shredded meat with a little salt, tamarind water and sugar. Heat the oil in a wok and add the shredded chicken. Stir-fry over a low heat until dry and golden brown.

At this stage you have produced a soft abon. If you want it crisp, add some oil to the wok, and continue stir-frying until the abon is crisp. Serve straight away. It will become less and less crisp as it is stored longer.

Goreng bawang
Crisp-fried onions

Fried onions are suggested as garnish for a number of recipes in this book. You can, of course, buy them ready-made: Scandinavian fried onions are sold in plastic tubs in most supermarkets, and Thai shops make them from the little red onions, not quite shallots, that are found in many Asian countries. These have much less water in them than big European onions, so they fry crisp without the addition of flour. To make crisp-fried onions from your own home-grown shallots, proceed as follows.

---

1 kg/2 lb 3 oz/9 cups shallots, thinly sliced

285 ml/1/2 pint/11/4 cups peanut or sunflower oil

It is easier to make these fried onions in a wok, but a frying pan will do. Heat the oil until a sliver of onion dropped into it sizzles immediately. Fry the shallots in three or four batches, stirring all the time, for 3–4 minutes each time or until they are crisp and lightly browned. Remove with a slotted spoon to drain in a colander lined with absorbent paper. Let them cool, then store in an airtight container; they will keep crisp and fresh for about a week.

Acar campur
Mixed cooked vegetables in piquant sauce

This is sometimes called acar kuning, yellow acar; the colour comes from turmeric. Acar is normally eaten cold, but this version can be served hot as a side-dish with hot vegetables. For serving cold, on the other hand, it can be made several days in advance, and kept in the fridge in a covered container. It is also suitable for freezing. Thaw it out completely before serving it cold, or reheating it gently in a saucepan for 3–4 minutes.

For 4–6 people

112 ml/4 fl oz/^{1}/$_{2}$ cup water
10–12 small pickling onions, peeled (optional)
225 g/8 oz/2 cups French beans, topped and tailed and each cut into 3 pieces
4 medium carrots, peeled and cut into sticks the same length as the beans

170 g/6 oz/1^{1}/$_{2}$ cups cauliflower florets
1 tsp mustard powder
1 tsp sugar
1 tbsp white distilled vinegar
10–12 small red or green chillies, left whole (optional)
Salt to taste

For the paste:
2 shallots, chopped
2 cloves garlic, chopped
3 candlenuts, or 5 blanched almonds
1–2 small red chillies

1 tsp ground turmeric
2 tbsp white distilled vinegar
2 tbsp peanut oil
^{1}/$_{2}$ tsp salt

Put all the ingredients for the paste into a blender, and blend until smooth. Transfer this to a saucepan and simmer for 4 minutes, stirring often. Add the pickling onions, if used, and continue to simmer for 2 more minutes. Pour in the water, and simmer for about 5 minutes. Then put in the beans, and cover the pan for 2 minutes. Uncover, and add the carrots. Cover the pan again, and continue to simmer for 2 more minutes. Once again uncover the pan and add the cauliflower and the rest of the ingredients. Stir them around and put the cover back, and continue cooking for 3–5 more minutes. Uncover the pan for the last time, adjust the seasoning and turn the vegetables over again for a few seconds. Transfer to a warm serving dish, if the acar is to be served hot; otherwise leave it to get cold, then refrigerate to be served a few hours or a few days later.

Acar mangga dan kobis
Mango and cabbage acar

A cabbage acar without mango is sold in jars in the Netherlands, labelled, in the old spelling as usual, *atjar*. This Dutch product is often available in Britain, in large delicatessens or supermarkets. I like it with sour green unripe mangoes, available in the West in ethnic street markets or in Indian and Thai shops. They are quite small; if you can't get them, substitute hard green apples, such as Granny Smiths.

For 6–8 people

340 g/12 oz/3 cups white cabbage, finely shredded	*3 small green mangoes or apples*
	3 tbsp salt
For the dressing:	
100 ml/3¹/₂ fl oz/scant ¹/₂ cup white distilled vinegar	*Several thin slices of ginger*
	1 tsp salt
2 shallots, very finely chopped	*2 tbsp castor sugar*
2–5 bird chillies, each cut in half	*56 ml/2 fl oz/4 tbsp warm water*

First, put the cabbage in a large bowl and sprinkle with 2 tablespoonfuls of salt. Mix the salt well into the cabbage. Peel the mangoes or apples and cut them into matchsticks. Put them into another bowl and mix in the remaining 1 tablespoonful of salt. Leave the cabbage and mangoes or apples with the salt for 1–2 hours. Then rinse them well to get rid of all the salt. You can now mix them to drain in a large colander.

Put all the ingredients for the dressing in a large glass bowl. Stir to dissolve the sugar. Adjust the seasoning. When the cabbage and mangoes or apples are well drained, put them into the bowl with the dressing. Mix all these well in the bowl and keep in a cool place for at least 1 hour before serving.

You can also keep this acar in a large glass jar or bowl, tightly covered, in the fridge for several days.

COOKING RICE

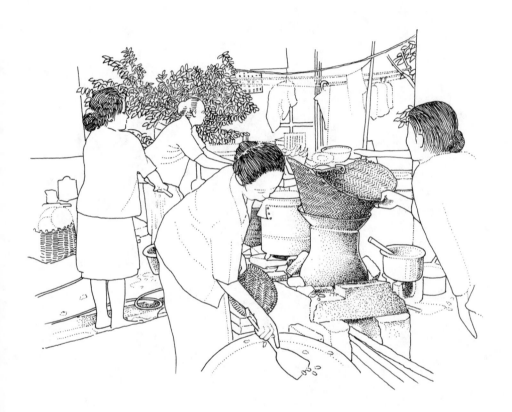

Not everyone in Indonesia eats rice all the time, but it is by far the most popular staple food and most people regard it as the basis of any proper meal. Despite the rush to the towns, a high percentage of the population still grows rice on tiny farms. When I was researching *The Rice Book*, this was one of the few countries where I found farmers who wanted their sons to stay on the land. Today, the government is officially encouraging people to eat more rice and less foreign food. One reason is that Indonesia now produces, in most years, a small rice surplus. This is a big change from the 1960s and early 1970s, when large amounts had to be imported. The change has come about partly through a more efficient storage and distribution network, but largely through better farming methods, better irrigation, and of course the planting of new varieties of rice – the product of scientific breeding.

The first high-yielding rice varieties had poor cooking and eating qualities. If you talk to Indonesian farmers today, you will get conflicting opinions about the taste and texture of what they are growing, but most of them seem to think that the new rice now compares pretty well with the old. Certainly the top-quality rice in any pasar or supermarket is still very good indeed, and prices, as far as I could observe, are pretty much the same in any part of the country and any kind of shop.

What qualities do Indonesians look for in rice? For everyday eating, it must be long grain, highly milled and polished so that it is perfectly white. Cooked rice must be, as the Javanese say, pulen: soft and succulent but the opposite of soggy. If there is any hardness in the kernel, if it is at all al dente, the rice is undercooked. In the pasar, rice – beras – is normally sold loose, by weight. In a store or supermarket, it is bagged and labelled according to its variety and quality. Brand names for rice are starting to appear and will no doubt take an increasing share of the market, but for the moment you can still buy bags stencilled or printed with messages such as *Beras Cianjur Slijp Kepala*. Slijp is a Dutch word indicating that the grains are milled and highly polished; kepala, the Indonesian for 'head', shows that this is 'head rice', the grains are unbroken. Cianjur, in West Java, has long been regarded as the home of the very best rice, and I cannot believe that all the rice thus labelled actually comes from there.

In Britain, Indonesian rice is still pretty well unobtainable, but rice from Thailand is plentiful and has very similar qualities. My own favourite is Thai Fragrant or Jasmine rice. It is relatively expensive, but worth the extra pennies. (One reason for the higher price is that rice imported into the European Community pays duty; this is substantially

235

higher on milled than unmilled rice.) This is not to say that you can't eat Indonesian food with other kinds of rice. Convenience rices, ready-cooked, parboiled, boil-in-the bag, cook-in-the-fridge, pudding rice, glutinous rice, red, brown, black rice, Basmati, Arborio, French, Spanish, Brazilian, American, Australian – all are fine. I am only saying that not all of them have the eating quality Indonesians prefer. The finest Basmati, for instance, is too unsticky for us, I suppose because we were brought up to eat with our fingers, rolling the rice into a ball.

A white rice grain is principally starch, with a little protein in the spaces between the cells. In cooking, the starch absorbs water and swells. On your plate, the grains continue to soak up sauces and cooking juices; this is one reason why rice tastes so good, although real rice-lovers will eat plain boiled rice by itself or with a little chilli. Nutritionists now say that cooked rice, like bread, contains a useful amount of 'resistant starch', which acts like fibre in the digestive system. In Australia, rice is marketed as a health food, targeted especially at athletes and people whose jobs need plenty of physical energy, because the starch is converted at a steady rate into glycogen and taken into the muscles as fuel.

Food allergy to rice is extremely rare. Quite a lot of people, on the other hand, are allergic to the gluten in wheat and bread. Rice contains no gluten whatever; so-called 'glutinous' rice is likewise completely gluten-free.

Brown rice is gaining popularity in the West as a health food. I like it, but Indonesians generally don't eat it; they regard it as food for invalids and babies. The bran is good for you, particularly because of the fibre it contains, but if you are eating a normal diet your body does not really need the extra proteins and vitamins.

Storing rice

Uncooked rice will keep, in dry, reasonably cool conditions, for a long time. There should be little or no loss of quality for the first three years, though the grains dry out and will absorb more water when cooked. Thereafter, the flavour will deteriorate, but even ten-year-old rice may be quite eatable. I don't imagine anyone is going to store rice for ten years, anyway.

Cooked rice is another matter. It quickly gets infected by a bug, *Bacillus cereus*, which is not likely to kill anyone but can give you a nasty stomach upset. *B. cereus* dies at temperatures below 4°C/40°F and above 60°C/140°F. If you want to store leftover rice overnight, therefore, put it in the fridge, and reheat it, in a steamer, saucepan, or microwave, before you eat it. Electric rice cookers automatically reheat rice as long as the power is left on, so the bacillus has no chance. But rice that is continually reheated starts to dry out and tastes less attractive. I may say that in a lifetime of eating rice I have never had a moment's difficulty from this bug.

Cooking Plain White Rice

This section describes several ways of cooking plain white boiled rice. Fortunately, cooking rice to perfection is much easier than some people seem to think. If you have an electric rice cooker, good results are pretty well guaranteed, but you can cook rice beautifully in an ordinary saucepan.

If you are using good rice, let its flavour speak for itself – don't cook it with salt. Plain white rice, eaten from a separate bowl, is regarded in Asia as a symbol of purity; salt and spices belong in the other dishes on the table. (There are, of course, recipes in which rice and salt are used together with other ingredients.)

Most cooking methods allow you to uncover the pan and taste a grain or two of rice to see if it's done. Bite it gently – this will show if the centre is still unacceptably hard. Slightly overcooked rice is not a disaster, but undercooked rice is not very pleasant to eat.

How much to cook?

Rice absorbs a lot of water as it cooks: 450 g/1 lb/2 cups of uncooked rice will soak up at least 570 ml/1 pint/$2^{1}/2$ cups of water. This would feed my family of four adults. We are moderate rice-eaters; the same quantity would be, perhaps, not quite enough for two hungry Indonesians, but ample for eight English people who don't eat rice often and therefore find it more filling.

Washing

In Indonesia, we wash rice in several changes of water before cooking. Put it in the pan, pour on enough cold water to cover it, swirl it around with your fingers, and pour it away, seeing that the water takes with it

237

any bits of husk or discoloured grains that have not been taken out by the miller. (Packeted rice in supermarkets is rigorously screened before it reaches you, so you won't find much.) You can repeat this process once or twice if you wish. The last time, pour away as much of the water as you easily can – there is no need to drain off every last drop.

Measuring

If you use an electric rice cooker, or the 'absorption' method in a saucepan, it is important to measure the water (or other liquid) accurately.

You will need, for example, 280 ml/10 fl oz/1¼ cups of water to 225 g/8 oz/1 cup of rice. If your rice is a dry variety, like Basmati, or if you like it rather soft, add a little more water; up to 340 ml/12 fl oz/1½ cups of water to 225 g/8 oz/1 cup of rice. The same quantity of brown rice may require 420 ml/15 fl oz/scant 2 cups of water.

But if your rice is to be fried afterwards, don't use any more water than you have to; cooked rice for frying must be fairly dry and fluffy.

Cooking rice in an electric rice cooker

Put in the rice with the right amount of water (see above, and of course see also the instructions that come with the cooker), and switch on. Do not add any salt. When the rice is done, the cooker will switch off automatically. The rice is ready to serve. You can take the cooker to the table, or transfer the rice to a serving bowl. The cooker automatically switches itself on again at intervals to keep the rice hot. This process is safe (the temperature is high enough to kill bacteria), but an hour or so of continual reheating starts to make the rice rather dry.

The electric cooker also cooks brown rice and glutinous rice correctly; it takes a little longer, but the machine looks after this.

Cooking rice in a saucepan: the absorption method

450 g/1 lb/2 cups long grain rice, white or brown   *570 ml/1 pint/2½ cups water*

Put the rice and water in a saucepan, put the saucepan on a moderate

238

heat and bring to the boil. Stir once with a wooden spoon. Let the rice simmer, uncovered, until all the water has been absorbed. This will take about 10 minutes (brown rice, perhaps 15 minutes).

There are four ways to finish cooking – take your pick.

Traditional method

The traditional Oriental way is to keep the rice in the saucepan and put the lid on as tightly as possible. If the lid isn't tight-fitting, you can put a layer of aluminium foil between the lid and the pan. A tea-towel is better still – it stops steam condensing inside the lid and dripping back into the rice. Turn down the heat as low as possible, and leave the rice to cook undisturbed for 10 or 12 minutes. (The time for brown rice is the same as for white.) Don't take off the lid. Take the pan off the heat and set it on a wet tea-towel on your draining board. Leave the rice to rest for 5 minutes, still with the lid on. (The wet cloth will stop the bottom layer of rice sticking to the pan.) Then serve.

The layer at the bottom of the pan: intip

With white rice, you will find that there is a layer of rice grains, about 1/2 cm/1/4 inch thick, stuck together on the bottom of the pan like a thin cake. Don't throw this away! In Indonesia, we call this rice cake *intip*. Dry it in the sun, or in the oven as if you were drying bread for breadcrumbs. Then break it into smallish pieces and store in an airtight container. When you have a worthwhile quantity, deep-fry the pieces of intip until they become slightly coloured. Sprinkle them with a little salt, and you have an unusual and delicious quick snack to serve with drinks. (With brown rice, the intip is so thin and brittle that you can just mix it in with the rest of the boiled rice.)

If you don't want to eat this crusty bottom layer, don't stand your saucepan on a wet cloth while it rests at the end of cooking. The bottom layer will stick to the pan, and you can soak it off and throw the rice away.

Note that the other three methods of finishing off boiled rice (see below) do not give any bottom layer.

Steaming

Transfer the rice from the pan to a double saucepan or a rice-steaming pan with a metal 'basket' to hold the rice, and steam for 10 minutes (brown rice, 15 minutes). The lid should be kept on while the rice is steaming, but it doesn't matter if you take it off to see if the rice is done. The best test for doneness is just to eat a few grains. If the centres are still noticeably hard and resistant to the teeth, give the rice a few minutes longer.

In many parts of South-East Asia, we use a special pan for this process, called in Indonesian a dandang. The dandang is a metal pot which narrows a little near the top. In this narrow neck rests a basket, called a kukusan, woven from strips of bamboo. Steam from the dandang percolates through the woven basketwork and cooks the rice in the kukusan.

Oven method

Transfer the rice from the pan to an ovenproof dish. Cover the dish with buttered greaseproof paper, then with aluminium foil. Cook in a pre-heated oven at 180°C/350°F/Gas Mark 4 for 15–16 minutes (brown rice, 16–20 minutes).

Microwave method

Transfer the rice from the pan to a container which can be microwaved. Cover it with clingfilm, set the microwave to full power, and cook for 4–5 minutes (brown rice, 6–7 minutes). (This assumes a 650-watt microwave; you may need to experiment a little.)

Lontong.
Compressed rice

Lontong is always eaten cold, for example with satay; it soaks up the hot satay sauce, and its coolness and soft texture contrast with the hot spices and the meat. In Indonesia, the rice is cooked in a cylinder of banana leaf, or else in a little woven packet of coconut fronds. The latter is called ketupat. Ketupat are particularly associated with Lebaran festivities.

It is possible to use aluminium foil instead of banana leaf, but much the easiest way of cooking lontong is to use a bag made of muslin (or heatproof perforated paper, if you can get it). Boil-in-the-bag rice ought to be ideal, and the bags themselves are indeed excellent. Unfortunately, almost all boil-in-the-bag rice nowadays is parboiled, and this makes it hopeless for lontong because the grains cannot compress and merge together. If you can find boil-in-the-bag rice that is not parboiled, by all means use it. The cooking instructions will then be exactly as given below.

For 8–10 people

225 g / 8 oz / 1 cup long grain rice, washed and drained	*or heatproof perforated paper*
2 bags, about 15 cm / 6 inches square, made from muslin	*1.75 litres / 3 pints / 7 1/2 cups hot water, and more later*
	A pinch of salt

Fill each bag one-third full with rice. Sew up the opening. Boil the water with the pinch of salt. When boiling, put in the bags of rice and let the water bubble gently for 75 minutes. Add more boiling water as required during cooking; the bags of rice must always be submerged. When finished, take out the bags, which are now like plump, rather hard cushions, and drain them in a colander. When they are cold, keep them in the fridge until they are to be eaten.

To serve, just cut up the 'cushions' into chunks or slices about 3 cm (1 inch or a little more) on a side. Use a large, sharp knife wetted with water. Discard the bags.

Nasi gurih
Coconut rice

Nasi gurih, also known as nasi uduk, is rice cooked in coconut milk. Coloured with turmeric, it becomes nasi kuning (see next recipe). In Indonesia, we do not always soak the rice first, nor do we stir-fry it in oil or butter. However, the method I suggest here will appeal to people in the West, because it ensures that the rice does not become too soft and clingy.

For 4–6 people

---

450 g/1 lb/2 cups long grain rice, soaked for 1 hour, washed and drained
2 tbsp olive oil or clarified butter

670 ml/24 fl oz/3 cups coconut milk
1 tsp salt

In a saucepan, stir-fry the rice in the butter or oil for 3 minutes. Add the coconut milk and salt. Bring to the boil and cook until the rice has absorbed all the liquid.

Then lower the heat, cover the pan tightly, and cook for a further 10–12 minutes undisturbed. Alternatively, the rice can be 'finished' by steaming in a rice steamer, or by cooking in the oven or in a microwave (see page 240). Serve hot.

Nasi kuning
Yellow savoury rice

Yellow, perhaps because it is the colour of gold, is associated all over South-East Asia with gods, royalty and feasts. Any thanksgiving or celebration party, even if the event celebrated is a very mundane one, is likely to have a large dish of yellow rice at the centre of the table.

For 4–6 people

450 g/1 lb/2 cups long grain rice, soaked for 1 hour, washed and drained	1/2 tsp ground cumin
	670 ml/24 fl oz/3 cups coconut milk or stock
2 tbsp vegetable oil	1 stick of cinnamon
3 shallots or 1 small onion, sliced finely	2 cloves
	1/2 tsp salt
1 tsp ground turmeric	1 kaffir lime or bay leaf
1 tsp ground coriander	

Heat the oil in a saucepan. Stir-fry the sliced shallots or onion for 2 minutes. Add the rice, turmeric, coriander and cumin. Stir-fry for another 2 minutes, then add the coconut milk or stock, then all the other ingredients. Boil the mixture, uncovered, stirring it once or twice with a wooden spoon, until the rice has absorbed all the liquid. Then steam for 10 minutes.

Instead of steaming, you can cover the saucepan tightly, and cook undisturbed on a low heat for 10 minutes; or you can finish off the cooking in the oven or microwave, as described on page 240 for plain cooked rice.

Transfer the rice to a serving dish, discard the cinnamon, cloves, and kaffir lime or bay leaf. Serve hot to accompany meat, fish and vegetables.

COCONUTS

I suspect that most Westerners think coconuts grow wild, being self-seeded and needing no maintenance. This is quite wrong; some palms may grow wild, but the vast majority, even on the remotest and most idyllic beach, have been planted and are cared for by someone. Coconuts need a light soil that allows air to circulate around their roots, and moist winds to keep their fronds from drying out in the sun. Hence their presence on sandy beaches cooled by the sea wind; but inland they are planted among the village houses to provide shade, fresh nuts, decorative fronds, raw materials for making household implements and weaving containers of all sizes, juice from the flowers to be fermented and distilled into a potent liquor, and eventually fence-posts and fuel. In a landscape of wet rice fields, you may pick out the villages from afar as islands of shady coconut palm and bamboo.

Isaac Henry Burkill, author of the massive *Economic Products of the Malay Peninsula*, explains why coconuts are something of a botanic freak. They collectively make up one member of a family of four, the other three all being natives of the Americas. How did they cross the ocean, and at what stage in their evolution? And *Cocos nucifera* is virtually the only member of its branch of the family, with relatively few races: very different from the hundreds of varieties and races of the rice plant.

Apart from its usefulness, the coconut – kelapa in Indonesian – is also a luxury. Most Indonesians, and notoriously the Javanese, love sweet things, and coconuts contain a lot of natural sugar. One of the pleasures of living in the tropics is to stop by the roadside on a hot afternoon and drink the juice of a young coconut, which is then roughly chopped open so that you can scoop out and eat the soft flesh. This coconut water is considered to have no commercial value, and most of it goes to waste; but it contains some vitamin A as well as proteins and sugars. Very ripe nuts usually do not have much water left in them, or if they have it is salty and unpleasant to drink. Much more valuable, especially for the cook, is santen, the milk that is extracted by squeezing the shredded flesh of the older nut in water. This contains the same proteins, sugars and salts, but in stronger concentration. Most important, it also contains some coconut oil as an emulsion. This oil is essential in cooking a great many Indonesian dishes, and even – as with rendang (page 40) – allows you to start a long cooking process by boiling (in the milk) and end it by frying (in the oil, after all the water has been driven off or absorbed by the meat).

You can, of course, make your own coconut oil, minyak kelapa, by boiling a pan of santen until all the water has been driven off. This process produces another luxury, a semi-solid residue called blondo, which is used in various recipes to impart a characteristic and delicious flavour; mixed with peanuts, for example, in a kind of peanut sauce, or with spices in cooking chicken.

Indonesians are health-conscious people, many of them with tendencies towards faddiness, and they are well aware nowadays of the risks that lurk behind the attractions of the coconut: a high level of cholesterol and saturated fats as well as a great deal of sugar. Maybe we shall see the luxury consumption of coconuts diminish over the next ten or fifteen years. But, like butter in the cuisines of France, coconut oil will hold its necessary place in Indonesian cooking, because there is really nothing which can adequately replace it. Locally produced oils, such as soya bean oil, lack the characteristic flavour. The ubiquitous margarine, which now seems to be one of the principal legacies of the Dutch to their former colonies, has very limited uses in good cooking. Olives do not grow in Indonesia, or not in sufficient numbers; and the dairying industry is only just getting started. I no longer believe the old story that Asians lack the enzymes needed to digest dairy products. Indonesians are taking to ice cream and milk shakes with enthusiasm. But, quite apart from any health considerations, butter will always cost far more than coconut oil, and food cooked with it will always taste different.

Kopyor

Generally speaking, from the cook's point of view, all that matters about a coconut is its age; otherwise, all coconuts are the same. However, there is one 'sport' or oddity that is highly valued because it makes the most delicious ice cream. This is what we call kelapa kopyor, and the ice cream is es krim kopyor. For a long time I thought this was a variety of coconut grown specially to make this delectable ice cream. Fortunately, before I had time to dream of becoming rich by cultivating kelapa kopyor for export, I was told that these nuts grow on ordinary coconut trees. But only a tiny proportion of trees produce any kopyor nuts at all, and those that do bear them produce maybe one kopyor among a hundred ordinary coconuts. Some people say these nuts are diseased, because the flesh is loose and already mixed with the coconut water – ready, in fact, to go straight into the ice cream churn. I daresay genetic engineering will soon give us a coconut tree that guarantees kelapa kopyor every time.

Cooking with Coconuts

In places where coconuts grow in abundance, such as almost all the islands of Indonesia, cooks take great care to select a coconut at exactly the right stage of maturity, because different recipes need coconuts of different textures.

Very young coconuts contain little flesh but plenty of water. In many parts of Indonesia these are sold by the side of the road; the customer asks the vendor to open the nut so that the water, which is still plentiful and sweet, can be drunk straight from the shell, usually with a straw. The flesh is still too young and too thin to scrape out and eat. In a warung or a small restaurant, however, the coconuts tend to be just that little bit older, so the flesh can be scraped out with a spoon. Most restaurants prefer to mix coconut water with highly coloured sugar syrup, red, green, or yellow, and the coconut flesh is then divided among several glasses. This gives an excessively sweet drink, very popular with Indonesians. Most tourists prefer the real thing, undiluted, because that way you can be sure it has not been contaminated, and no fly has a chance to taste it before you do.

At the next stage, the coconut water is ideal as a tenderizer for meat and poultry. It is normally mixed with spices and used as either a marinade or a cooking medium. In the famous ayam mBok Berek (page 149), the chicken is boiled in coconut water. At this stage the flesh has become thicker but is still not thick enough to grate. It is used, chopped up or sliced, for cake mixes or ice cream. The most delicious ice cream is made with kelapa kopyor (see page 248).

Indonesians call the next stage kelapa mengkal or kelapa setengah mateng. The water is still good for drinking, marinating and cooking, but the flesh can now be grated. The brown rind is quite pale, and some people don't bother to remove it, although if you want the grated coconut to be perfectly white you should peel it off with a potato peeler or a sharp knife. This grated coconut is used for salad dressing (see the recipes on page 170), and to decorate sticky cakes. The coconut flesh is still young and soft, and definitely not fibrous or chewy. However, it is not old enough for making coconut milk.

The final stage is kelapa tua – old coconut. These are the coconuts we can buy in the West. The water, although much less plentiful than in a young nut and not particularly nice to drink, is still very good for marinating and cooking. The flesh is thick and firm, even hard; from it are made desiccated coconut and good thick santen or coconut milk, and this is the coconut milk that is used to make coconut oil.

Using coconuts

Young coconuts, which are full of water and have very soft flesh, do not concern us here, as they are not available in the West. Old fresh nuts, which have brown, hard, hairy shells, are easily obtainable almost anywhere and are the best for cooking. Hold the nut to your ear and shake it gently; you should hear liquid sloshing about inside. If you do, the nut is probably all right. If not, it may be very old and stale.

To open the nut, tap it smartly all over with a heavy blunt instrument to loosen the outer shell from the flesh. Then give it a few firm blows to crack the shell. (To prevent mess and keep all the fragments together, you may prefer to put the nut in a strong plastic bag.) If you are clever and lucky, you may be able to remove the outer shell and leave the flesh intact. Usually, the water spills out as the globe of flesh inside cracks open. Assuming the flesh is still sticking to the fragments of the shell, prise it away carefully with a short-bladed, blunt knife.

The white flesh has a brown outer skin. For making coconut milk, this is left on when the flesh is grated, but for light-coloured dishes (especially sweets) it must be peeled off and discarded.

Coconut products

Creamed coconut: This is like a hard, whitish margarine. It has its uses, but I would not recommend it for any of the recipes in this book, unless a very small amount is needed near the end of cooking in order to thicken the sauce.

Desiccated coconut: Very useful for making coconut milk (see below). Packeted brands bought in supermarkets are good, but expensive if you need a large quantity. Most Asian shops sell unsweetened desiccated coconut in large bags, much more cheaply. Sniff the bag before you buy; if it has been in store for too long, it will smell rancid, even through the plastic.

250

Santen
Coconut milk for cooking

This is *not* the water that you drink from a fresh nut. It is a white, milky liquid that is easily extracted from coconut flesh with hot water, and it is essential for much South-East Asian cooking. You can buy it in cans from most Asian shops, or you can buy 'instant' powder and simply mix it with water; these are both quite all right, but they do not get results as good as fresh milk you have made yourself from either a fresh nut or (just as good) desiccated coconut.

This is how to make 570 ml/1 pint/2^1/2 cups of thick 'first extraction' milk. If you need more or thinner milk, repeat the process with fresh hot water but the same coconut flesh. If you mix the two, you will have about 1.1 litres/2 pints/5 cups of average milk.

From fresh coconut

---

1 coconut

Grate the flesh, pour hot water over it and leave it to cool till it is hand-hot. Then squeeze handfuls of the grated flesh through a fine sieve, pressing out the last drop. (You can also do this in a blender – see below.)

From desiccated coconut

---

340 g/12 oz/3 cups desiccated coconut

With a blender. The water should be fairly hot. Put the desiccated coconut and half the water into the blender. Blend for 20–30 seconds, then squeeze and sieve the resulting mush. Put the squeezed coconut back into the blender with the rest of the hot water, and repeat.

Without a blender. Simmer the desiccated coconut and water in a pan for 4–5 minutes. Allow to cool a little, then sieve and strain as above.

251

Storing and using coconut milk

This milk will keep in the fridge for not more than 48 hours. During this time, a thick 'cream' may come to the top; this can simply be stirred back into the liquid below.

Coconut milk cannot be frozen. If you are cooking for the freezer, omit the coconut milk until you thaw the dish ready to reheat and serve it. Rendang (page 40) is an exception – the milk is totally absorbed into the meat, therefore rendang and kalio can be frozen.

Minyak kelapa, blondo
Coconut oil, coconut oil sediment

This is not strictly a recipe, but some notes about what happens when you boil coconut milk. I shall describe these products together, because when you make one, you make the other also. Making them at home takes time, but is very easy; it can be done while you are cooking other things in the kitchen.

Most traditionally minded Indonesians cook with coconut oil, as until recently that was more or less the only oil they could buy. My grandmother used it, though only if it was made by herself or a member of the family. The oil gets rancid very quickly, and when rancid it will ruin any food that is cooked with it.

Blondo is the sediment left at the bottom of the pan or wok when the coconut milk has become oil. In the Minahasa region of North Sulawesi it is called tai minyak, and is usually served as a relish or sambal, mixed with spices – chilli predominantly – and perhaps some garlic and onion. In Java, it is used as a creamy coconut topping with gudeg (page 145) and kue Bugis (page 203). It is used sparingly, as the taste is very rich indeed, and it is more often used by professional food producers, because it takes time to make.

From 1.4 litres/2½ pints/6¼ cups of very thick coconut milk, that is from 'first extraction' milk made from freshly grated or desiccated coconut (page 251), you will get about 112 ml/4 fl oz/½ cup of oil and about 112 g/4 oz of blondo.

Boil the coconut milk in a wok or deep frying pan, stirring occasionally. It must boil for about 2 hours before the sediment can be easily separated from the oil.

White blondo

While the coconut milk is still separating from the oil, the sediment is white or off-white in colour. The oil is not quite ready yet if you want to use it for deep-frying, though a small quantity can be used for sautéing or stir-frying vegetables.

The most likely reason for stopping at this stage is that you may want to use the blondo to make some kind of relish or sambal, or to put on top of a traditional Yogya gudeg or kue Bugis.

In either case, it is better to make only a small quantity. If you stop at this point, the oil will get rancid much more quickly, though it will still stay good in the refrigerator for about 2 weeks.

Brown blondo

If you want to use the oil for frying or deep-frying, you need to keep stirring until the blondo becomes golden brown. This golden brown blondo can also be used for cooking, for example, in gulai bagar (page 43) to replace the roasted grated coconut. It is often mixed with other ingredients to make a bumbu (spice paste). It can be used to give extra flavour to sambal kacang (page 222), especially if the peanut sauce is going to be used for bumbu gado-gado (people in West and Central Java are particularly fond of this). Alternatively, if you mix some crushed chilli or sambal ulek into it, with some crushed garlic and juice of lime, you have a very tasty sambal.

Storing coconut oil

The oil can be stored in the fridge for between 2 and 4 weeks, depending on the extent to which it has separated from the milk (see blondo, below).

Coconut oil will become as stiff as lard when stored in a cool place. To melt a whole jar of it straight from the fridge, just put the jar in a bowl of hot water and it will melt in no time. If you need only a few spoonfuls of the oil, then leave the jar at room temperature for a few minutes, and spoon the thick oil from the top straight into the wok or frying pan. Remember to put the jar back in the fridge.

Storing blondo

Blondo will stay in good condition in the fridge for about 8–10 days. It will become hard (the browner the blondo, the harder it becomes), but can easily be made soft again by heating.

GLOSSARY

Ingredients and Techniques

Indonesian words which are explained in the text may not be listed here but usually can be found in the Index.

I have assumed that my readers will be more familiar with English than with Indonesian; therefore, explanations and instructions accompany English headwords (e.g. TAMARIND) and the Indonesian word (ASAM) is simply cross-referenced to the English equivalent. However, if there is no commonly used English form, the Indonesian word is used as the headword (e.g. JENGKOL).

Pronunciation. Indonesian *c* is always pronounced like English *ch* in *Church*; *j* is always as in *judge*. A final *k* is a glottal stop. The letter *e* has two pronunciations: 'strong', as in English *pen*, and 'weak', as in *open*. In this Glossary, every 'strong' *e* in Indonesian words is marked with an accent, e.g. kedelé (pronounced k'd'lay). (But note that in modern printed Indonesian no accents are used.)

ADAT Custom, customary law, tradition.

AGAR-AGAR A substance extracted from certain species of seaweed (e.g. *Gelidium cartilagineum* and others), which acts like gelatine.

AIR (two syllables: ay-er) Water, liquid.

AIR KAPUR See LIMEWATER.

ALMOND Almonds are somewhat similar, in flavour and texture, to KENARI nuts, and either can be substituted for the other in cooking.

AMBU-AMBU *Euthynnus affinis* or related species; mackerel tuna or little tunny. Also known as TONGKOL.

ASAM See TAMARIND.

ASINAN Something salty; see asinan Jakarta, page 190.

AUBERGINE/EGGPLANT Terong or terung.

AVOCADO Advokat, adpokat, pokat.

AYAM Chicken.

BABI Pig, pork.

BAIN-MARIE A reservoir of boiling water placed in the oven, in which are placed pans or bowls of the food to be cooked. A deep baking tin makes a suitable reservoir.

BAKAR Grilled.

BANANA *Musa sapientum*; pisang. Bananas imported into Europe are virtually all of one race, the Gros Michel. Bananas in Indonesia are of about forty races, from small golden yellow ones to large pale ones. They are eaten raw, boiled, fried, candied, or sliced and dried in the sun, as appropriate. The banana tree is a very large, fast-growing herb, and lives only for one year, producing long glossy leaves that are quickly shredded to ribbons by the wind, and a single large purple flower. Young leaves, having very tough fibres, are used as wrapping materials. The heart-shaped flower, jantung pisang, is cooked and eaten as a vegetable.

BASIL (1) *Ocimum basilicum*, (2) *O. gratissimum*; kemangi, selasih. These are the two species of basil available in South-East Asia and in the West: (1), with light-green leaves and white flowers, is the English sweet basil; (2), with purplish stems is flown to Britain from Thailand and is sold in Thai shops.

BEAN-CURD See SOYA BEAN.

BEANS FRENCH BEANS, Kacang buncis; MUNG BEANS, Kacang hijau; SOYA BEANS, Kacang kedelé; YARD-LONG BEANS, Kacang panjang. See also PETÉ.

BEANSPROUTS Taogé. Unless otherwise marked, beansprouts sold in Britain are usually the sprouts of mung (green gram) beans. They can easily be grown at home from seed; they are ready to eat after about four days. They consist mostly of water, but the texture is agreeable for salads and garnishes. If you have time and patience, break off the brown root of each sprout; this improves the appearance of the dish.

BÉBÉK Duck.

BELIMBING WULUH *Averrhoa bilimbi* This plant used to grow in all parts of Java, and was often used instead of tamarind to give sourness in cooking. Where belimbing wuluh are specified by recipes in this book, I have suggested using rhubarb as an alternative. Even in Indonesia, and especially in big cities and towns, belimbing wuluh has now become a rarity.

BENGKUANG   See JICAMA.

BERAS   Uncooked rice, normally white and polished, as opposed to PADI (rice as grown and harvested) and NASI (cooked rice).

BERLADA   With LADA, chilli; hot and spicy.

BIRD PEPPER   *Capsicum frutescens;* cabé rawit. See CHILLI.

BITTER GOURD, BITTER CUCUMBER   *Momordica charantia;* peria, paria. These can be bought in Britain in Indian shops and street markets; most are imported from India, Thailand, or China.

BREM   Balinese rice wine.

BUKA   Open. The meal eaten immediately after sunset during the Muslim fasting month.

BULUH, BULU   Bamboo.

BUMBU   A mixture of herbs and spices, often a paste or a sauce, used to flavour a cooked dish.

CABÉ RAWIT   See CHILLI.

CAKALANG   Skipjack; *Katsuwonus pelamis.*

CANDLENUT   *Aleurites moluccana;* kemiri. The English name comes from the oil which these nuts produce, which was once used as lamp oil. The nutshells are extremely tough, and the kernels are therefore extracted before being done up in packets for export. They can be bought in Oriental shops in the West. They are often broken when the shells are opened, so in a recipe 'a candlenut' may mean, in practice, fragments equal to one nut – a whole nut is about the size of a walnut kernel. Raw candlenuts are mildly toxic and should not be eaten, but they become perfectly harmless when cooked. If you cannot find any, MACADAMIA NUTS or, at a pinch, ALMONDS make satisfactory substitutes.

CARDAMOM   (1) *Elettaria cardamomum,* (2) *Amomum* (various species); kapulaga. Because of the demand for this spice, a number of plants are used as sources and cardamoms therefore come in different colours: (1) is regarded as the best, but colour depends on how the fruit was processed – green, white, brown, or almost black, the green being the top quality; (2) is a member of the same family as ginger.

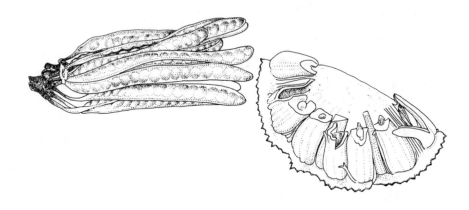

CASSAVA *Manihot utilissima* or *M. esculenta*; ubi kayu (in Java, ketéla or singkong). This unexciting but valuable tuber was brought to Asia from South America. It will flourish in very dry conditions. It consists mostly of starch, but also contains a form of prussic acid, and the flesh is therefore grated, washed, pressed and finally baked to make it safe. Further processing produces tapioca. However, ordinary boiling makes cassava completely safe. Cassava leaves are also used in cooking: see page 55, 112.

CHILLI (1) *Capsicum annuum*; cabé. (2) *C. frutescens*; cabé rawit (bird pepper). Chillies were taken from Central and South America to Asia. Today they are grown in a vast range of shapes, sizes, colours, flavours and degrees of hotness. Flavour is more important to the cook than mere heat. Generally, the smaller the chilli, the hotter. The hottest part is the seeds, so removing these reduces heat but retains flavour. Handle hot chillies with respect: wash your hands immediately after handling them, and keep hands away from eyes while working. If you do get chilli in your eye, wash it with plain cold water; it will sting, but do no harm. If you get a mouthful of unbearably hot chilli, plain boiled rice or cucumber are the best antidotes.

CINNAMON *Cinnamomum zeylanicum*; kayu manis. These small trees are a characteristic sight in hilly parts of Indonesia. The rolled-up 'quills' are segments of bark, cut very thinly and allowed to roll up as it dries. Quills can be stored for a long time, but powdered cinnamon quickly loses its flavour.

CLARIFIED BUTTER See GHEE.

CLOVE *Eugenia aromatica*; cengkéh.

COBÉK A mortar, in which to grind spices, etc., with an ulek-ulek, or pestle.

COPRA Dried coconut flesh, usually exported as the raw material from which coconut oil is commercially extracted.

CORIANDER *Coriandrum sativum*; ketumbar. Indonesian cooks principally use the seeds, either ground or whole; Thais use the leaves and roots. This is an important difference between the two cuisines.

CORNFLOUR/CORNSTARCH Literally, tepung jagung, but a common brand name is Maizéna and in Indonesia it is usually called tepung Maizéna. The fine white powder, almost pure starch, made by grinding maize/corn kernels. It is used in making porridge, sweet puddings and cookies. Cornstarch, tepung kanji, is used to starch clothes after washing.

CUMIN *Cuminum cyminum*; jinten (also used for caraway). Sold in Indian shops as jeera.

DAGING Meat, flesh.

DAUN Leaf or leaves.

DAUN JERUK PURUT Kaffir lime leaf; the leaf of *Citrus hystrix*. The peel and the juice of the fruit are used in cooking, but only the leaves are called for in recipes in this book. Fresh and dried leaves are sold in most Oriental shops. Bay leaves can be used as a substitute, but are stronger-tasting, so use one bay leaf instead of two or three kaffir lime leaves. Remove the leaves before serving the dish.

DAUN MELINJO See MELINJO and page 227.

DAUN PANDAN Pandanus leaf; the young leaf of *Pandanus odorus* or screwpine, used to add flavour and a green colour to some cakes and sweets. Available in the West in most Oriental shops.

For flavouring, put a section of leaf about 10 cm/4 inches long into the pan during cooking; remove before serving. For colouring, cut a section of leaf into smallish pieces and blend with about half a cupful of warm water, then strain; mix the liquid with the ingredients to be coloured. For stronger colour, use more leaf.

DAUN SALAM   See SALAM LEAF.

DÉNDÉNG   Meat sliced thin, spiced, cooked and dried in the sun, partly to preserve it but also to make it taste good.

DRIED SHRIMPS   Ébi. In Britain, these are sold only in Asian shops, where they may also be labelled dried prawns. They are sold in packets, already shelled, salted and roasted. The flavour is strong – use sparingly.

DURIAN   *Durio zibethinus*; duren. A remarkable and justly celebrated South-East Asian fruit. Fresh durian are flown to London from Thailand, but are extremely expensive. Even in countries where they grow, they are not cheap because demand is always high. The received wisdom is that the smell is dreadful, the taste divine. In fact the durian tastes as it smells; the flavour is extremely complex, and it has been suggested that every tree is unique. The smell is certainly strong, and annoying in a confined space. A good mature durian looks like a large green rugby football covered with sharp pyramidal spikes. The thick rind, when split open, reveals four or five compartments, each with one or more large seeds, each seed covered with a thick soft layer of flesh, yellow as custard and approaching the same consistency.

ÉBI   See DRIED SHRIMPS.

FERNSHOOT, FIDDLEHEAD   Paku or pakis. The Indonesian word just means 'fern', and there are dozens of species that in one place or another are cooked and eaten. The only edible ones I have been able to find in Britain are in glass jars, imported from Canada.

FLOUR   Tepung. Tepung jagung is CORNFLOUR/CORNSTARCH, tepung terigu wheat flour, tepung beras RICE FLOUR.

GALINGALE   *Languas galanga*; laos (in Malaysia, etc., lengkuas; in Thailand, ka). This is a rhizome, which looks like a pinkish ginger root. It is used in cooking to add a slightly bitter note to a savoury dish. Treat fresh galingale as ginger: peel and chop. Fresh and powdered galingale can be bought in Oriental shops in Western countries. Dried slices are also sold; these should be soaked in cold water before use and discarded before the dish goes to table.

GARUPA   Grouper, sea perch, or sea bass; various species of the family Serranidae; also called, in Indonesia and Malaysia, kerapu.

GHEE   The principal cooking medium of much of India, but relatively uncommon in Indonesia, where until very recently milk and butter were almost unknown. Ghee is very like clarified butter, though its flavour is stronger because it is made of buffalo milk. Real ghee is difficult to make at home but easy to buy from Indian shops almost anywhere. To clarify butter, heat it gently until it stops frothing and a thin sediment (sugar and milk protein) falls to the bottom. Strain the liquid through fine muslin.

GINGER   *Zingiber officinale*; jahé. Use fresh ginger, not powdered. Cut off a chunk of root, peel it, and then grate, chop, or whatever the recipe directs.

GOGO RANCAH   A variety of upland, or dry, rice, reputed to be among the best of all rices; the island of Lombok sometimes calls itself Bumigora, meaning roughly 'the land of gogo rancah'.

GORÉNG   Fried.

GULA   See SUGAR.

GULAI   A stew of meat, fish, or vegetables, with a lot of sauce, usually made with coconut milk.

GURAMI   A large freshwater fish, often raised in tanks for food.

HARI RAYA   Literally, 'the great day' – the holiday at the end of the Muslim fasting month. Also called Lebaran and, as a religious festival, Idul Fitri.

IKAN   Fish.

IKAN ASIN   Salted fish; still traded and eaten in huge quantities in Indonesia, and until recently a major source of protein for everybody who did not have access to meat or fresh fish.

IKAN BAKAR   Grilled fish.

IKAN BAWAL   Pomfret; *Stromateus cinereus* and related species.

IKAN BELIDA *Notopterus notopterus* or *N. chitala*. Large river-fish. In Britain, I use tilapia.

IKAN KAKAP Sea perch; *Lates calcarifer*, saltwater fish living in estuaries.

IKAN LÉLÉ Catfish; *Clarias melanoderma* and other species. Burkill says that catfish, being able to breathe in air, are easily transported to market alive and fresh. They are regarded as sacred in various freshwater springs and pools in Indonesia.

IKAN MAS Carp or goldfish; *Carrassius auratus* or *Cyprinus carpio*.

IKAN TERI Anchovy or whitebait; *Stolephorus heterolobus*, etc. Very small ikan teri (also called ikan bilis) are sold in packets in Chinese shops, dried and salted. If their heads are still on, it is better to remove these before cooking, but they can also be bought without heads.

JACKFRUIT *Artocarpus integra*, nangka. Jackfruit can sometimes be bought fresh in London from Indian shops. They are very large, shapeless fruit, covered in rough green skin. Ripe jackfruit are eaten as fruit, not cooked. If you have to cut up a fresh jackfruit, beware the sticky juice (getah), which is difficult to remove from hands and almost impossible to get off clothing. Green unripe jackfruit, weighing about 1 kg/2 lb, are best for cooking, and are an essential ingredient of gudeg (page 145). However, canned green jackfruit can be easily bought from most Oriental shops and is much easier to handle.

JAGUNG See MAIZE.

JAHÉ See GINGER.

JÉNGKOL *Pithecellobium jiringa*. The fruit of this tree is used as a vegetable, boiled or fried, and in West Sumatra (where it is called jaring) it is made into rendang. Eaten raw, or in large quantities even if cooked, it is somewhat toxic.

JERUK A general word for any type of citrus fruit, of which Indonesia has many varieties. See DAUN JERUK PURUT.

JICAMA Yam bean; *Pachyrrhizus erosus*; bengkuang.

KACANG A general word for BEANS and small nuts. For kacang kedelé, see SOYA BEAN. For kacang panjang, see YARD-LONG BEAN.

KALAMANSI *Citrus retusa*; jeruk sundai, jeruk sambal, jeruk Cina, etc. A small green citrus fruit, sold in the West in Oriental shops, usually under its Filipino name, kalamansi.

KAMBING Goat or sheep; goats are much commoner than sheep in Indonesia, so the word usually refers to the former.

KANGKUNG See WATER SPINACH.

KEDONDONG *Spondias cytherea*. This looks like a green plum; its flesh is firm, it can be peeled like an apple, and it has a single spiny seed. It can be eaten raw or stewed, when it makes a tropical substitute for apple sauce.

KELAPA Coconut; *Cocos nucifera*; see pages 247–253.

KEMANGI See BASIL.

KEMIRI See CANDLENUT.

KENARI *Canarium commune*. These tall, shade-giving trees are often planted to shelter nutmeg trees and roadsides. The nuts are similar to ALMONDS and either can replace the other in cooking.

KENCUR *Kaempferia galanga*. A strongly flavoured aromatic rhizome. Use sparingly.

KEPITING Crab.

KERBAU Buffalo (in old books sometimes called carabou); *Bos bubalus*.

KLUWEK *Pangium edule*. The seeds of a large tree, dark red or black inside, an important ingredient of rawon (page 158) and some other dishes. Dried kluwek can be bought in Holland; these must be soaked for 30 minutes before being ground up. Fresh kluwek can contain hydrocyanic acid, which must be made harmless either by repeated boiling and washing, or by heating for 10–15 minutes in the embers of a fire.

KRECEK The Javanese name for krupuk jangat, buffalo skin, which is made into sambal goreng and eaten with gudeg.

KUAH Sauce or soup, as in ikan kuah asam (page 92).

KUÉH Biscuit or sweet cake.

KULIT Skin, peel, outer covering.

KUNING Yellow.

KUNYIT See TURMERIC.

LADA Pepper (but see also BERLADA).

LALAB Raw or plain boiled vegetables, usually served with a chilli sauce.

LAOS See GALINGALE.

LEBARAN The festival at the end of Ramadan.

LEMANG Sumatran compressed glutinous (sticky) rice, cooked in bamboo segments. See page 23.

LEMON GRASS *Cymbopogon citratus*; seréh, serai. Fresh lemon grass can be bought in most large towns in the West, and is usually to be preferred to dried or powdered forms, though these will do well enough. It is worth trying to get a stem to root; it makes an attractive house plant.

To make a lemon grass brush, cut off and discard about 1 cm/$^{1}/2$ inch from the hard root-end of a stem of fresh lemon grass. Beat the cut end, not too hard, with the handle of a knife or a steak hammer until the fibres fray and make a flexible brush. Use this to brush on sauces while grilling or barbecuing; it will give a delicious extra aroma instead of the smell of roasting nylon.

LIMEWATER Air kapur. This is used in Java in the making of sweetmeats from sticky rice flour; it gives them a slightly chewy, elastic texture and prevents them from being too soft. But it is also used all over Indonesia by people who chew betel leaves, because it is an essential ingredient of the betel leaf parcel; for this purpose, it is called kapur sirih. Air kapur is used in making MANISAN, the best known of which is MANISAN PALA. The effect of air kapur is to make the fruit crisp during its lengthy boiling in sugar syrup.

According to Tom Stobart in *The Cook's Encyclopaedia*, 'Limewater can be made by stirring 2–3 tbsp slaked lime in hot water'. Slaked lime can be bought at a chemist's, or from most Indian shops, where it is labelled 'Chuna Edible Lime'.

MACADAMIA NUT *Macadamia ternifolia*. These excellent nuts originated in Australia but are grown on a commercial scale mainly in Hawaii. They are good to eat by themselves, and are a satisfactory substitute for CANDLENUTS in recipes in this book.

MACE   See NUTMEG.

MAGRIB   The hour of late afternoon prayer for Muslims.

MAIZE   *Zea mays*; jagung. Another valuable and widespread introduction from the Americas.

MAKANAN   Food. MAKANAN KECIL, literally 'small food', are snacks.

MANIS   Sweet.

MANISAN   The opposite of ASINAN, sweet instead of salty; a useful way to preserve fruit by boiling it in plenty of sugar syrup.

MANISAN PALA   The candied flesh of the nutmeg fruit. The whole fruit is about the size and shape of an apricot, in colour more green than yellow. The fruit must be fully ripe if the mace and nutmeg are to be ready for the market. Considering how expensive nutmeg and mace are in the West, and how keen Indonesia is to export them, I am astonished to find a recipe for manisan pala in an Indonesian-language cookery book published in Jakarta in 1957. It starts: 'Peel the fruit very thinly, then carefully cut it in half, and *throw away* the hard stone inside' (that is, the nutmeg and mace – my italics). Thereafter, proceed as follows. Soak the fruit halves in plenty of salted water for 2 hours. (This recipe is for about half a kilo/1–1½ lb of the flesh.) Drain, and cut each half into ribbons, but do not cut all the way: leave the skin intact at one end, so that the flesh can be spread into fan shapes. Then dilute 2 teaspoonfuls of limewater in a bowl of water, and soak the fruit in it overnight. The next day, drain the fruit in a colander, and rinse well under a cold tap. Discard the limewater. Boil 1.5 kg/3 lb 4 oz/6½ cups of granulated sugar in 1.1 litres/2 pints/5 cups of water. Stir to dissolve. Put in the fruit and bring the sugar syrup back to boil. When boiled, turn the heat off. Leave the fruit in the sugar syrup overnight. The next day take them out with a wire scoop and drain them in a colander. Heat the sugar syrup to a boiling point and put the fruit back in. Bring back to boil, then take them off the heat, and leave to get cold. Repeat this process twice more. On the last time, drain the fruit after the sugar syrup comes back to the boil. Spread more sugar on a tray, and spread the drained fruit on the sugar, coating them well with the sugar. Now spread them on a mat and dry in the sun for a few hours. Stored in an airtight container, the manisan pala will stay good for several months. This process is also good for making manisan jahé, crystallized ginger, from fresh ginger.

MARKISAH Passion fruit; *Passiflora quadrangularis* or *P. laurifolia*.

MELINJO *Gnetum gnemon*. A tree whose leaves are occasionally used in cooking (see page 168). Melinjo nuts are the raw material of emping (page 227).

MÉRAH Red.

MINUMAN Drink.

MIRIN Sweet Japanese rice-based cooking wine.

NANGKA See JACKFRUIT.

NASI Cooked rice. See BERAS and PADI.

NANAS, NENAS Pineapple.

NUTMEG *Myristica fragrans*; pala. This tree probably originated in eastern Indonesia, where it still grows, though people there in the past valued its fruit more as medicine than as flavouring for food. However, we have always enjoyed eating the inner 'wall' of the fruit, which is soaked, boiled in sugar and candied to make MANISAN PALA, which is delicious. The next layer is the bright red mace, itself a valuable spice. At the centre of the fruit is the dark-coloured seed, the nutmeg itself. It retains its flavour for a long time as long as it is not powdered; therefore, many people keep nutmeg graters in their kitchens. All these parts of the nutmeg are *pala* in Indonesian.

Burkill says: 'The fate of part of the fruit-walls, where crops of nuts are grown, is to be thrown away. In Banda the decaying heaps of these supply a mushroom, greatly relished, and called "kulat pala" in the local Malay. In Malaya there is often a bigger demand for the fruit-walls than the supply can meet.' Burkill wrote this in the 1930s. In my recent trip to Banda, in early 1993, I didn't see any decaying heaps – not of nutmeg skins, anyway – nor did I learn about the mushroom.

OIL Minyak. The most commonly used cooking oil in Indonesia is coconut oil (page 252). Much oil is sold under the brand name Palmolie. Peanut, corn and soya bean oil are also used. Olive oil is imported, but is too expensive for most people to use; it is sometimes suggested in recipes in this book because it is likely to be preferred by Western cooks. Peanut oil is often labelled 'groundnut oil'.

PADI Rice growing in the field, or harvested but not yet threshed and milled. Hence, of course, the English word paddy for a rice field.

PAKIS, PAKU See FERNSHOOT, FIDDLEHEAD.

PALA See NUTMEG.

PALM SUGAR See SUGAR.

PANDANUS See DAUN PANDAN.

PAN-FRY Fry in shallow oil.

PAPAYA *Carica papaya*; katés. This is another American tree, brought to Malaysia by Spaniards or Portuguese. It is one of the easiest fruits to grow, and delicious, if a little lemon or lime juice is squeezed over it. Papaya leaves are used for tenderizing meat, and during the war we used to drink the juice of young leaves as a prophylactic against malaria. Burkill says that the papaya 'does not lend itself to transport', but it is often available nowadays in the West. Unfortunately, it has to be shipped green and ripened artificially, hence the rather uninteresting flavour of English supermarket fruit.

PARSLEY, FLAT-LEAF *Petroselinum vulgare*; selédri. This is flat-leaf or 'continental' parsley, whose leaves resemble coriander/cilantro leaves in shape but not in smell.

PEANUT *Arachis hypogaea*; kacang tanah. These Central American plants have been grown in Java for over two hundred years. Sir Thomas Stamford Raffles said they were grown near towns for the sake of their oil, which was used for cooking, as it still is. The Javanese also make a fermented peanut paste called oncom which is something like TÉMPÉ. NOTE: Peanut oil is often sold under the name 'groundnut oil'.

PEDAS, PEDIS Chilli-hot.

PEPPER *Piper nigrum*; lada, merica.

PETÉ *Parkia speciosa*. A rather bitter-tasting bean, obtainable in Thai shops; each bean is prominent inside the long ribbon-like pod. Beans packed in brine (peté asin) are sold by Conimex. Pods of young fresh peté are often topped and tailed, the stringy edges are trimmed off, and the whole bean is sliced thin and fried; or the beans are taken out and cooked after each has been skinned with a sharp knife.

PETOLA *Luffa acutangula* or *L. cylindrica*; also called oyong, or in English the bottle gourd. The botanical difference between these plants is not very important, as the fruit have to be eaten young, before their internal structure hardens. (*L. cylindrica*, when late-middle-aged, provides the bath loofah.)

PINEAPPLE Nanas, nenas.

PISANG See BANANA, PLANTAIN.

PLANTAIN *Musa paradisiaca*; pisang. These are green or yellow, unripe or ripe. They are available in supermarkets and Indian shops. Green ones are sliced thin and fried to make plantain crisps. In this book, ripe plantains are specified as a substitute for pisang kepok, an Indonesian cooking banana used in cakes, etc.

PRAWN Udang.

PUASA The Indonesian name for Ramadan, the Muslim fasting month. The Indonesian word means simply 'fasting'.

RAGI Any yeast, mould, or fungus used for fermenting or otherwise altering the chemistry of a plant product.

RICE POWDER   Rice flour and rice powder can be bought in any Asian shop. Powder is finer than flour, and for some recipes (e.g. rempéyék, page 227) the difference is important.

ROTI   Bread.

SAGO   *Metroxylon sagus* or *M. rumphii; sagu.* A palm tree whose trunk, at an age of between nine and fifteen years, produces a large amount of starch in preparation for flowering. At this point it is felled, the outer skin of the trunk is cut off, and the soft, woody interior is processed into a kind of coarse sawdust. This is repeatedly washed and strained to extract the starch itself – the sago. Other parts of the palm can also be eaten, as can the grubs that soon infest a felled tree, though it is only in certain areas that these are considered delicacies.

SAGUER   A sweet drink tapped from the sugar palm (see page 84).

SALAM LEAF   *Eugenia polyantha,* daun salam. Not a 'curry leaf' and not a kaffir lime leaf or DAUN JERUK PURUT, but an aromatic leaf that, like them, can be replaced by a bay leaf if necessary. Dried salam leaves are sold in some Asian shops in London and elsewhere.

SAMBAL, SAMBEL   A spiced chilli sauce or paste, used either as a condiment or as an ingredient in cooking.

SANTEN   Coconut milk; see page 251.

SAPI   Cow.

SAUR   (two syllables: sa-oor)   The meal eaten immediately before dawn during Ramadan.

SAWAH   Wet rice land, paddy fields.

SAYUR-SAYURAN   A general term for vegetables.

SEA BASS   Several species of the Serranidae family; see GARUPA.

SELAMATAN   In Javanese society, a quasi-religious family or neighbourhood feast to mark or celebrate some important occasion (see page 173).

SELUDANG MAYANG   The hard sheath from which a coconut flower and eventually the coconuts develop. It is sometimes used to wrap food for cooking (see pages 126, 255).

SERÉH   See LEMON GRASS.

SHALLOT Bawang mérah. The small red onions sold in Thai and some other Oriental shops in the West are similar to shallots. These are my first choice. The shallot flavour is distinct from that of onion, but shallots are seasonal in temperate climates. Small onions will just about do at a pinch.

SHRIMP Udang.

SHRIMP PASTE Terasi (also known as trassie, and balachan or blachen in Malaysia). This is easily available in Oriental shops. It is sold in hard blocks, weighing about 250 g/8 oz, or in slices. The slices are individually packed, weigh about 50 g/2 oz, and have been roasted or fried, ready for use. Shrimp paste is extremely strong-smelling and extremely salty, and must be used very sparingly. If in doubt, use less rather than more. A quarter of one of the small slices is enough for one recipe. If you buy a large block, cut it into, say, 12–14 slices. Wrap these in a double layer of aluminium foil and bake in the oven at 100°C/210°F/Gas Mark 1/4 for 10–15 minutes. When cold, the paste can be crumbled, so you can measure it with a teaspoon. Kept in an air-tight container, the paste, whether baked, grilled, or raw, will last indefi-nitely.

Most recipes in this book specify crumbled shrimp paste, but if a *piece* is called for, that means a piece about 1/2-cm/1/4-inch thick and the size of a small postage stamp. Use the raw paste only if it is an ingredient of a paste that is going to be fried or sautéed before being added to other ingredients. In many recipes, shrimp paste is optional, but its use is highly recommended.

SIMMER Keep liquid at a temperature very close to boiling point, so that it gently seethes and is agitated but does not reach a 'rolling boil'.

SKILLET A small, shallow frying pan.

SOTO Soup with plenty of meat and vegetables in it. There are many regional variations.

SOYA BEAN *Glycine maximus*; kacang kedelé. Though Indonesia is justly proud of being self-sufficient in rice, she still has to import large quantities of soya beans, mainly from North America. Soya beans can be simply boiled and eaten – we used to nibble them on our way to school when I was a small girl – but much of their food value is then lost because humans do not have the right enzymes to digest these beans properly. In any case, the interest of soya beans lies in what they become when fermented, particularly as SOY SAUCE and TÉMPÉ, or when the 'milk' is extracted and made into TOFU (Indonesian, tahu).

SOY SAUCE   Kécap (whence the English word ketchup). The making of this sauce is a complex industrial process, involving fermentation with *Aspergillus oryzae* fungus and a period of soaking in brine, which is presumably what gives soy sauce its saltiness. In Britain, the best all-purpose soy sauce is probably Kikkoman, but other brands – Amoy, Pearl River Bridge, and so on – are very good. Some recipes distinguish between light (salty) and dark ('sweet') soy, though this is really a matter of degree of saltiness. Indonesian kécap manis, sweet soy, is thick and black. One reason for using light soy is that it does not colour the food, as dark soy is apt to do.

SQUASH   *Cucurbita*; labu. Indonesians grow and eat several varieties of squash. In Europe, the butternut squash is generally available in supermarkets and performs well in dishes described in this book. Pumpkins are sometimes called labu kuning, 'yellow squash'.

SQUID   Cumi-cumi.

STAR ANISE   *Illicium verum*; bunga lawang or adas Cina. This South Chinese spice is used in Indonesia mainly in dishes that show strong Chinese influence. It is easily obtainable in Oriental shops in the West, and easily recognized by its dry, brown, fragile eight-pointed star.

STEAMING   A very healthy and convenient way of cooking. If the food is in ramekins or small cups, these can be steamed in a conventional steamer, a rice steamer, or a double saucepan. A large saucepan or wok is also suitable. Put a trivet or some other firm support in the bottom, and place on it whatever is to be steamed. Pour boiling water into the pan or wok, to a reasonable depth – obviously this water must not come into contact with the food. If steaming continues for a long time, the water may have to be replenished with boiling water straight from the kettle.

STROOP   (Dutch)   Syrup, treacle; a thick, often brightly coloured sweet syrup added to coconut water or used for making soft drinks.

SUBUH   Dawn, the hour of the first prayer for Muslims.

SUGAR   As well as growing and consuming vast amounts of refined granulated cane sugar, Indonesians also value palm sugar, which we call gula aren (from the sugar palm, *Arenga pinnata*) or gula Jawa (from the coconut palm). These are particularly used in cooking. A general name for both is gula mérah, red sugar. Gula Melaka (Malaya) and jaggery (Burma) are very similar. All are sold in very hard blocks, from which you scrape or grate or chip what you require. Gula mérah can be bought in Oriental shops anywhere.

SWEET POTATO   *Ipomoea batatas*; ubi jalar, ketéla rambat. This is one plant that made the crossing of the Pacific before 1492; its pre-Columbian presence in Polynesia and New Zealand was one of Thor Heyerdahl's reasons for his voyage in *Kon-Tiki*.

TAHU   See TOFU.

TAMARIND   *Tamarindus indica*; asam, asem, asem Jawa. This is one of our many sources of sourness in cooking. In tropical countries, the pods are sold freshly picked from the tree. If the tamarind is already ripe, the skin is likely to be cracked, and is easily peeled off. In the West it is sold already pulped and packed in dark brown blocks. At the time of writing, fresh tamarind is available in Thai and Indian shops in Britain, and in the food halls of some large department stores in London.

Some recipes specify a small piece of tamarind pulp, about the size of a walnut, which is to be grilled, or heated in a heavy iron pan or skillet, until slightly charred all over. In all other cases, use tamarind water. Break a piece of pulp from the block, or the tamarind seeds from one whole pod, and place in a small bowl. Add 3–4 tbsp warm water, then squeeze and press with your fingers or a spoon, so that the water becomes thick and brown. Repeat the process until you have as much tamarind water as you need. Pass the water through a sieve and discard the solids. As a guide, 30 g/1 oz of tamarind will make about 170 ml/6 fl oz/³/4 cup of tamarind water; if the recipe specifies thick tamarind water, use twice as much tamarind.

If you use tamarind water often, it is worth making a small stock of it. Crumble the whole 450-g/1-lb block of tamarind pulp into a saucepan, add 1.1 litres/2 pints/5 cups of water, and simmer until the water has reduced to half its volume. Pass this through a sieve and simmer for 10 more minutes to purify it further. Leave the liquid to get cold. It can then be stored in the fridge for at least 2 weeks, or can be frozen for up to 3 months. One tamarind-water ice cube is the equivalent of 2 tbsp of thick tamarind water.

Similar to tamarind, from the cook's point of view, are:

TAMARIND SLICES *Garcinia atroviridis*; asam gelugur. This resembles asam kandis (below), but the fruit is rather larger. To prepare it for use in cooking, it is thinly sliced and then dried in the sun. In this form, usually labelled 'Tamarind Slices', it can be bought in the West, at Oriental or Chinese stores. The slices are more practical if you are making a sauce, which already has a lot of liquid. Put in one or two slices, and they will give the same delicate sourness as tamarind water. They will swell up during cooking, and you need to discard them before serving.

Garcinia globulosa, *G. nigrolineata*; asam kandis. This is a small, round, thin-skinned fruit, about 1 centimetre (less than $1/2$ inch) in diameter, which is often used in cooking instead of tamarind. It is easy to find in Indonesia, especially in Sumatra, where it is more commonly used, e.g. in pangék (page 52). It is still, in 1993, difficult to get in Europe, except perhaps in Holland. The pulp of this fruit is sweet but the skin, which is the part used in cooking, is bitter. After picking, the fruit is split down the middle and the half-skins are dried in the sun so that what comes to

275

market is a hard, black, wrinkled fragment. It goes into the pot with all the other ingredients, as does asam gelugur (above). All solids should, of course, be removed before serving.

TANAH, TANA Land, country, area. The standard form has the final 'h', but in some dialects – e.g. that of Tana Toraja – it is silent and tends to be omitted in writing.

TAPÉ Soft sticky rice, or cooked CASSAVA, fermented with a mould, or ragi, to produce a slightly sour-tasting and very mildly alcoholic food. Other starchy foods are also used as a basis for tapé, which is found in many forms all over Indonesia. The mould is often an *Aspergillus*, which may also be used for making TÉMPÉ.

TARO Also called dasheen, eddo, and other names. *Colocasia esculenta*; keladi, talas, tales. This root has been grown and eaten in tropical Asia for a long time, longer (in many areas) than rice. The best Indonesian taro comes from Bogor in West Java, as do the best pineapples. Taro is prepared and boiled like potato; when boiled, it may also be sliced thin and sautéed. It is used in cakes, and the big glossy leaves are used as edible wrappers, as in buntil (page 169).

TÉMPÉ, TÉMPÉH A preparation of boiled soya beans, held together by a mould which digests parts of the beans that the human digestive system cannot cope with and also gives the tempé a mild, nutty flavour. Témpé is made and sold in slabs or cakes about 2.5 cm/1 inch thick. It must be boiled or fried before being eaten, and is rather tasteless by itself, but it makes an excellent basis for a wide variety of savoury and sweet dishes, hamburgers, sauces, dips, ice creams, etc. In Java and some other parts of Indonesia it is a valuable source of protein, but in the past, because it was associated with hard times and poverty, its status as a food was very low. It is becoming moderately popular in the USA and Europe as a vegetarian and health food, and can be bought, usually frozen, from organic and health food shops. It is also quite easy to make témpé at home if you have a supply of the ragi, or starter. The usual starter is a yeast called *Rhizopus oligosporus*. Instructions are given in William Shurtleff and Akiko Aoyagi's *The Book of Tempeh* and in my *The Rice Book*.

TERASI See SHRIMP PASTE.

TERONG Aubergine/eggplant.

TOFU   Bean curd; tahu. See SOYA BEAN. A thick curd made from soya 'milk', very nutritious, very bland in taste and texture but delicious when cooked with flavours that it readily absorbs. Fresh tofu is sold in many Asian shops, certainly in all that deal in Chinese or Japanese food-stuffs; it is packed and stored in cold water, and must be stored in the fridge and used within 3 days at most. Branded fresh tofu is now manu-factured and distributed in UK supermarkets (e.g. Cauldron brand, which may be 'original' or 'smoked'); this, too, has a limited fridge life. Fried tofu is sold in Japanese and some other Asian shops. You can also make your own by deep-frying cubes of plain tofu, about 2.5 cm/1 inch on a side, until the surface is slightly browned. The inside remains white and soft. Fried tofu from a shop may be rather oily. Remove excess oil by pouring water over the cubes and lightly pressing or patting them with absorbent paper. Deep-fried tofu can be stored in the fridge for up to a week, but not frozen.

TONGKOL   Frigate mackerel, mackerel tuna, little tunny, tuna; a name applied to several fish of the Scombridae family.

TUAK   Spirit distilled from palm wine (page 84).

TURMERIC   *Curcuma domestica*; kunyit (in Java, kunir). This has long been popular in South-East Asia for its pungent flavour as well as its vivid colour. By turning boiled rice yellow, the colour of royalty, it cre-ates an air of festivity. In the West it is usually sold as a powder, but if you can get fresh turmeric, the rhizome, cut off a small piece, peel it, and crush or blend it with the other spices.

UDANG   Prawn or shrimp.

UDANG BESAR   Lobster.

ULEK   Pounded in a mortar.

ULEK-ULEK   A pestle.

VINEGAR   Cuka is a colourless vinegar used for cooking in Indonesia. Distilled colourless malt vinegar is the nearest equivalent to it in the West.

WATERCRESS   *Nasturtium officinale*; selada air. Burkill says this was introduced to Malaysia by Europeans and spread to Java in the early nineteenth century.

WATER SPINACH Swamp cabbage; *Ipomoea aquatica* or *I. reptans*; kangkung. A common vegetable in Indonesia; available in the West in Thai and Chinese shops. Its place in cooking can usually be taken by ordinary spinach.

YAM BEAN See JICAMA.

YARD-LONG BEAN *Vigna sinensis sesquipedalis*; kacang panjang. These green beans, when cut up, somewhat resemble French beans, but they do in fact grow to as much as a yard (90 cm) long. They can be bought in Thai and other Oriental shops, usually coiled up like lengths of green rope.

BIBLIOGRAPHY

General

From the vast stock of books on Indonesia, these are a few that will be useful for travellers or for people who simply want to have a clearer view of the country and its background. There are three excellent series of guidebooks, published by Insight Guides, Lonely Planet and Periplus; the last of these is my own favourite. Raffles' book is perhaps one for the antiquarian, but Merle Ricklefs' *Modern Indonesia* is a fine piece of historical writing as well as authoritative. The standard Indonesian/English dictionary is by Echols and Shadily; Labrousse is more comprehensive and includes many common but non-standard Indonesian words. A pocket version for travellers is available.

Cummings, Joe, and others, *Indonesia: A Travel Survival Kit* (Hawthorn, Victoria: Lonely Planet, 1990)

Deane, Shirley, *Ambon, Island of Spices* (London: John Murray, 1979)

Geertz, Clifford, *The Religion of Java* (Chicago: The Free Press, 1960)

Geertz, Clifford: *Negara: The Theatre State in Nineteenth-Century Bali* (Princeton, NJ: Princeton University Press, 1980)

Labrousse, Pierre: *Indonésien-Français: Dictionnaire Général* (Paris: Association Archipel, 1984)

Mason, Anthony, and Felicity Goulden, *Bali* (London: Cadogan Books, 1989)

Muller, Kal, *Maluku: The Spice Islands* (Berkeley, Calif.: Periplus Indonesia Travel Guides, 1990)

Oey, Eric M. (ed.), *Sumatra* (Singapore: Periplus Indonesia Travel Guides, 1991)

Raffles, Sir Thomas Stamford, *History of Java* (London: 1817; repr. Oxford University Press)

Reid, Anthony, *Southeast Asia in the Age of Commerce*, Vol. 1 (New Haven, Conn., and London: Yale University Press, 1988)

Ricklefs, M. C., *A History of Modern Indonesia* (London: Macmillan, 1981)

Schnitger, *Forgotten Kingdoms of Sumatra* (Leyden. 1938; repr. Singapore, 1989)

Volkman, Toby Alice, and Ian Caldwell (eds), *Sulawesi* (Berkeley, Calif.: Periplus Indonesia Travel Guides, 1990)

Food and Cookery

There is not a great deal in print on Indonesian food. Alan Davidson's fish books are invaluable, because Indonesians eat so much fish. Jill Norman and Tom Stobart are excellent for reference, and Burkill and Herklots are indispensable. Cherry Ripe's *Cringe* is a perceptive and entertaining account of contemporary Australian food and attitudes.

Bissell, Frances, *Sainsbury's Book of Food* (London: Webster's Wine Price Guide Ltd for Sainsbury, 1989)

Burkill, I. H., *A Dictionary of the Economic Products of the Malay Peninsula* (1935; repr. Kuala Lumpur: Ministry of Agriculture and Co-peratives, 1966)

Davidson, Alan, *Fish and Fish Dishes of Laos* (Tokyo: Charles E. Tuttle, 1975)

Davidson, Alan, *Seafood of South-East Asia* (Singapore: Federal Publications, 1977; London: Macmillan, 1978)

Davidson, Alan (ed.), *The Cook's Room* (London: Macdonald, 1991)

Departemen Pertanian, *Mustikarasa* (Jakarta: 1967)

Herklots, G. A. C., *Vegetables in South-East Asia* (London: Allen & Unwin, 1972)

Latief, Tuty, *Resep Masakan Daerah* (Surabaya: P. T. Bina Ilmu, 1977)

Norman, Jill, *The Complete Book of Spices* (London: Dorling Kindersley, 1990)

Ortiz, Elisabeth Lambert, *Caribbean Cooking* (London: Deutsch, 1975; Penguin, 1977)

Owen, Sri, *Indonesian Food and Cookery* (London: Prospect Books, 1980 and 1986)

Owen, Sri, *Indonesian and Thai Cookery* (London: Piatkus, 1988)

Owen, Sri, *The Cooking of Indonesia, Thailand and Malaysia* (London: Martin Books for Sainsbury, 1991)

Owen, Sri, *Exotic Feasts* (London: Kyle Cathie, 1991)

Owen, Sri, *The Rice Book* (London: Doubleday, 1993)

Owen, Sri, 'Three staples of Indonesia: rice, coconuts, tempeh', in *Proceedings of the Oxford Symposium on Food and Cookery, 1989* (London: Prospect Books, 1990)

Owen, Sri, 'Introducing children to food and table manners in Java', in *Food, Culture and History*, ed. Gerald and Valerie Mars (London: The London Food Seminar, 1993)

Owen, Sri, and Roger Owen, 'Public eating, public manners in Asia', in *Proceedings of the Oxford Symposium, 1991* (London: Prospect Books, 1992)

Ripe, Cherry, *Goodbye Culinary Cringe* (St Leonards, NSW: Allen & Unwin, 1993)

Shurtleff, William, and Akiko Aoyagi, *The Book of Tempeh* (New York: Harper & Row, 1979)

Skrobanek, Detlef, with Suzanne Charlé and Gerald Gay, *The New Art of Indonesian Cooking* (Singapore: Times Editions; London: Ward Lock, 1988)

Stobart, Tom, *The Cook's Encyclopaedia* (London: Batsford, 1980)

Index

Page references to recipes are **in heavy type**. Page references to illustrations are in italics. Some items described in the Glossary are not listed in the Index.